The Social Roots of Asian American Partisanship

The Social Roots of Asian American Partisanship

From Political Learning to Partisan Leanings

TANIKA RAYCHAUDHURI

Oxford University Press is a department of the University of Oxford.
It furthers the University's objective of excellence in research, scholarship,
and education by publishing worldwide. Oxford is a registered trade mark of
Oxford University Press in the UK and in certain other countries.

Published in the United States of America by Oxford University Press
198 Madison Avenue, New York, NY 10016, United States of America.

© Oxford University Press 2025

All rights reserved. No part of this publication may be reproduced, stored in a retrieval system, transmitted, used for text and data mining, or used for training artificial intelligence, in any form or by any means, without the prior permission in writing of Oxford University Press, or as expressly permitted by law, by license or under terms agreed with the appropriate reprographics rights organization. Inquiries concerning reproduction outside the scope of the above should be sent to the Rights Department, Oxford University Press, at the address above.

You must not circulate this work in any other form
and you must impose this same condition on any acquirer.

CIP data is on file at the Library of Congress

ISBN 9780197826539
ISBN 9780197826577 (hbk.)
DOI: 10.1093/9780197826560.001.0001

The manufacturer's authorized representative in the EU for product safety is
Oxford University Press España S.A., Parque Empresarial San Fernando de Henares,
Avenida de Castilla, 2 – 28830 Madrid (www.oup.es/en or product.safety@oup.com).
OUP España S.A. also acts as importer into Spain of products made by the manufacturer.

For my parents, Arundhati and Dipankar, and my husband, Alexander.

Contents

List of Figures	ix
List of Tables	xi
Acknowledgments	xiii
About the Companion Website	xvi

1. The Political Influence of Diverse Asian American Communities — 1

PART I. LOCAL CONTEXT, PEER INFLUENCE, AND ASIAN AMERICAN PARTISAN PREFERENCES

2. Social Transmission and the Partisan Influence of Peers — 25
3. Local Partisan Context and Vote Choice in Asian American Communities — 68
4. The Relative Partisan Influence of Peers and Family — 94

PART II. PEER POLITICAL INFLUENCE ON COLLEGE CAMPUSES

5. Interactions with College Peers and Political Learning on Campus — 127
6. Political Endorsements from Peers in Campus Social Networks — 156
7. Conclusion and Implications for Asian American Political Incorporation — 177

Appendix A: Interview Methodology and Houston Case Study Information (Chapter 2) — 190
Appendix B: NAAS Cross-Tabulations and Additional Survey Results (Chapter 3) — 193

Appendix C: OAAS Cross-Tabulations and Additional Survey
  Results (Chapter 4) 197
Appendix D: Additional CIRP Survey Results (Chapter 5) 201
Appendix E: Additional Experimental Results (Chapter 6) 202

References 217
Index 241

List of Figures

1.1	Growth of Asian American population and national origin groups (2005–2022)	2
1.2	Democratic vote share in presidential elections by race (1992–2024)	10
1.3	Democratic vote choice in 2016 and 2020 by Asian American national origin	11
2.1	Asian American population and general voting trends in Harris County (1980–2020)	44
2.2	Asian American population and general voting trends in Fort Bend County (1980–2020)	45
3.1	Intended Democratic vote choice among likely Asian American voters	76
3.2	Democratic vote share in counties of residence	77
3.3	Democratic vote share in counties of residence by national origin	79
3.4	Asian American vote choice by local partisan context	80
3.5	Asian American population percentage in counties of residence	81
3.6	Asian American population percentage in counties of residence by national origin	82
3.7	Asian American vote choice by local Asian American population context	83
3.8	Associations between local context measures and vote choice	85
3.9	Likelihood of Democratic vote choice across local partisan contexts	87
3.10	Likelihood of Democratic vote choice among immigrants across local partisan contexts	91
4.1	Partisan preferences among Asian Americans by national origin	108
4.2	Partisan preferences among Asian Americans by generational status	108
4.3	Frequency of political discussion with family and peers by national origin	110
4.4	Comparing the frequency of political discussion with family and peers (83.4% CIs)	111
4.5	Association between political discussion measures and partisan outcomes (95% CIs)	117
4.6	Association between discussing American politics more frequently with peers than family and partisan outcomes (95% CIs)	118
4.7	Frequency of political discussion with family and peers by generational status (83.4% CIs)	121

4.8 Association between political discussion with peers and partisan outcomes by generational status (95% CIs)   123

5.1 Percentage of recent high school graduates enrolled in college (1989–2022, three-year rolling averages)   129

5.2 Changes in aggregate political views from freshman to senior year   141

5.3 Association between interactions with peers of a different race and the political views of students across racial groups   144

5.4 Association between interactions with peers of a different race and the political views of Asian American and white students by campus ideology   147

5.5 Political views by college attendance across racial groups   150

5.6 Political views by importance of peer groups in political learning for Asian Americans and Latinos   151

5.7 Political views by partisan composition of social network for Asian Americans   152

6.1 Peer social endorsement treatment effects on policy outcomes (95% CIs)   169

6.2 Peer social endorsement treatment effects on changes in party ratings (95% CIs)   170

6.3 Peer social endorsement treatment effects on partisanship (95% CIs)   170

6.4 Peer social endorsement treatment effects on perceptions of the parties (95% CIs)   171

List of Tables

3.1	Summary of Hypotheses	73
3.2	Effects of Social Transmission Predictors on Vote Choice, by Levels of Political Interest	89
3.3	Effects of Social Transmission Predictors on Vote Choice, Weighted Model	90
4.1	Summary of Hypotheses	104
4.2	Average Ratings of Democratic Party Across Levels of Political Discussion with Peers	113
4.3	Cross-Tabulation of Political Discussion with Peers and Identification as a Democrat or Leaner	114
4.4	Average Ratings of Democratic Party Across Levels of Political Discussion with Family	115
4.5	Cross-Tabulation of Political Discussion with Family and Identification as a Democrat or Leaner	115
4.6	Association Between Discussing American Politics with Family or Peers and Any Partisan Identification	119
5.1	Summary of Hypotheses	135
5.2	Changes in the Crystallization of Political Views During College	139
6.1	Overview of Experimental Conditions	159
6.2	Moderating Effects of Race on Change in Republican Party Ratings	173
A.1	Metropolitan Statistical Areas with Largest Asian American Populations	190
A.2	Demographic Profile of Houston-Area Asian American Interview Respondents	192
B.1	Asian American Vote Choice by Local Partisan Context	194
B.2	Asian American Vote Choice by Local Asian American Context	195
B.3	Association Between County Partisan Context and Vote Choice	196
C.1	Democratic Party Ratings Across Levels of Political Discussion	197
C.2	Democratic Partisans and Leaners Across Levels of Political Discussion	197
C.3	Cross-Tabulation of Political Discussion with Peers and Any Partisan Identification	198
C.4	Cross-Tabulation of Political Discussion with Family and Any Partisan Identification	198

C.5	Association Between Discussing American Politics with Family or Peers and Partisan Outcomes	198
C.6	Association Between Discussing American Politics with Asian or Non-Asian Peers and Partisan Outcomes Across Generational Subsets	200
D.1	Changes in Aggregate Political Views from Freshman to Senior Year	201
E.1	Sample Size Across Experimental Conditions	202
E.2	Balance Across Experimental Conditions	202
E.3	Manipulation Check Results (Study 1)	203
E.4	Manipulation Check Results (Study 2)	204
E.5	Treatment Effects on Change in Support for Debt Forgiveness Policy (Study 1)	205
E.6	Treatment Effects on Willingness to Sign Petition (Study 1)	206
E.7	Treatment Effects on Change in Republican Party Feeling Thermometer Ratings (Study 1)	207
E.8	Treatment Effects on Change in Democratic Party Feeling Thermometer Ratings (Study 1)	207
E.9	Treatment Effects on Partisan Identification (Study 1)	208
E.10	Treatment Effects on Change in Viewing Republican Party in a Positive Light (Study 1)	208
E.11	Treatment Effects on Change in Viewing the Democratic Party in a Positive Light (Study 1)	209
E.12	Treatment Effects on Democrats Represent People "Like Me" (Study 1)	209
E.13	Treatment Effects on Republicans Represent People "Like Me" (Study 1)	210
E.14	Treatment Effects on Parties Represent People "Like Me" (Combined Measure) (Study 1)	210
E.15	Treatment Effects on Change in Support for Pell Grant Policy (Study 2)	211
E.16	Treatment Effects on Willingness to Sign Petition (Study 2)	212
E.17	Treatment Effects on Change in Republican Party Feeling Thermometer Ratings (Study 2)	213
E.18	Treatment Effects on Change in Democratic Party Feeling Thermometer Ratings (Study 2)	213
E.19	Treatment Effects on Change in Partisanship (Study 2)	214
E.20	Treatment Effects on Viewing the Republican Party in a Positive Light (Study 2)	214
E.21	Treatment Effects on Viewing the Democratic Party in a Positive Light (Study 2)	215
E.22	Treatment Effects on "Republicans Represent People Like Me" (Study 2)	215
E.23	Treatment Effects on "Democrats Represent People Like Me" (Study 2)	216

Acknowledgments

This book was born out of my interest in understanding how immigrants learn about the political system in a new country. As a child of South Asian immigrants growing up in suburban New Jersey, I rarely saw the experiences of my family, friends, and community members represented in social and political narratives about American life. Since then, I have joined a community of scholars working to fill this gap so that our collective understanding of American politics reflects the perspectives of an increasingly diverse citizenry. This book represents one contribution toward that end.

I began working on this research in my dissertation at Princeton University. My advisor, Tali Mendelberg, encouraged me to explore Asian American vote choice in my research. Her advisement and willingness to read many iterations of my work helped me to identify the research questions underlying this book, articulate the theoretical argument, and develop research designs to test them. I am deeply grateful to Dara Strolovitch, who provided keen theoretical insights, detailed handwritten notes on my dissertation chapters, and advisement as I developed ideas for this manuscript. This book would not be published without Dara's supportive mentorship and willingness to help me navigate the publication process.

I am also indebted to several other faculty members I met at Princeton who helped me to develop this project, including Christopher Achen, Rafaela Dancygier, Andrew Guess, Martin Gilens, LaFleur Stephens-Dougan, Ali Valenzuela, and Omar Wasow. Many friends, cohort-mates, and colleagues offered helpful insights, including Stephanie Chan, Chaya Crowder, Cassandra Emmons, Dayna Judge, Katherine McCabe, Rachael McLellan, Andrew Proctor, Daniel Tavana, Adam Thal, Matthew Tokeshi, and Elsa Voytas. Financial support from the Center for the Study of Democratic Politics and the Program in American Studies at Princeton was essential for completing some of the research presented in this book. I also appreciate kindness and support from Michele Epstein and Helene Wood at the Center for the Study of Democratic Politics.

I am grateful to the participants of my interviewees in Houston, whose time and insights were crucial to the development of the theoretical perspective. The Chao Center for Asian Studies at Rice University was an invaluable resource during my fieldwork in the summer of 2017. I also thank the Higher Education

Research Institute at UCLA for providing access to the Cooperative Institutional Research Program's Freshman and Senior surveys.

In the intervening years, I received guidance on this project from many other mentors and colleagues. Conversations with Michael Jones-Correa during my postdoctoral fellowship at the University of Pennsylvania were formative for framing the project and developing this research into a book manuscript. I am grateful for his continued mentorship and for insights from other scholars at UPenn, including Daniel Hopkins and Michele Margolis. I continued to develop this project in my first tenure-track position at the University of Houston, where I received funding from the College of Liberal Arts and Social Sciences; detailed feedback from supportive colleagues, including Allison Archer, Jason Casellas, Jeffrey Church, Scott Clifford, Jae-Hee Jung, Michael Kistner, Brandon Rottinghaus, and Elizabeth Simas; and research assistance from Aparajita Datta, Lucia Lopez, and Silky Joshi. I am also grateful for feedback and support from colleagues at Rice University, including Jaclyn Kaslovsky, Rithika Kumar, Ashley Leeds, Erik Peterson, Kaitlyn Robinson, Leslie Schwindt-Bayer, and Matthew Tyler, as well as research assistance from Niél Arroyo and Madison Hering.

I held a book workshop in June 2023, funded by the American Political Science Association's MSI Virtual Book Workshop Project. The workshop was generously organized by Niambi Carter and Heath Brown and attended by Angela Chnapko, Lauren Davenport, Taeku Lee, and Janelle Wong. I received detailed and constructive feedback from these incredible scholars, which helped guide my revisions and strengthen this manuscript.

Allison Anoll, Jane Junn, Pei-te Lien, Christopher Ojeda, Efrén Pérez, Karthick Ramakrishnan, Nicholas Valentino, and the participants of seminars and workshops at UC Berkeley, Indiana, UC Merced, Northwestern, Vanderbilt, and Rice provided feedback as the project developed. Monthly check-in meetings with Andrew Proctor and Elsa Voytas offered intellectual and emotional support during the writing process. Nathan Chan also offered guidance and feedback throughout the process. I also received support from a wider community of scholars of Asian American politics, including Andrew Aoki, Sonya Chen, Chinbo Chong, Nicole Filler, James Lai, Vivien Leung, Jae Yeon Kim, Fan Lu, Christian Dyogi Phillips, Okiyoshi Takeda, Paru Shah, and Sara Sadhwani.

I am grateful to Angela Chnapko, Andrea Smith, and the editorial team at Oxford University Press for publishing this manuscript. Angela saw potential in this project early on and guided me through the publication process, offering detailed feedback and helpful suggestions. I would also like to thank the two anonymous reviewers for their deep engagement with my manuscript and many insights that helped to improve it. I am deeply appreciative of Claire Ma, a friend, colleague, and artist, who illustrated the book's cover and brought the manuscript's central arguments to life.

My friends and family have also supported me throughout the process of writing and publishing this book. Jiajia, Wendy, Niki, Megan, and Rebecca offered inspiration and moral support over the years. I am grateful for encouragement from my family, including my brother, Mayukh, sister-in-law, Meghan, and my niece, Veda, a third-generation Asian American who constantly inspires me. My parents, Arundhati and Dipankar, encouraged me to pursue a career in academia and explore topics I am passionate about in my work. Finally, my husband, Alexander, has been a constant source of love and support, having patiently listened to countless presentations about this research and edited many iterations of my work. I would not have been able to complete this project without him.

About the Companion Website

www.oup.com/us/socialrootsasianamericanpartisanship

Oxford has created a website to accompany *The Social Roots of Asian American Partisanship*. Materials that cannot be made available in the book, including detailed interview protocols and extended statistical tables, are provided at the URL listed above. The reader is encouraged to consult this resource in conjunction with the book chapters. Examples available online are indicated in the text with Oxford's symbol ⊙.

1
The Political Influence of Diverse Asian American Communities

Anne Le and Nicole Phan, two Asian American residents of Gwinnett County, Georgia, felt compelled to vote for Democratic candidates in the 2020 general elections. In an interview with *NBC News*, Anne, who did not vote in the previous presidential election, said: "Clearly, it's a big deal and it does make a big difference. The last four years had shown that not voting in 2016 was a mistake one does not want to make again" (Yam 2020). Nicole, a recently naturalized citizen and first-time voter, claimed that she wanted to "vote out the person and party that has been threatening the livelihood of women and people of color" (Yam 2020). Both voters were part of a coalition of Asian Americans who helped propel two Georgia Democrats, Raphael Warnock and Jon Ossoff, to the US Senate during hotly contested run-off elections several months later.

The perspectives of these two Georgia voters reflect the growing importance of Asian Americans' political choices for American politics as the electorate diversifies. Asian Americans[1]—a diverse and predominantly immigrant group comprising those who trace their national origin to countries in East, Southeast, and South Asia—are currently the fastest-growing racial or ethnic group in the US electorate (Budiman 2020; Budiman and Ruiz 2021b). The six largest national origin groups within this pan-ethnic community are Chinese Americans, Indian Americans, Filipino Americans, Vietnamese Americans, Korean Americans, and Japanese Americans, who collectively account for about 85% of the Asian American population (Budiman and Ruiz 2021b). In the aggregate, Asian Americans represent about 6% of the US population and nearly 5% of eligible voters (Budiman 2020; Budiman and Ruiz 2021a).

These numbers reflect the remarkable growth of the Asian American population, which has nearly doubled over the past two decades due in large part to immigration. Figure 1.1 illustrates the size of the Asian American population

---

[1] This book focuses on diverse national origin groups within the Asian American community. I define the term "Asian American" as including people with ethnic origin from regions of East, Southeast, and South Asia. Pacific Islanders and Native Hawaiians are often included under umbrella terms such as "AANHPI" (i.e., Asian American, Native Hawaiian, Pacific Islander). I do not include Native Hawaiian and Pacific Islander groups along with Asian Americans in this research because they experience qualitatively different histories of colonialism, migration, and racialization in the US (Aoki and Nakanishi 2001; Grieco 2001; Hall 2015; Phan and Lee 2022).

The Social Roots of Asian American Partisanship. Tanika Raychaudhuri, Oxford University Press.
© Oxford University Press (2025). DOI: 10.1093/9780197826560.003.0001

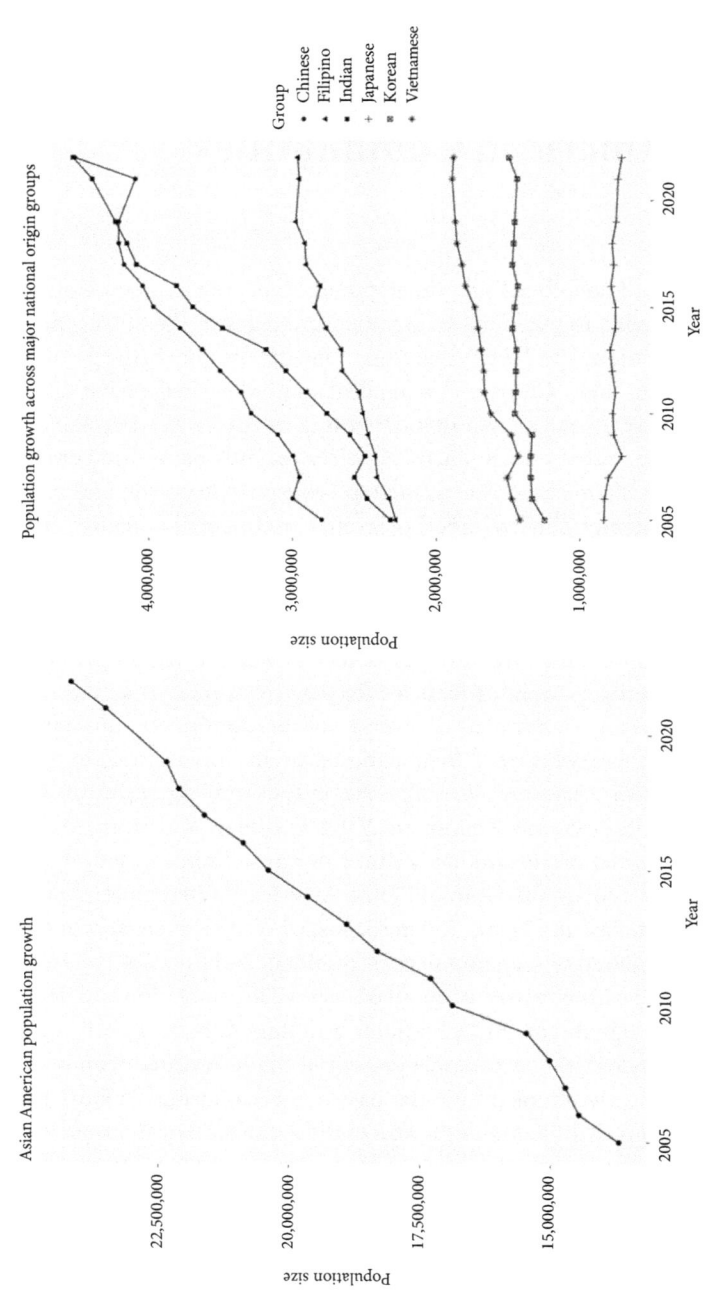

Figure 1.1 Growth of Asian American population and national origin groups (2005–2022)

Source: The data are drawn from American Community Survey one-year estimates collected between 2005 and 2022 (US Census Bureau 2024a). Asian American population totals from 2012 to 2022 reflect those who identify as Asian American alone or in combination. Asian American population totals prior to 2012 reflect those who identify as Asian alone or in combination with the following racial groups: white, African American, Native American, Native Hawaiian, or other race.

and the six largest Asian national origin subgroups between 2005 and 2022. As of 2022, approximately 24.2 million people identified as Asian alone or in combination with some other race, reflecting nearly a twofold increase from 13.6 million in 2005 (US Census Bureau 2024a). This growth is reflected unevenly across Asian American subgroups. As Figure 1.1 shows, Chinese American and Indian American populations have grown rapidly, while Filipino American, Korean American, and Vietnamese American populations have grown at slower rates. Only the Japanese American population has declined in recent years, reflecting an earlier history of immigration than other Asian origin groups (Takaki 1998). Overall, rapid population growth across multiple subgroups within the Asian American community is notable in an era of heightened partisan polarization in American politics. As elections become closer and are increasingly determined on razor-thin margins, Asian American voters from diverse national origin groups may play a central role in shaping their results.

Asian Americans live in a diverse range of communities nationwide, many of which are politically competitive, like Atlanta, Georgia (Gebellof et al. 2021; Shah and Ramakrishnan 2018). The Pew Research Center estimates that about 45% of Asian Americans live in the West, 12% in the Midwest, 24% in the South, and 19% in the Northeast (Budiman and Ruiz 2021b). Across these regions, some Asian Americans live in electorally competitive districts, including Orange County in Southern California; Clark County in Nevada (home to Las Vegas); Fort Bend County in the suburbs of Houston, Texas; and Gwinnett County in suburban Atlanta (Shah and Ramakrishnan 2018). A 2018 analysis conducted by AAPI Data found that Asian Americans represented at least 5% of eligible voters in 27 toss-up congressional districts spanning 11 states (Shah and Ramakrishnan 2018). An earlier analysis found that as of 2008, 31% of Asian Americans lived in presidential swing states and 27% lived in electorally competitive counties (Wong et al. 2011, 109).

The 2021 US Senate run-off elections in Georgia offer one example of the centrality of Asian Americans' partisan preferences and vote choices to contemporary American electoral politics. These elections were notable because they occurred in the wake of President Joe Biden's historic 2020 win in Georgia, leading to a Democratic majority in the US Senate and sending two Georgia Democrats to the Senate for the first time in nearly two decades. The elections also came after a period of rapid growth for Asian American communities in the state of Georgia. Nearly half a million Asian Americans lived in Georgia as of the 2020 Census, accounting for about 4.5% of the state's population, compared to just 3.3% in 2010 (Asian Americans Advancing Justice-Atlanta and Asian American Advocacy Fund 2022). This growing Asian American community includes a diverse range of ethnic subgroups. While Indian Americans account for over a third of Asian American residents of Georgia, other subgroups with a large presence in Georgia include Vietnamese Americans, Chinese Americans, and Filipino Americans (Asian Americans Advancing Justice-Atlanta and Asian American Advocacy Fund 2022).

Although many Asian Americans supported Democrats in elections across the nation for several decades, the Georgia run-offs represent one of the first times that Democratic candidates' campaigns centered Asian American voters in mobilization efforts. In recognition of Asian American population growth ahead of a close election, both Senators Jon Ossoff and Raphael Warnock hired specialized campaign staff, ran campaign ads in Asian languages, and held events that targeted Asian American voters (Kenny et al. 2020). This suggests an intentional effort to incorporate Asian Americans into the Democratic Party's diverse coalition of voters that developed in the post–1965 era, including African Americans, Jewish Americans, and the LGBTQ community (Proctor 2022; Schickler 2016).

While it is difficult to say whether a particular group is decisive in the outcome of a close election, these targeted mobilization efforts, high turnout, and strong support for the Democratic senatorial candidates among Asian Americans from many national origin groups suggest they played an important role in Senators Ossoff's and Warnock's victories. Asian Americans in Georgia also voted at higher rates during both the 2020 presidential and 2021 senate run-off elections than they did in 2016. This increase in voting participation was fueled by an estimated 63,000 new Asian American voters in Georgia (Noe-Bustamante and Budiman 2020). Local advocacy organizations found that about 55% of Asian American voters in Georgia supported Biden in the 2020 presidential election and over two-thirds supported the Democratic candidates in the senate run-off elections several months later (Asian Americans Advancing Justice-Atlanta and Asian American Advocacy Fund 2022; Asian American Legal Defense and Education Fund 2021).[2]

Asian American politicians and organizers in Georgia credited the Democratic candidates' victories to high turnout and strong Democratic support within the community. For example, in an interview with the *L.A. Times* ahead of the special elections, Sam Park, a Democrat in the Georgia state legislature, observed that "the surge in Asian American turnout—especially amongst first-time, younger Asian American voters—helped Biden flip the state. If Reverend Warnock and Jon Ossoff are to be successful, turnout amongst the Asian American community will be critical" (Jarvie and Haberkorn 2020). Neil Makhija, of Indian American Impact, went a step further in an interview with

---

[2] While the 2020 presidential election poll of Asian Americans in Georgia did not include a national origin breakdown, the AALDEF 2021 senate run-off poll included Indian American (23%), Korean American (29%), Vietnamese American (14%), Chinese American (13%), Bangladeshi American (8%), Pakistani American (4%), and other Asian American (8%) respondents (Asian American Legal Defense and Education Fund 2021).

Politico, stating: "The Democratic Party couldn't win the presidency or the Senate without Asian Americans" (Barrón-López 2020). Finally, Margaret Fung, the former executive director of the Asian American Legal Defense and Education Fund, noted, "Asian American voters played a critical role in electing Warnock and Ossoff in two extremely close races that will result in Democratic control of the US Senate. Asian American voters must no longer be ignored in the political process" (Asian American Legal Defense and Education Fund 2021). Fung's quote echoes the claims of political scientists who argue that both major parties have failed to engage contemporary immigrant groups and have ignored new voters who are finally exerting political power and influence in electoral politics (Hajnal and Lee 2011; Wong 2006).

While the 2020 Georgia run-offs represent a turning point in which mainstream political actors finally turned their attention to Asian American voters, that race offers just one example of how Asian Americans are transforming the dynamics of electoral politics in ways that may benefit candidates across the partisan spectrum. For example, news articles published before the 2018 midterm elections described Asian Americans as "the Democrats' fastest-growing new constituency," who may shape election outcomes in places like Southern California, Michigan, and Pennsylvania (Desai 2018; Merica 2018). In response to strong support for Democratic candidates among Asian American voters nationwide, Democrats formed Justice Unites Us, a new political action committee with plans to spend millions of dollars on mobilizing Asian Americans to vote for Democrats in future elections across the country (Seitz-Wald 2022).

However, Asian Americans do not uniformly support Democrats. In fact, they may be contributing to the victories of Republican candidates in some localities. For example, media accounts indicate that Asian American voters played an important role in electing Michelle Steel, a Korean American Republican, to Congress in Southern California's 45th district in a highly competitive race against Jay Chen, a Taiwanese American Democratic challenger, during the 2022 midterms (Lai 2022b). Although Representative Steel's district includes many older Vietnamese voters with ties to the Republican Party, her electoral success stands in contrast to expectations that Asian Americans would uniformly "turn Orange County blue" (Lai 2022b; Nyugen 2018).

Moreover, this example may reflect a broader national trend of movement toward Republicans at the margins in recent elections. In fact, analyses of Asian American voting patterns during the 2022 and 2024 election cycles indicate increases in Republican voting, especially in constituencies where Asian Americans make up a large majority of the population, such as Brooklyn's Chinatown and Westminster in Orange County, California, which falls within Representative Steel's congressional district (Leonhardt 2023; Stamm and Zitner 2022; Rubinstein and Chen 2024).

These dynamics highlight the complexities underlying the development of contemporary partisan preferences among Asian Americans, simultaneously reflecting a trend of Democratic support and challenging assumptions about the natural affinity of immigrant groups to the Democratic Party in the decades following the racial realignment of the political parties. In their foundational book *Issue Evolution: Race and the Transformation of American Politics*, Edward Carmines and James Stimson (1989) argue that both political parties historically held similar stances on race and civil rights, with Republicans taking somewhat more racially egalitarian positions. However, the parties realigned on these issues in the aftermath of the passage of the Civil Rights Act of 1964, which received strong support from President Lyndon Johnson and Democrats in Congress (Carmines and Stimson 1989).

Several scholars point to this moment as a "critical juncture" after which Democrats replaced Republicans as the more progressive party on racial issues in the post–1965 era (Abramowitz 2018; Carmines and Stimson 1989; McAdam and Kloos 2014). Although prior accounts center party leaders as the primary political actors driving this process, more recent work argues that party elites were responding to a longer-term grassroots shift in the core constituencies of the Democratic Party's coalition, which began as early as the 1930s (Lee 2002; Schickler 2016). This effort, primarily led by civil rights and labor activists, resulted in a diverse base of support for the Democratic Party, including African Americans, organized labor, Jewish people, and eventually other minority groups like Latinos and LGBTQ Americans (Schickler 2016; Proctor 2022). This historical coalition of Democratic minority groups was diverse but largely omitted Asian Americans, even as they were becoming politically active at the time (Le Espiritu 1992).

An important question as the American public diversifies is whether predominantly immigrant groups like Asian Americans will become incorporated into the contemporary Democratic Party's coalition of supporters. As Zoltan Hajnal and Taeku Lee (2011) describe in *Why Americans Don't Join the Party: Race, Immigration, and the Failure (of Political Parties) to Engage the Electorate*, the moment of "racial realignment" on civil rights issues coincided with the passage of the Immigration and Nationality Act of 1965, which fundamentally changed American immigration law and the demographic composition of immigrants entering the US. The shift from a quota-based system to a system prioritizing skilled labor, family reunification, and refugee resettlement allowed large numbers of Asian immigrants to enter the country after many years of exclusion, directly leading to the rapid growth and diversification of the Asian American community in the decades following (Hajnal and Lee 2011).

Although many Asian Americans and other immigrants entered the United States around the time of partisan racial realignment, their support for the Democratic Party was not a foregone conclusion (Hajnal and Lee 2011). In fact, in the period following World War II, both parties made inroads with immigrant groups as permissive immigration policies passed during periods of divided government (Tichenor 2002). For example, the Immigration Reform and Control Act of 1986 was passed by a Democratic majority in Congress and signed by President Ronald Reagan in a bipartisan effort (Calavita 1989). This bill made it illegal for employers to knowingly hire unauthorized workers but provided amnesty to tens of thousands of undocumented immigrants already in the country (Tichenor 2002). In the following election cycle, both parties briefly mentioned permissive immigration policies in their 1988 platforms, highlighting the potential for incorporating Asian Americans and other immigrants into their political constituencies ("1988 Democratic Party Platform" 2023; "Republican Party Platform of 1988" 2023). However, the parties have polarized sharply on immigration policy since the late 1980s (Khalid 2019).

As a growing ethno-racial minority group that supports Democrats in large numbers and is increasingly represented among elected officials, will Asian Americans become incorporated into the Democrat Party's political coalition? To what extent have their partisan views reflected the party realignment in the post–1965 era? While prior work centers "political capture" by the comparatively racially egalitarian Democratic Party as an explanation for Democratic support among other ethno-racial minority groups in the US, including African Americans, little is known about whether these accounts extend to Asian Americans (Frymer 2010; Frymer and Skrentny 1998).

Some scholars argue that as late as the mid-1990s and early 2000s, both parties faced electoral incentives not to include Asian Americans in their political coalitions. For example, Michael Chang's (2004) analysis of the 1996 "Asian Donorgate" scandal, a controversy regarding Democratic fundraising efforts allegedly orchestrated by China, points to the marginalization of Asian American political actors and campaign donors by both major parties because they were perceived as unassimilable foreigners (Chang 2004). Thomas Kim (2007, 4) builds on this work, arguing that "the political logic of the two-party system" compels party elites to strategically exclude Asian Americans, whose status as political and cultural outsiders is a liability, when it comes to building winning electoral coalitions.

Despite these exclusionary dynamics, research on Asian Americans' political preferences suggests that their views on a range of issues, including immigration, healthcare, education, and the economy align with the contemporary Democratic Party's policy stances, suggesting a clear fit into the Democrats' diverse coalition (Ramakrishnan 2016). However, Asian Americans' issue-based alignment with Democrats may not result in full incorporation into the party for several reasons. First, as described above, the Republican Party historically supported immigration reform and has made inroads with Asian American voters in recent years, suggesting that the Democratic trend in vote choice in this community may erode in the future. Second, both parties may also have incentives to strategically exclude Asian Americans from national political coalitions (Chang 2004; Kim 2007). Third, many Asian Americans who vote for Democratic candidates in elections do not identify as Democratic partisans, indicating that contemporary voting patterns may not translate into long-term attachments to the political party (Hajnal and Lee 2011; Phan and Garcia 2009). Moreover, large numbers of Asian American immigrants are not naturalized citizens and are thus ineligible to vote. For example, recent Census estimates indicate that over a quarter of Asian Americans living in the US are not American citizens (Monte and Shin 2022).[3]

These dynamics of contemporary Asian American politics raise several important questions for research in political science. First, does recent support for Democrats in places like Georgia reflect national trends in Asian American vote choice? If so, what explains these voting patterns? Why do most Asian American voters favor Democratic over Republican candidates in national elections? Moving beyond a narrow focus on voting, how do new Asian American immigrants, including those who are not eligible to vote, develop partisan preferences? What partisan options are available to Asian American noncitizens as they navigate a new political system that privileges the voting eligible? More broadly, how do Asian Americans make their vote choices and develop preferences for and attachments to the political parties at different stages in the process of immigrant incorporation?

This book comprehensively explores these questions, developing an explanation for political learning and partisan acquisition among diverse Asian American subgroups that centers social connections. This account of political learning, which I call the theory of social transmission, foregrounds the role of equal-status peer groups in local contexts in contrast to traditional explanations focusing on the family, political parties, and civic institutions. Next, I describe contemporary partisan trends in the Asian American community and national origin subgroups before offering a detailed overview of the theoretical account.

Trends in Vote Choice: Strong Support for Democrats with Recent Republican Inroads

National polls indicate that in the aggregate, most Asian American voters supported Democratic candidates over the past two decades, mirroring recent patterns in Georgia and many other localities across the country. According to English-language national exit polls conducted by a consortium of media

---

[3] This estimate applies to those who identify as Asian alone from a five-year American Community Survey (2017–2021) (Monte and Shin 2022).

companies and news divisions, most Asian Americans voted for Democratic candidates in every presidential election since 2000, although there has been some movement toward Republicans during the past few election cycles ("How Groups Voted" 2025).

Figure 1.2 shows the percentage of voters across the four major racial groups who voted for the Democratic candidate in the US in every presidential election since 1992. Focusing on Asian American vote share in recent elections, approximately 62% of Asian Americans voted for Barack Obama in 2008, 73% voted for Obama in 2012, 65% voted for Hillary Clinton in 2016, 61% voted for Joe Biden in 2020, and 55% voted for Kamala Harris in 2024.[4] While Asian American support for Republicans has increased over the past 12 years, these data indicate that Asian Americans have consistently voted for Democrats at much higher rates than white Americans and at comparable rates to other racial minorities since 2000 (Figure 1.2). Although there are questions about the extent to which English-language exit polls reflect the political attitudes of geographically concentrated minority groups, especially in the early years of exit polling focused on Asian Americans, a range of surveys and polls analyzed by *AAPI Data* confirm patterns of consistent support for Democrats and recent movement toward Republicans at the margins among Asian Americans (Ramakrishnan 2020; 2021).

Although the Asian American community is internally diverse, one factor uniting many of its national origin groups is that a majority of voters supported Democrats in recent national elections. Figure 1.3 presents the percentage of Asian Americans who voted for the Democratic presidential candidate in 2016 and 2020, separately for major national origin groups represented in national surveys which over-sampled Asian Americans. These include the 2020 Asian American Voter Survey (AAVS), the 2016 Collaborative Multi-Racial Post-Election Survey (CMPS), and the 2016 National Asian American Survey (NAAS) (AAPI Data 2020; Frasure et al. 2016; Ramakrishnan et al. 2016).

As Figure 1.3 shows, a majority of Bangladeshi American, Cambodian American, Chinese American, Filipino American, Indian American, Japanese American, Pakistani American, Korean American, and Vietnamese American respondents to the 2016 NAAS and 2016 CMPS reported voting for Clinton in 2016. A similar pattern held for the national origin groups surveyed in 2020. Across three surveys, Vietnamese American respondents to the 2020 AAVS were the only subgroup of Asian American voters for which a minority supported a Democratic candidate.

---

[4] Multilingual polls indicate that as many as 70% or even 80% of Asian Americans voted for the Democratic candidates in 2016 and 2020 (Asian American Legal Defense and Education Fund 2017; Asian American Legal Defense and Education Fund 2020). However, these polls were conducted in cities and states with rapidly growing Asian American populations and may not reflect the perspectives of Asian Americans nationwide (Ramakrishnan 2020).

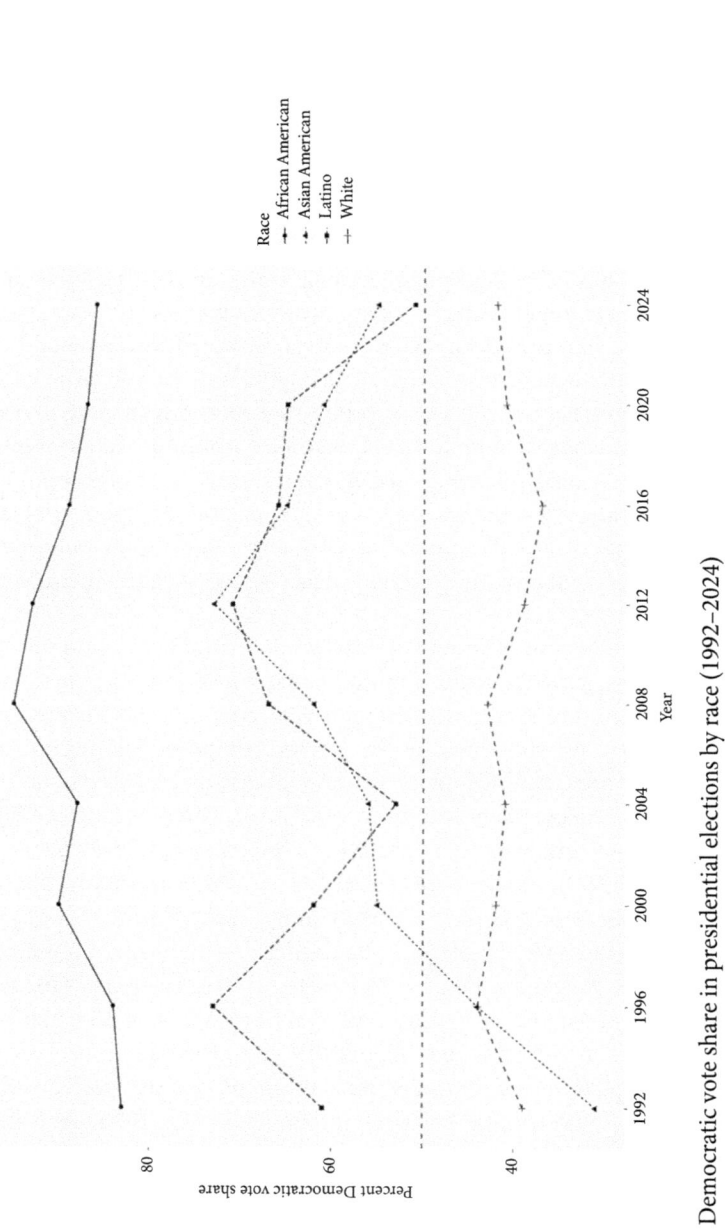

Figure 1.2 Democratic vote share in presidential elections by race (1992–2024)

Source: The data are drawn from national exit polls of Americans ("How Groups Voted" 2025). The timeseries begins in 1992, the first year in which national exit polling data were collected separately for Asian Americans. Between 1992 and 2000, the polls were conducted by "Voter Research and Surveys" (1992) and "Voter News Service" (1996 and 2000). Beginning in 2004, the polls were conducted by Edison Research for "The National Election Pool" and other national exit polls.

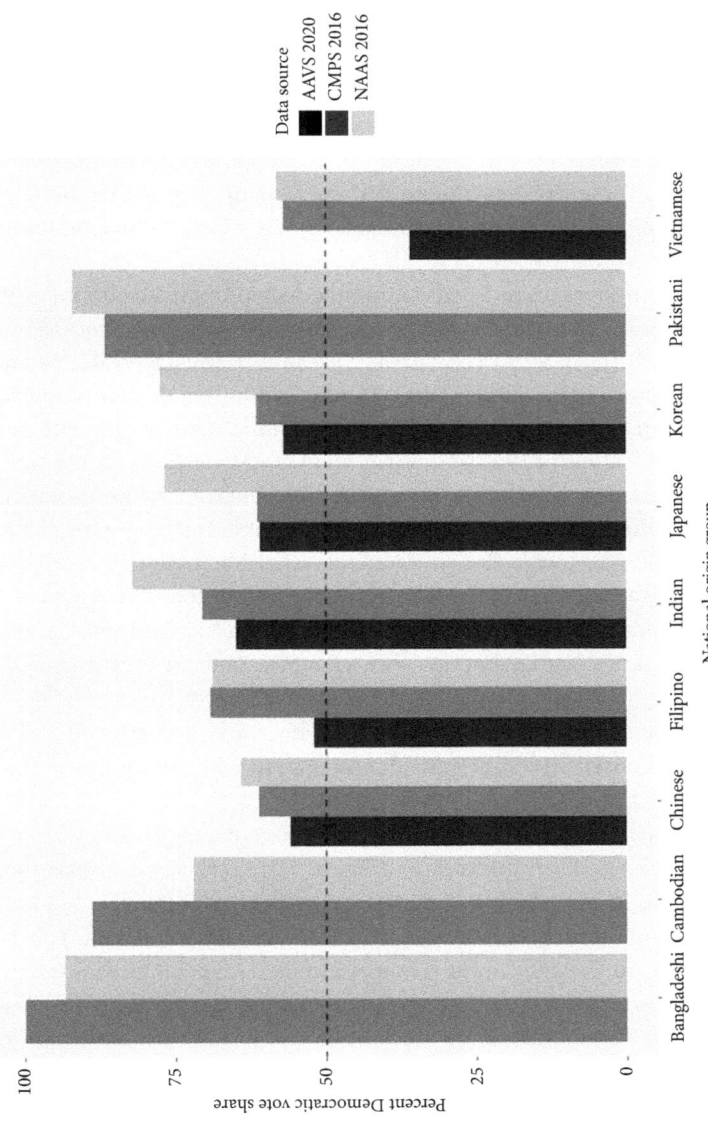

Figure 1.3 Democratic vote choice in 2016 and 2020 by Asian American national origin

Source: The data are drawn from the 2016 NAAS post-election survey, 2016 CMPS post-election survey, and 2020 AAVS pre-election survey. AAVS estimates reflect intended vote choice and are drawn from publicly available toplines (AAPI Data 2020). CMPS and NAAS estimates were calculated for respondents who voted in the 2016 presidential election (Frasure et al. 2016; Ramakrishnan et al. 2016).

Most Asian American voters support Democratic candidates in contemporary national elections. However, many Asian Americans—a group that also includes nonvoters and noncitizens—do not identify as Democratic partisans (Hajnal and Lee 2011; Phan and Garcia 2009). Foundational research conducted by Zoltan Hajnal and Taeku Lee (2011) indicates that Asian Americans identify with partisan labels at lower rates than African Americans and whites. Other research on Asian American political behavior confirms this point, finding lower rates of Democratic partisan identification than vote choice in national surveys of this diverse pan-ethnic community (Masouka et al. 2018; Raychaudhuri 2020; Wong et al. 2011). These findings suggest that the development of Democratic partisan leanings among Asian American voters may not translate into long-term partisan attachments.

Taken together, these partisan trends within the Asian American community reflect a puzzle worthy of further investigation. First, the strong and consistent voting preference for Democrats is surprising because in the aggregate, Asian Americans have some characteristics that typically lead to Republican support. For example, Asian Americans are a high socioeconomic status group with an average household income of $94,903 in 2020, compared to $67,521 for the typical American household (US Census Bureau 2020b).[5] In fact, Asian Americans have reported the highest average household income of all racial groups since the mid-1980s, when data were first collected for Asian Americans (US Census Bureau 2020b). Also, many Asian Americans immigrated to the US from countries with a communist or authoritarian history, including Vietnam and China. In turn, they may associate Democrats with extremist policies they migrated to escape (Lien et al. 2004). Finally, many Asian Americans are members of conservative religious denominations. For example, nearly a quarter identify as Evangelicals, a conservative Christian denomination with strong ties to the Republican Party (Wong 2018).

Second, accounting for national origin diversity does not unveil major within-group differences in partisan preferences (Figure 1.3). This suggests that the strong Democratic leaning within the Asian American community persists across a diverse range of subgroups from East, Southeast, and South Asia. Third, the movement toward Republicans in recent elections is surprising considering how discrimination against Asian Americans increased during the COVID-19 pandemic (Han et al. 2023). Prior work finds that social exclusion pushes Asian Americans toward the Democratic Party and would predict higher rates of Democratic support in 2020 and 2024 (Chan et al. 2022; Kuo et al. 2017).

---

[5] There is a great deal of variation in income across Asian American national origin subgroups (Budiman and Ruiz 2021c). To offer two examples highlighting this disparity, the median household income of Indian Americans was $112,000 per year in 2019, compared to $44,000 among Burmese Americans (Budiman and Ruiz 2021c).

These partisan trends raise the following questions. Why do many Asian Americans support Democrats despite relative economic prosperity, some conservative social predispositions, and high levels of internal diversity? In contrast, why do others within the community support Republicans in an era of increasing discrimination? To what extent do trends in Asian American vote choice and partisan support manifest into long-term partisan attachments? More generally, how do Asian Americans learn about American politics and develop partisan preferences? In this book, I consider and systematically answer these questions alongside those raised earlier in the chapter, analyzing the process of political learning within diverse Asian American immigrant communities.

The Social Transmission of Partisan Views in Peer Networks

The central argument of the book is that Asian Americans develop partisan views through interactions with peers in local contexts, which have varied partisan dynamics. This account, which I call the theory of social transmission, both builds on and departs from standard explanations of political socialization in the American context that are focused on the family and political parties[6] as well as recent explanations for Asian American partisanship rooted in experiences of discrimination and exclusion. In the empirical chapters, I test the social transmission account alongside alternative explanations, drawing evidence from in-depth interviews, large-scale national surveys of Asian American adults, a national panel survey of college students, and several original experiments. While I test these explanations for Asian Americans as a broad pan-ethnic group, where possible, I also break down the Asian American community by national origin and generational status to explore the extent to which social transmission applies to diverse subgroups.

The conventional wisdom about political socialization in the United States was developed over 50 years ago, well before the American electorate diversified across lines of race, ethnicity, and generational status. At the time, scholars argued that most people learned about American politics and developed partisan preferences through the influence of their parents in early childhood and young adulthood (Davies 1965; Greenstein 1965; Jennings and Niemi 1968; 1974; 1981). Despite the many changes in people's social environments and experiences over the course of their lives, scholars found that the partisan attachments developed early in life were nearly impervious to change (Campbell et al. 1960).

---

[6] In Chapter 2, I discuss research which centers the role of political parties in the development of political views for immigrants who arrived in the US in the first half of the twentieth century (Allswang [1977] 2019; Andersen 1979; Cornwell 1960). Recent scholarship suggests that the parties do little to mobilize contemporary Asian American immigrants (Hajnal and Lee 2011; Wong 2006).

Although developed half a century ago, these accounts of partisan acquisition apply quite well to the present-day cohort of US-born Americans whose parents were also raised in the United States (Jennings et al. 2009). However, the demographics of the American electorate have changed significantly since these explanations were developed, in large part due to immigration from Asia, Africa, the Caribbean, Latin America, and the Middle East. Currently, naturalized citizens account for one in every 10 eligible voters (Budiman et al. 2020). Many other new voters are the children of immigrants and represent the first generation of their families to come of age in the United States.

While theories of familial influence may explain the development of partisan attachments among Americans with long family histories in the United States, they may not extend to the growing number of voters from predominantly immigrant groups, including Asian Americans. I argue that social connections outside of the family play an important role in the process of political learning because many Asian Americans experience limited discussion of American politics at home during childhood, regardless of whether they grew up abroad or in the US (Carlos 2018; Hajnal and Lee 2011; Raychaudhuri 2018). This is because their parents may not have a deep understanding of the American political system or strong partisan attachments to pass along to their children (Hajnal and Lee 2011). Given a lack of political discussion with family during childhood, Asian Americans are open to the partisan influence of equal-status peers, extended family members, and other social contacts outside of the home. In turn, I argue that Asian Americans develop partisan views through interactions with such peers in local contexts, including neighborhoods, schools, colleges, workplaces, churches, and informal social gatherings. The empirical chapters offer evidence supporting these arguments.

Social transmission explains why many Asian Americans support Democrats despite background characteristics that typically predict Republican partisanship. This argument stems from an observation about residential settlement. Asian Americans tend to settle in liberal metropolitan areas, where they are more likely to interact with Democratic than Republican peers. For example, 55% of Asian Americans live in just five states: California, New York, Texas, New Jersey, and Washington (Budiman and Ruiz 2021b). Within these states, most Asian Americans live in suburban and urban neighborhoods in left-leaning metropolitan population centers (Gebeloff et al. 2021; Gelman 2012; Logan and Zhang 2013). This geographical context may shape Asian Americans' political socialization, providing pro-Democratic cues while they are still relatively unfamiliar with the political parties.

This explanation is also flexible enough to explain recent erosion in Democratic support and gains among Republicans. By this account, many Asian Americans vote for Democrats because they live in liberal social environments. However, those who live in conservative areas or are embedded into Republican social networks may develop pro-Republican views. Republican socialization is less common, since most Asian Americans settle in liberal communities. However, it is possible, especially if the partisan dynamics of Asian Americans' social networks reflect more conservative perspectives.[7] Moreover, because Asian Americans have weaker attachments to the political parties than others in their communities, they may be particularly responsive to changing partisan dynamics within local communities. This could explain shifts in partisanship that align with local (and in some cases national) dynamics.

Social transmission is a compelling explanation for the partisan socialization of Asian Americans because they are a predominantly immigrant group that gains little political exposure through the family across generations. The Pew Research Center estimates that 71% of Asian American adults (compared to just 17% of the general adult population) are first-generation immigrants (Budiman and Ruiz 2021b). In addition, many Asian Americans born in the United States are the direct descendants of immigrants. Data from the Pew Research Center indicates that Asian Americans account for nearly 12% of all second-generation Americans but less than 1% of third-generation Americans (*Second Generation Americans* 2013). Immigrants often enter local environments in the United States without partisan preferences passed down through their families. Their children's generation may have a similar experience, growing up in immigrant households with limited discussion of American politics, particularly during the formative years of early childhood and young adulthood (Kiang 2001). Therefore, interactions with peers in local contexts may be an important source of political information and partisan socialization across generations.

Since race is a central force shaping social experiences in the United States, the social transmission account also considers whether variation in the racial composition of Asian Americans' peer groups influences the development of partisan preferences. While peer political influence is a universal mechanism, I argue that the racial composition of peer groups varies across generations, with implications for political socialization.

Most Asian American immigrants have racially homogeneous social networks, primarily composed of other immigrants from their own national origin group (Ruiz et al. 2023b). For example, a 2023 survey conducted by the Pew Research Center found that 56% of Asian American immigrants reported that "all or most of their friends" are from their own ethnic group (Ruiz et al. 2023b). The percentage of Asian American immigrants with mostly co-ethnic friends increases to 60% among those who have been in the US for less than 10 years, but is only 10 percentage points lower, at 50%, among those who immigrated

---

[7] According to the Cooperative Election Study (CES), Democratic vote share in the 2016 and 2020 presidential elections in the average county in which Asian American respondents lived was 63% (Ansolabehere and Schaffner 2017; Schaffner et al. 2021).

over 20 years ago (Ruiz et al. 2023b). Accordingly, the social transmission account predicts that Asian American immigrants are most likely to learn about American politics and develop political views through interactions with Asian peers.

In contrast, Asian Americans who come of age in the US (e.g., transitional-, second-, and third-generation) have more diverse peer groups who they meet in education settings (Hitti et al. 2013). For example, just 38% of US-born Asian American respondents to the same Pew survey reported that most of their friends were from their own ethnic group (Ruiz et al. 2023b). Relatedly, research in psychology suggests that Asian Americans are more likely to develop cross-racial friendships than similarly positioned white and African Americans, particularly in college settings (Bowman and Park 2014; Tran and Lee 2011). Qualitative evidence from focus groups suggests that the children of Asian American immigrants are more open to establishing relationships with people from different racial groups than their parents' generation (Plummer et al. 2016). In line with these prior findings, the theory of social transmission predicts that the children and grandchildren of Asian American immigrants may learn about American politics and develop partisan views by interacting with both Asian and non-Asian peers.

In this book, I offer a systematic account of the development of Asian Americans' partisan views that explains both high levels of Democratic support and variation in partisanship based on patterns of residential settlement and social interaction among Asian Americans. This is notable against the backdrop of existing scholarship on this topic, which puts forward few theoretical explanations for partisan acquisition among Asian Americans. Some recent work explores whether racial discrimination leads Asian Americans to support Democrats (Chan et al. 2022; Hopkins et al. 2020; Kuo et al. 2017). However, this research results in mixed findings, suggesting that factors like discrimination, which may repel Asian Americans from the Republican Party, cannot fully explain Democratic voting trends. Moreover, explanations that center social exclusion or discrimination overlook factors that might attract Asian Americans to the Democratic Party. Social transmission is an important complement to existing theories because it considers how social experiences might draw Asian Americans toward each political party.

Defining and Understanding the Asian American Community

In the opening pages of this chapter, I define the Asian American community as a pan-ethnic group of people who trace their origin to countries in East Asia, South Asia, and Southeast Asia. As of the 2020 Census, an estimated

20.6 million people identified as Asian American alone, and 24 million people identified as Asian American in combination with some other race (Monte and Shin 2022). The six largest national origin groups are Chinese American, Indian American, Filipino American, Vietnamese American, Korean American, and Japanese American (Budiman and Ruiz 2021b). However, the Asian American community includes people from many other countries, such as Bangladesh, Pakistan, Taiwan, Cambodia, Laos, Malaysia, and Indonesia.

The pan-ethnic category of "Asian American" emerged through a process of coalition building across a diverse range of Asian ethnic groups. Much of this work was the product of political organizing by student activists in California in the 1960s who advocated for an ethnic studies curriculum that acknowledged their groups' histories and experiences (Le Espiritu 1992). These activists realized that individual Asian national origin groups were too small to be recognized on their own but found they could gain representation as a pan-ethnic community. Although the category of Asian American emerged within the group, many immigrants first learn about it when they arrive in the United States and perceive it as an ascribed identity (Võ 2004).

Currently, about 68% of all Asian American adults—including 83% of Indian American, 74% of Vietnamese American, 72% of Chinese American, 69% of Korean American, 61% of Filipino American, and 30% of Japanese American—are foreign-born (Ruiz et al. 2023b). These numbers indicate that immigrants comprise the majority of adults within many Asian American ethnic groups, which may have implications for political learning and partisan acquisition. Prior research finds that immigrants face many barriers to political incorporation, including the naturalization process, language access, a lack of exposure to the American political system, and low rates of civic education (Cho 1999, DeSipio 1996; Lien 1997; Ramakrishnan 2005; Wong 2006).

Despite these barriers, recent work shows that Asian American immigrants tend to vote at similar rates to their US-born counterparts (Ramakrishnan 2017). For example, in an analysis of Asian American turnout in 2016, Karthick Ramakrishnan (2017) finds that 52% of foreign-born and 48% of native-born Asian Americans voted in the presidential election. He explains that "this continues a pattern evident since the 2000 presidential election, and is largely related to the fact that, among Asian Americans who are eligible to vote, the native-born population is younger than the foreign-born population" (Ramakrishnan 2017). Despite the potential intervening role of age, this analysis highlights differences in voting eligibility and turnout rates across generations within the Asian American community.

As the previous discussion suggests, generational status is relevant to many of the analyses presented throughout the book. I use several terms to refer to the generational cohorts within the Asian American community. These include "first generation," "transitional generation," "second generation," and "third generation and beyond." "First generation" refers to immigrants who arrived in the US as adults. "Transitional generation" is a term I use in previous work to refer to immigrants who arrived in the US as children (Raychaudhuri 2018). "Second generation" refers to those born in the US with at least one foreign-born parent, and "third generation and beyond" refers to those with two US-born parents.

As described at the beginning of this chapter, Asian Americans are currently the fastest-growing racial group in the US. The Asian American population grew from 10.5 million to 18.9 million between 2000 and 2019 (Budiman and Ruiz 2021a). Turning to the future, demographers project that the Asian American population will reach nearly 36 million by 2060 (Budiman and Ruiz 2021a). Much of this growth is fueled by immigration, as most Asian Americans are first-generation immigrants, but the population of Asian Americans born in the US is also growing steadily (Vespa et al. 2018).

While the Asian American community is internally diverse, meaningful generalizations can be drawn about the group's political behavior because subgroups within the community share several common experiences. First, "Asian" or "Asian American" is a commonly used racial category and the primary racial identity choice for people of Asian descent on many official forms, regardless of country of origin (Junn and Masuoka 2008). Second, nearly all ethnic groups within the Asian American community are primarily composed of immigrants and children of immigrants. Third, upon arriving in the United States, many Asian American immigrants settle in metropolitan areas (Logan and Zhang 2013). Finally, Asian Americans experience common patterns of racialization. Across national origin groups, Asian Americans are often stereotyped as hard-working "model minorities" who are more successful than other minority groups but are still seen as outsiders who are unable to assimilate into American culture (Kim 1999). Taken together, these points of commonality suggest that although "Asian American" may not be the main locus of personal identity for most members of the community, it is a relevant social and racial marker with important political implications (Lien et al. 2004).

Chapter Outline

This book explores the process of partisan acquisition among Asian Americans using varied forms of evidence and diverse methodological approaches. I draw evidence from in-depth qualitative interviews of Asian American citizens and noncitizens, cross-sectional national surveys of Asian Americans, a national two-wave survey of college students, and original survey experiments. I use a multimethod approach to investigate Asian American partisanship despite challenges associated with studying "hard-to-survey" populations, including immigrants and ethno-racial minorities (Tourangeau et al. 2014). The chapters complement each other and collectively offer a comprehensive examination of the research questions.

To briefly summarize the structure of the book, the chapters in Part I (Chapters 2 through 4) present the central argument and explore whether local partisan context and political discussion with peers and family members influence Asian Americans' partisan views using evidence from national surveys[8] and in-depth interviews. The chapters in Part II (Chapters 5 and 6) build on the foregoing findings with a case study exploring whether Asian Americans who come of age in the US develop partisan views through the influence of peers in college.[9] Chapter 7 concludes the book with a discussion of implications for various aspects of American politics. I describe each chapter in further detail below.

Chapter 2 presents the theory of social transmission and describes its implications for the development of Asian Americans' partisan preferences. This argument is presented in relation to standard explanations for partisan political socialization in American politics which focus on the family and political institutions, as well as social exclusion, the dominant theory offered to explain Asian Americans' partisan views in recent work. I use in-depth interviews with a diverse group of Asian American citizens in mixed-partisan Houston to inductively develop the theory and illustrate the key mechanisms underlying the argument. These include limited discussion of American politics at home during childhood and peer partisan influence in local environments.[10] The interviews also illustrate how the racial composition of Asian Americans' peer groups varies across generations and the implications of these differences for partisan acquisition. The experiences of political socialization reflected in the interviews provide a detailed picture of the mechanisms that may drive social

---

[8] These include an existing nationally representative survey, the 2008 National Asian American Survey (Ramakrishnan et al. 2008), and an original national survey of Asian Americans called the 2020 Omnibus Asian American Survey (Leung et al. 2020). These surveys are useful because they represent the perspectives of Asian Americans nationwide and include questions about social and political experiences.

[9] College students are a useful population for this research because most Asian Americans raised in the US attend college, an important setting for social interaction with peer groups (Digest of Education Statistics 2023).

[10] Houston is a useful case for studying Asian American political socialization because it has a large Asian American population but is mixed in terms of partisanship, unlike many other cities with large Asian American populations, which are strongly Democratic (AAPI Data 2022). I use evidence from qualitative interviews to develop the theory because these data offer detailed personal accounts of political learning and partisan acquisition.

transmission, complementing the empirical breadth of the quantitative analyses with theoretical depth.

Next, Chapter 3 provides the first empirical test of the theory, exploring whether local partisan norms influence Asian Americans' voting decisions. This chapter tests the hypothesis that living in predominantly Democratic areas increases Asian Americans' likelihood of voting for Democrats, relative to living in Republican areas. Analyses of over 2000 likely voters who responded to the 2008 NAAS demonstrate that living in majority-Democratic counties significantly increased Asian Americans' likelihood of voting for Obama in the 2008 presidential election. This relationship between local context and vote choice holds when accounting for a range of potential alternative explanations including local Asian American population size and across the six largest national origin subgroups within the Asian American community.

Chapter 4 explores the individual-level mechanisms that drive the powerful effects of local partisan context on vote choice within the Asian American community. This chapter directly compares peer influence—the book's hypothesized mechanism of partisan socialization—to familial influence, the mechanism of partisan acquisition presented in established accounts. Analyses of an original national survey of over 1500 Asian Americans indicates that across generations and ethnic groups, Asian Americans discuss American politics more frequently with peers during adulthood than with family during childhood. In turn, discussing American politics with peers shapes partisan views, typically increasing support for Democrats among Asian Americans. This suggests that peers substitute for the family in the process of partisan socialization. This chapter also shows that the racial composition of politically formative peer groups varies across generations, as the theory of social transmission predicts.

Chapter 5 explores whether Asian Americans who were raised in the US but received limited political information from their parents develop political views through interactions with college peers. One prediction I consider is whether Asian American students are open to political influence from non-Asian peers, who enter college with political views developed through the family. I test this expectation using a large nationwide longitudinal survey of Asian American, African American, Latino, and white college students. These data come from a two-wave survey, which interviews students at the beginning and end of college. I first demonstrate that Asian Americans (as well as African Americans and Latinos) enter college with less crystallized views than their white peers. Next, I show that social interactions with non-Asian peers shift the political orientations of Asian Americans in a liberal direction. In contrast, interacting with peers of a different race is not strongly associated with changes in the political views of African American and Latino students. Among white students, interactions with nonwhite peers also push political orientations in a liberal direction, but to a lesser degree. I supplement this analysis with a short follow-up focused on a diverse group of young Americans using evidence from the 2016 CMPS.

Chapter 6 details the results of original experiments that offer a direct causal test of social transmission. Does receiving partisan cues endorsed by peer networks influence Asian Americans' partisan views, compared to similar partisan messages without a social endorsement? The experiments test whether learning that many other undergraduate students at their university support a policy proposal attributed to either the Democratic or Republican Party makes Asian American college students express support for the party and policy in question. The experiments were conducted with Asian American and non-Asian students at a large public university and over 200 colleges nationwide. Participants were presented with an infographic treatment describing a policy to make higher education more affordable. I randomly manipulated if the policy proposal was attributed to Democrats or Republicans and whether the infographic stated that most undergraduates on campus supported the proposal. Across both studies, comparing the impact of the infographic with and without the peer group endorsement offers evidence of peer partisan influence when the policy was attributed to Republicans. This suggests that peer endorsements shape Asian Americans' partisan views and may contribute to recent voting patterns. Moreover, the peer influence effect is weaker among non-Asians, suggesting that Asian Americans are particularly open to partisan cues from peers. These studies complement the observational analyses with causal evidence of social transmission.

Chapter 7 broadens the lens, drawing conclusions from the book's findings and discussing its implications for political mobilization, the future of electoral politics, and politics outside the Asian American community. This chapter draws several conclusions based on the book's findings. First, it sums up the key empirical takeaways and discusses the implications for understanding Asian American partisan choices. Second, it considers the practical implications of this research as it relates to campaigns and political organizations that intend to mobilize Asian Americans. Third, it discusses the implications of this research for the future of Asian American political incorporation as the voting-eligible population grows. Finally, it considers the extent to which social transmission offers a compelling explanation for political socialization among other groups, including Latinos and LGBTQ youth.

Conclusion

Returning to the example of the 2021 senate run-off election in Georgia, Asian Americans are playing an increasingly important role in American electoral politics. In recent elections, many Asian American voters have supported Democratic candidates and contributed to close Democratic victories. Yet there has been a small but noticeable rightward shift in voting patterns over the past few years, particularly in areas with large Asian American populations (Stamm and Zitner 2022; Leonhardt 2023). Moreover, several high-profile Asian American political candidates, including Nikki Haley and Vivek Ramaswamy, emerged as stars in the 2024 Republican presidential primary, though some co-ethnic voters were ambivalent about their candidacies (Ulloa 2023).

As this group becomes a critical electoral constituency, political scientists must be able to explain how Asian Americans think about politics and contribute to American political life, whether they are recent immigrants, naturalized citizens, or born in the United States. Why do Asian American voters favor Democratic or Republican candidates? To what extent are Asian Americans' political views represented by the major parties? Why should Asian Americans, not just those who are citizens and voters, identify with the Democratic Party or Republican Party? Do similar patterns apply across diverse subgroups within the Asian American community?

This book offers one of the first comprehensive accounts exploring these questions, developing and testing a theory of Asian American voting behavior and partisan acquisition that explains strong support for Democrats within this diverse, pan-ethnic community. More generally, it provides insight into how political socialization works within a predominantly immigrant community. To that end, this book has implications for understanding Asian American political behavior, political learning in immigrant communities within and beyond the Asian American community, and electoral politics in a diversifying nation.

The findings also offer insights to political candidates and campaigns as the Asian American community grows into a political force. As Janelle Wong articulates in her foundational book *Democracy's Promise: Immigrants and American Civic Institutions* (2006, 5), "today's immigrants will become tomorrow's citizens and voters," and "America's mainstream political parties are missing an opportunity to win these people over as constituents." Almost two decades later, some senatorial and presidential candidates facing tight elections are heeding this warning, attempting to mobilize Asian Americans through a variety of methods, including targeted campaign ads, hiring AAPI campaign staff, and specialized meetings and events (Kenny et al. 2020; Venkatraman 2023).

A practical implication of this work is that candidates may mobilize these new constituents by drawing on a diverse range of social networks and peer groups in Asian Americans' local communities. By engaging trusted peer networks in immigrant social networks, church groups, and student groups on college campuses, political parties, candidates, and civic organizations may engage Asian Americans from diverse generational and national origin groups as they exercise their political power.

PART I
LOCAL CONTEXT, PEER INFLUENCE, AND ASIAN AMERICAN PARTISAN PREFERENCES

The chapters in the first part of the book present a detailed overview of the social transmission account and explore whether Asian Americans develop partisan preferences through the influence of peers in local contexts. These chapters draw on a range of empirical evidence, including in-depth qualitative interviews and national surveys.

What factors shape political learning and the development of partisan views among Asian Americans? How does this process compare to long-standing explanations for political socialization in research on American politics? Do local partisan norms shape Asian Americans' vote choices in contemporary elections? What role do peer groups and family members play in the development of Asian Americans' partisan preferences? How do these patterns vary across subgroups within the Asian American community? Part I explores these questions, inductively developing the theoretical account and testing it using evidence from large-scale national surveys of diverse Asian American communities.

2
Social Transmission and the Partisan Influence of Peers

Immigrants and their children present a distinctive case when it comes to political learning and partisan acquisition. In this chapter, I argue that peer groups in local contexts play a central role in the political socialization of Asian Americans. As Alexander Kuo, Neil Malhotra, and Cecilia Mo note in their article "Social Exclusion and Political Identity": "Immigrant political identity does not fit neatly within existing paradigms of American political behavior, such as theories that conceive of party identification as largely a product of early socialization or parental attitudes" (2017, 17). As this observation suggests, the process of partisan acquisition among first- and second-generation Asian Americans departs from the predictions of standard theories, which center the family during childhood, political parties, and civic institutions.

Since existing explanations cannot fully explain this divergence from standard accounts of political socialization, new theories are required to understand partisan acquisition in the Asian American community. This chapter initiates this process, bridging existing research on political socialization in the United States with insights about the social and political experiences of diverse Asian American groups. The argument centers the role of social interactions and political discussion with equal-status peer groups in local contexts, an explanation for political learning in immigrant communities that has received limited attention in extant political science literature.

In this chapter, I present a detailed overview of social transmission, a new explanation for political learning in the Asian American community.[1] By this account, Asian Americans develop partisan preferences through social interactions with peers in local environments. This process often leads to Democratic partisan views as a byproduct of Asian American settlement patterns. Many Asian Americans reside in liberal local environments where they primarily interact with peers who support Democrats rather than Republicans. However, when Asian Americans settle in conservative local environments or become integrated

---

[1] This chapter is derived in part from my article published in *Politics, Groups, and Identities* (Raychaudhuri 2018).

into conservative social networks, the theory predicts that social influence from peer groups leads to Republican views.

Although I argue the social transmission account applies across the Asian American community, there may be differences in how peer partisan influence operates across generational and national origin subgroups within it. First, there are important differences in the racial composition of Asian Americans' peer groups across immigrant generations. Asian American immigrants mostly interact with other immigrants from their own ethnic group, while those who are raised in the United States develop more racially diverse social networks (Mok et al. 2007; Qian et al. 2001; *Second-Generation Americans* 2013; Zhou and Xiong 2005).

There also may be differences in the extent to which this explanation applies across national origin groups. I argue that the social transmission account applies most readily to rapidly growing Asian American ethnic subgroups with large immigrant populations, such as Indian Americans and Chinese Americans (Budiman and Ruiz 2021b). In contrast, peer groups may play a less prominent role in political socialization for more acculturated subgroups, such as Japanese Americans, who are well established in the US and may develop political attitudes through the family (Budiman and Ruiz 2021b).

This chapter begins with a brief overview of research on the development of partisan identities among ethno-racial minorities and immigrants in the United States. Next, I discuss the book's theoretical contributions in relation to a rich literature on Asian American civic engagement, vote choice, and partisan acquisition. Third, I outline the major existing explanations for political socialization in the United States, which center the family during childhood, political parties, candidate-centric campaigns, and community organizations. After situating the book's contribution in existing literature, I present the theory of social transmission and several hypotheses focused on how Asian Americans develop partisan views. I present a general overview of this theoretical perspective and consider the extent to which it applies across generations and national origin groups. I also consider how a range of factors related to immigrant socialization, such as age, length of residency, country of origin, reasons for migration, political transnationalism, and pre-migration socialization shape this process.

Throughout this discussion, I use in-depth interviews conducted with Asian American residents of Houston, Texas to illustrate the mechanisms underlying the main argument. Houston is a useful case because it has a large and diverse Asian American population but is mixed in terms of partisanship, unlike most coastal immigrant hubs which are solidly Democratic. Houston's partisan composition also reduces concerns about residential selection. Given the mix of partisan perspectives represented in Houston, people are unlikely to settle in this area because it is a strongly Democratic environment. The in-depth interviews allowed for inductive theory building, a method used to develop rich theoretical arguments in the social sciences (Anoll 2022; Charmaz and Belgrave 2012; Mosley 2013). Subsequent chapters test this account using a diverse range of empirical evidence.

The Development of Partisanship among Ethno-Racial Minorities and Immigrants in the US

Foundational research on the development of partisanship among ethno-racial minorities focuses on the African American community. Much of this work centers social connections. In the landmark book *Behind the Mule: Race and Class in African-American Politics,* Michael Dawson (1995) argues that African Americans remain unified in their partisan choices despite increasing socioeconomic diversity due to perceptions of shared group interests. This in turn leads many Black voters to make political decisions based on their perceptions of what is best for their racial group, which they use as a proxy for their individual interests. While the book aims to explain strong contemporary support for Democrats in the Black community, Dawson (1995) notes that this group-based dynamic also explains African American support for the Republican Party after emancipation, and for third parties during moments when the major parties ignored the interests of African American constituents. Recently, Ismail White and Cheryl Laird revisit this question in *Steadfast Democrats: How Social Forces Shape Black Political Behavior* and claim that "racialized social constraint" or pressure from tightly knit African American social networks, rather than perceptions of shared fate, leads Black voters to support Democrats in the contemporary period (2020, 15).

These explanations for partisan identification are rooted in the distinctive history of discrimination, group marginalization, and strong sense of community among African Americans (McClain et al. 2009). However, there is mixed evidence about whether concepts like group consciousness and linked fate translate neatly to pan-ethnic minority communities or explain political behavior among Latinos and Asian Americans (see Masuoka 2006; Junn and Masuoka 2008; McClain et al. 2009; Sanchez and Masuoka 2010; Sanchez and Vargas 2016; Wong et al. 2005).

Research on partisan acquisition among other ethno-racial minorities also considers a full range of partisan options, including nonaffiliation. For example, in *Why Americans Don't Join the Party: Race, Immigration, and the Failure (of Political Parties) to Engage the Electorate,* Zoltan Hajnal and Taeku Lee (2011) explore the development of partisan attachments across the four major ethnoracial groups in the US. The authors argue that partisanship is the product of "social identity, information, and ideology," factors which each have a different relationship with partisan acquisition across racial groups (2011, 21). For members of immigrant groups, accessing political information and developing an understanding of how their social identities or ideological perspectives translate into the American context requires political learning.

The authors find higher rates of identification as nonpartisan (e.g., Independent) and nonidentification with any partisan label among Latinos and Asian Americans than other racial groups, which they attribute to differences in the process of partisan acquisition for immigrant groups (Hajnal and Lee 2011). In turn, once Latinos and Asian Americans gain access to enough information about politics to develop attachments to a particular party, they make choices between parties based on ideological and identity-based concerns. Although some unaffiliated Latinos and Asian Americans do not vote, many vote for major party candidates, and very few support third party candidates (ibid. 267). These patterns extend to Native Americans and may lead to the adoption of partisan identities later in life among second-generation Latinos and Asian Americans (Carlos 2018; Koch 2017).

Despite high rates of nonaffiliation among Asian Americans and Latinos, many scholars explore the factors that drive partisanship in immigrant communities and propose a range of explanations. I briefly outline the robust literature on Latino partisanship and vote choice before discussing research on Asian American political behavior and partisan acquisition at length.

Although there is variation in partisan preferences within Latino communities, a majority vote for Democrats in most national elections, with recent movement toward Republicans ("How Groups Voted," 2025). One major explanation for the acquisition of partisanship (and often, for Democratic identification) among Latinos is immigrant incorporation, measured in terms of generational status and time spent in the US (Abrajano and Alvarez 2010; Cain et al. 1991; DeSipio 1996; Dutwin et al. 2005; Yang and de la Garza 2017). Others show that restrictive immigration policies pushed Latinos to support Democrats (Bowler et al. 2006; Street et al. 2015). Alternatively, Angel Saavedra Cisneros (2017) argues that social identity and economic policy views attract Latinos to Democrats. Yet other explanations include national origin, issue positions, local partisan context, and religious identification (Alvarez and Bedolla 2003; Fernandez and Dempsey 2017; Kelly and Kelly 2005; Segura 2012; Valenzuela 2014). Recent work suggests that class dynamics and ideological views contributed to a recent shift in Latino voting toward Republicans (Fraga et al. 2025). Literature on Asian Americans comports with some of these accounts and diverges with others.

Asian American Political Behavior: Questions of Civic Engagement and Partisanship

This book also builds on a rich tradition of scholarship on political behavior in the Asian American community.[2] As Pei-te Lien, Christian Collet, Janelle Wong, and Karthick Ramakrishnan describe in a foundational article, existing research addresses a range of questions related to civic engagement, including "How active are Asian Americans in the political process? What factors account for their involvement? What explains the 'puzzle' of low participation?" (2001, 625).

Several early studies show that Asian Americans turnout to vote at low levels, which is surprising given high levels of socioeconomic status and educational attainment in the community at large (Cho 1999; Jo and Roskin 1990; Junn 1999; Lien 1997; Nakanishi 2001; Rim 2009a). An important conclusion from this body of research is that socioeconomic theories of participation do not fully explain Asian American political engagement. Pei-te Lien and her co-authors (2001) highlight this contribution and argue that institutional barriers to voting and engagement in nonvoting political activities must be considered in future work.

To that end, subsequent research highlights barriers to political participation, civic engagement beyond voting, and diversity among Asian Americans. For example, Paul Ong and David Lee (2001) argue that the changing demographic profile of Asian Americans—from mostly US-born to foreign-born—led to a decline in voter turnout from the 1980s to the 2000s. In a case study of participation in 2006 immigration rallies, Kathy Rim (2009) finds that Asian Americans were less likely to protest than Latinos because they lacked political recruitment networks.

In their landmark book *Asian American Political Participation: Emerging Constituents and Their Political Identities* Janelle Wong, Karthick Ramakrishnan, Taeku Lee, and Jane Junn (2011) use the 2008 National Asian American Survey (NAAS) to comprehensively explore questions about Asian American civic engagement and partisanship. The authors analyze involvement in a range of political activities, including "voting, political donations, contacting government officials, working with others in one's community to solve a problem, and protest" (Wong et al. 2011, 20). In a wide-ranging exploration that includes nuanced analyses across national origin groups, they test the argument that Asian American political participation is shaped by "immigrant socialization;

---

[2] Janelle Wong and Karthick Ramakrishnan's (2023) annual review piece, "Asian Americans and the Politics of the Twenty-First Century," offers a detailed overview of research on Asian American politics as it relates to history, political behavior, and racialization.

residential contexts; party identification, mobilization, and political orientation; racial identity formation; and membership and involvement in civic associations" (27).

Yet other work indicates that claims of Asian American nonparticipation may be overstated. For example, when restricting analyses to registered voters, Asian Americans turn out at higher rates than non-Hispanic whites (Lien 2004a). In a get out the vote experiment, Janelle Wong (2005) finds that Asian Americans contacted by political organizations voted at higher rates than those who were not contacted. A rich line of research shows Asian Americans actively participated in historical protest activities (Le Espiritu 1992; Lien 2001; Nakanishi and Lai 2003; Nakanishi 2009). In addition, research focused on ethnic subgroups, such as Hmong Americans, indicates that they vote at higher rates than other Asian Americans, suggesting that social connections within Hmong communities cultivate a tradition of civic engagement (Wong 2017). Turning to contemporary electoral politics, Asian American turnout has increased substantially in recent elections as the voting-eligible population grows (Montanaro 2021; Ramakrishnan 2021).

A related strand of research focused on the representation of ethno-racial minorities in political office conveys that minority candidates often mobilize voters with a shared racial or ethnic identity. For example, Black and Latino candidates are most likely to be elected in districts where many residents are from their own ethno-racial group (Casellas 2010; Hardy-Fanta et al. 2016; Lublin et al. 2009). A similar logic may apply to Asian Americans, although Asian American political officials are particularly likely to represent districts with diverse minority populations or socially incorporated Asian American populations (Lai et al. 2001; Lien and Filler 2022; Kistner and Raychaudhuri 2025; Lublin and Wright 2024). The increased participation of co-ethnic voters may explain the link between district demographics and the election of minority candidates (Barreto 2007). For example, several behavioral studies find that Asian American voters are particularly likely to vote for AAPI candidates, particularly when they are from the same national origin group (Leung 2022; Sadhwani 2022).

Taken together, this research indicates that Asian Americans are an increasingly active political constituency that can be mobilized by political organizations, campaigns, and co-ethnic candidates. In turn, recent work has shifted from explaining nonparticipation to understanding how Asian Americans become politically engaged (Chan 2021; Chan et al. 2024; Wong and Ramakrishnan 2023). Next, I discuss existing research on vote choice and partisan identification in the Asian American community, the central outcomes of interest in this book.

A Democratic Trend in Asian American Vote Choice and Partisan Identification

Historical data indicate that in the aggregate, Asian Americans shifted from voting majority Republican to majority Democratic between the 1990s and 2000s (see Figure 1.2 in Chapter 1). While approximately 30% of Asian Americans voted for Clinton in 1992,[3] Democratic support increased steadily until nearly 75% of Asian Americans voted for Obama in 2012. Although the trend of Democratic vote choice persists, there has been an increase in voting for Republicans during the past decade. Research on voting trends in the Asian American community has focused on explaining these patterns in vote choice at different points in time.

For example, local studies conducted in California, as Asian American voting patterns were evolving in the 1990s and 2000s, conclude that national origin was an important predictor of Asian Americans' partisan preferences. For example, analyses of survey data on partisan identification in California show that Asian Americans who immigrated from countries with a communist or authoritarian history, like China and Vietnam, were more likely to identify as Republicans than those from democratic countries (Cain et al. 1991). In another study, Wendy Tam Cho and Bruce Cain (2001) characterize California Asian Americans as "median voters" without a strong preference for Democrats or Republicans.

Turning to nationwide trends, national surveys, including the 2000–2001 Pilot National Asian American Political Survey (PNAAPS), the 2008 and 2016 National Asian American Surveys (NAAS), the 2016 Collaborative Multiracial Post-Election Study (CMPS), and the 2020 Asian American Voter Survey (AAVS), provide a nuanced understanding of Asian Americans' partisan preferences. These surveys show a Democratic trend in vote choice for the community as a whole and across nearly all national origin subgroups since the early 2000s (AAPI Data 2020; Frasure et al. 2016; Lien 2001; Ramakrishnan et al. 2008; 2016).[4]

It is important to note that Democratic partisan identification lags Democratic vote choice among Asian Americans. For example, Pei-te Lien and her co-authors (2001) found that about 36% of Asian American respondents to the 2000–2001 PNAAPS identified as Democrats, and highlighted high rates of nonidentification. In *Asian American Political Participation*, Janelle Wong and

---

[3] Exit poll results from the 1990s are drawn from small (and likely unrepresentative) samples of Asian American voters using English-only instruments.
[4] See Figures 1.2 and 1.3 for more detailed discussion of voting trends across the Asian American community and key national origin subgroups.

her co-authors (2011) state that "the modal respondent" to the [2008] NAAS does not identify in partisan terms, a finding that applies across national origin groups but is higher among recent immigrants and the less educated (131–35). This point is echoed in other work (Hajnal and Lee 2011; Phan and Garcia 2009). As discussed in detail above, Zoltan Hajnal and Taeku Lee (2011) corroborate this claim, arguing that partisan acquisition is a multistage process that involves developing familiarity with the party labels prior to forming attachments to a particular party.

Several studies use national surveys to analyze Asian American partisan preferences, offering insight on the factors associated with Democratic voting and partisanship. For example, in a foundational study using the 2000–2001 PNAAPS, Pei-te Lien, Margaret Conway, and Janelle Wong (2004) find that region, linked fate with other Asian Americans, political interest, and ideology predict Democratic vote choice (121). In a detailed analysis of partisanship using the 2008 NAAS, Janelle Wong and her co-authors (2011) show that education and generational status shape whether Asian Americans identify with any party but do little to predict the direction of partisan acquisition (141). In a model directly comparing predictors of Democratic and Republican identification, the authors find that Asian American Republicans are more likely to be older, male, high income, American citizens, who have lived in the United States for many years (144).

In more recent work, Natalie Masuoka and her co-authors (2018) analyze the influence of various factors on support for Hillary Clinton in 2016 among Asian Americans using data from that year's CMPS. Their results indicate that voters who follow media coverage and have high levels of political efficacy were more likely to vote for Clinton (203). Taken together, these studies provide an in-depth profile of Asian American partisan preferences using high quality survey data. However, few consistent predictors of partisanship emerge across studies, making it difficult to draw strong conclusions about what drives these partisan trends.

An emergent strand of research investigates whether experiences of discrimination lead Asian Americans to support Democrats. These theories of social exclusion predict that experiencing discrimination leads Asian Americans to support Democrats, who they perceive as the more racially inclusive party in the contemporary period. Alexander Kuo, Neil Malhotra, and Cecilia Mo (2017) subject this argument to a causal test in a lab experiment that randomly exposed Asian American college students to a microaggression, asking them to confirm their US citizenship status prior to participating in the study. The authors find that Asian Americans exposed to the microaggression were more likely to express pro-Democratic attitudes than those who were not, relative to their white peers. Using panel data, Nathan Chan, Jae Yeon Kim, and Vivien Leung (2022) offer evidence that anti-Asian messages from Republican political elites during the

COVID-19 pandemic pushed Asian Americans to vote for Biden. Others show that perceptions of racial discrimination were associated with Democratic vote choice in 2020 (Chan et al. 2024).

In contrast, Dan Hopkins and his co-authors (2020) do not find a causal link between racial discrimination and Democratic preferences among Asian Americans. Multiple studies conducted on student and national samples provide no evidence that exposure to an article describing discrimination against Asian Americans influences partisanship or a range of alternative measures. Furthermore, the partisan views of Asian Americans have been stable between 2016 and 2020, despite increasing anti-Asian discrimination (Hopkins et al. 2023).

There are several potential explanations for these divergent findings. First, Hopkins et al. (2020) speculate that personal experiences of discrimination, rather than information about discrimination against Asian Americans as a pan-ethnic group, drive partisan preferences. Second, perhaps Asian Americans do not associate experiences of discrimination with their status as racial minorities. For example, Paul Ong and David Lee (2001) claim that "although Asian immigrants do experience discrimination, many attribute that discrimination to cultural and linguistic differences rather than race" (165). If Asian Americans are reluctant to identify instances of discrimination as linked to their racial identity, it is unlikely that these experiences alone lead to a rejection of the Republican Party on the premise of racial exclusion.

While this scholarship provides important insights into Asian American partisan acquisition, it leaves several aspects unexplored. Survey-based studies point to a range of demographic and political factors associated with Asian Americans' partisan views but offer few systematic explanations for these relationships. Also, recent studies that test theories of social exclusion offer mixed evidence, suggesting that discrimination alone cannot fully explain partisan trends among Asian Americans. Most importantly, existing research has not fully considered how exposure to the American political system influences the development of partisan preferences among Asian Americans. Accounting for the process of political learning in explanations of partisan acquisition is particularly important for Asian Americans because they are a predominantly immigrant constituency with limited prior exposure to American politics during childhood and young adulthood (Hajnal and Lee 2011).

Put in other terms, Asian American partisan acquisition implicates a process of political learning which may be distinctive to dynamics within immigrant families. To fully understand partisan acquisition among Asian Americans, it is important to consider the broader process of immigrant political socialization. Next, I draw on existing research on the role of the family, political parties, and local social ties in partisan acquisition as well as in-depth interviews with Asian Americans in Houston to develop one such account.

The Role of the Family in Standard Accounts of Political Learning and Partisan Acquisition

Scholars of American politics have long argued that the family plays a central role in partisan acquisition (Davies 1965; Greenstein 1965; Hyman 1959). Furthermore, partisan views developed during childhood and young adulthood are unlikely to change over the course of an individual's life (Berelson et al. 1954; Campbell et al. 1960). Another strand of empirical literature offers evidence of the intergenerational transmission of partisan attitudes within families. Across several longitudinal surveys, Kent Jennings and Richard Niemi uncover strong correlations between views expressed parents and children on political outcomes like partisan identification and vote choice (1968; 1974; 1981). Other scholars also provide evidence of intergenerational partisan transmission using panel surveys of parents and children (Hess and Torney 1967; Niemi et al. 1978).

Recent studies return to the role of the family in political socialization with increasing methodological sophistication. For example, in a follow-up to Kent Jennings and Richard Niemi's original 1968 study, Kent Jennings, Laura Stoker, and Jake Bowers (2009), consider whether similarities in partisanship extend to the next cohort of parents and their children. This study leverages data from a panel survey of three generations: the parent and child generations from the 1968 study, as well as the children of the original child generation. The new findings are consistent with the original results and support the authors' theory that children are especially likely to take on the political preferences of their parents if they come from families that frequently discuss partisan politics. Recent work offers evidence that young people have more polarized partisan views today than they did several decades ago and indicates that parents may play a role in this process (Tyler and Iyengar 2023).

Other scholars challenge theories of intergenerational political socialization that solely focus on political transmission from parents to children, arguing that socialization may take a different path in immigrant families. These accounts suggest that children influence their parents' political attitudes (McDevitt and Chaffee 2002; Wong and Tseng 2008). This "reversed" process of intergenerational political socialization is particularly likely in immigrant families because children often act as "translators and interpreters" for parents who do not speak English or are unfamiliar with the American political system (Carlos 2021; Wong and Tseng 2008, 158).

It is also possible that the family plays a smaller role in partisan socialization among immigrants than the population at large. Zoltan Hajnal and Taeku Lee (2011) make this point in a book investigating why immigrants are reluctant to identify with either political party. They argue that the acquisition of partisan identities is a two-stage process for immigrants, whose parents are unlikely to have attachments to American political parties. Immigrants must first become familiar with the political parties before choosing to identify with a particular party. Other research suggests that the poor fit of familial theories of political learning extends to the growing population of transitional- and second-generation Asian Americans who come of age in the US.[5] For example, second-generation Asian Americans may develop partisan preferences later in life than their counterparts whose parents were born in the US (Carlos 2018). Also, some Asian American high school students report limited political discussion with parents and learn about American politics through participation in student government (Kiang 2001). These studies suggest that standard familial explanations for political socialization may not apply well to Asian American children of immigrants.

The Role of Political Parties, Organizations, and Campaigns in Immigrant Mobilization

Moving beyond the family, historical accounts of immigrant political learning also center political parties, community organizations, and candidate-centered campaigns. For example, local parties historically played a major role in mobilizing European immigrants in major cities, often using incentives like jobs and material goods to gain political support (Allswang [1977] 2019; Andersen 1979; Dahl 1961; Wong et al. 2011). In a study of ethnic politics in Providence, Rhode Island, Elmer Cornwell (1960) claims that parties mobilized immigrants through various mechanisms, including offering "social services for the new arrivals [and] gradual admission of their representatives into the party organization at the ward and precinct level" (205).

In fact, many scholars argue that joining a political party was central to becoming incorporated into American society for European immigrants during the late nineteenth and early twentieth centuries. For example, both major parties appealed to Irish and Italian immigrants, eventually including them in local party leadership in cities where they made up a large proportion of the population (Archdeacon 1983; Cornwell 1960; Erie 1990). Steven Erie (1990) argues that New York's Tammany Hall urban machine facilitated naturalization for many Western European ethnic groups in exchange for political support.[6] While both major parties engaged in these efforts, Kristi Andersen (1979) claims Democrats were particularly focused on mobilizing less politically engaged

---

[5] Just 57% of Asian Americans overall (compared to 71% of Asian American adults) are foreign-born (Budiman and Ruiz 2021b).

[6] Demographic analyses of historical census data indicate that urban political machines likely facilitated naturalization on a smaller scale than such accounts suggest (see Bloemraad 2006).

groups like recently naturalized immigrants at the local level, contributing to the partisan realignment of the 1960s. This line of work suggests that through local mobilization efforts, political parties—especially the Democratic Party—played a central role in the political socialization of immigrants.

Although the major parties faced strong incentives to incorporate immigrants, a decline in immigration and the nationalization of the party system reduced their capacity for immigrant mobilization by the mid-twentieth century (Grieco 2014; Wong 2006). Legal restrictions standardized the naturalization process and sharply limited immigration, leading to a decline in the foreign-born population and making it more difficult for immigrants to become American citizens (Bloemraad 2006; Wong and Ramakrishnan 2023). These policy changes coincided with the centralization of the party system during the Progressive Era, such that urban machines and local party leaders played a smaller role in mobilizing potential voters (Erie 1990; Hopkins 2018; Sparacino 2021; Wong 2006). As Janelle Wong (2006) puts it in *Democracy's Promise:*

> Local political machines and political organizations formerly exhibited a consistent and committed interest in political mobilization at the neighborhood level but are no longer a vital presence... Those efforts have been replaced by the centralization of campaigns in the Republican and Democratic national headquarters, where technicalization, in the form of direct marketing and mass media campaigns, has become the norm (3).

As this quote suggests, the contemporary political parties have not centrally focused on engaging new immigrant constituencies since 1965 (Grieco 2014; Hajnal and Lee 2011). This is because recent immigrants are not eligible for citizenship for several years, and naturalization rates remain low among those who are eligible (Bloemraad 2006; Jones-Correa. 1998; Wong 2006). Zoltan Hajnal and Taeku Lee (2011) attribute low levels of partisanship among Asian Americans and Latinos to the fact that political parties do little to mobilize these groups. Instead, as Janelle Wong (2006) argues, contemporary political parties engage in a process of "limited mobilization," focusing recruitment on active political participants and existing supporters (9).

While Democrats have many advantages in mobilizing contemporary immigrant groups at the national level, they have not invested in organizational capacity at the local and state levels to the same extent as Republicans. On the one hand, Democrats have been proactive in providing multilingual campaign materials, focusing on issues that affect ethno-racial minorities, and recruiting more racially diverse political candidates (Fraga et al. 2020; Hassell and Visalvanich 2019). However, Republicans have focused on building local party capacity, while Democrats rode the coattails of Obama's national success at the expense of developing local and state organizations (Debeneditti 2017; Galvin 2016).

David Galvin (2009) argues that this reflects a broader trend. Since the Eisenhower administration, Republican presidents invested in their parties through fundraising, mobilization efforts at the local level, and investing in quality local and state candidates, while Democratic presidents have largely focused on national policy achievements (Galvin 2009). Along these lines, some local Democratic Party leaders blamed Obama's campaign team for massive losses on the state level between 2008 and 2016 (Debeneditti 2017). This suggests that Democrats lost the strategic advantage they once had in mobilizing immigrants on the local level (e.g., Andersen 1979), despite many other characteristics that make the party appealing to immigrants.

Although there have been potential missteps at the national level, informal party organizations and affiliated groups have played a role in a community-based strategy to recruit and engage with immigrant constituencies at the local level. For example, Democratic and Republican organizers engage with immigrants through student political groups on college campuses, where first- and second-generation immigrants accounted for nearly 30% of students nationwide in 2021 ("National Data on Immigrant Students" 2023). There is some evidence that Democrats are improving local outreach in college towns, which are becoming reliable liberal political strongholds, even in otherwise conservative parts of the country (Mahtesian and Alexander 2023). Both parties also leveraged youth-focused quasi-party organizations such as "Young Democrat" and "Young Republican" clubs to target young voters in cities and college campuses ahead of the 2024 presidential election (Kelly et al. 2024). Campus voter registration efforts, informational events, and social ties developed through these local level organizations may play an important role in the communication of political information.

Political parties may also work with labor unions, many of which serve increasingly diverse members and promote pro-immigrant policies (de Graauw and Gleeson 2021; Hamlin 2008; Milkman 2011). In research focused on immigrant labor organizing in California, Ruth Milkman (2006) and Rebecca Hamlin (2008) find that some unions recruited immigrants to strengthen their political power as membership declined, incorporating these members by focusing on labor issues affecting their communities. By working with these "immigrant-focused" unions, the parties may be able to mobilize lower- and middle-income immigrants who are unlikely to be reached through the party's national efforts.

As national party organizations have strengthened, candidate-centric campaigns also play a role in mobilizing and engaging partisan voters. Despite increasing polarization and partisan unity, Martin Wattenburg (1991) argues that candidates' personal characteristics are increasingly important to presidential vote choice since Ronald Reagan's election in 1980. Voters support candidates who they like and trust, and in turn, candidates aim to present themselves as dynamic, charismatic, likeable, and honest (Barker et al. 2006).

Although many immigrants are not strong partisans, recent work suggests that candidate-centered campaigns may impact their partisan acquisition. For example, James McCann and Katsuo Nishikawa Chávez (2016) find that exposure to candidate-centered advertisements for either major party presidential nominee in 2008 increased Mexican American immigrants' ratings of both candidates. However, only exposure to an Obama ad affected partisan identification, leading to movement toward the Democratic Party (McCann and Nishikawa Chávez 2016). Such appeals may be effective at garnering the support of acculturated immigrants who are already politically engaged, but many Asian American immigrants are not fluent in English or regular consumers of mainstream media, so they are unlikely to receive political mobilization messages (Masuoka et al. 2018; Wong and Ramirez 2006; Wong et al. 2011).

In addition to local partisan mobilization efforts and candidate-centric national approaches, nonprofits, civic organizations, and immigrant-serving community organizations play a major role in exposing immigrants to American politics. These organizations facilitate learning about the American political system in a variety of ways, including offering social services, helping immigrants to navigate the government bureaucracy, offering citizenship courses, holding political events, and encouraging voter turnout and other forms of civic participation (Brown 2016, Wong 2006). In some cases, immigrant-serving organizations also advocate for more inclusive immigration policies (de Graauw 2016).

AAPI-serving community organizations, particularly nonpartisan civic organizations, have grown rapidly in the past few decades. These organizations focus their programming on Asian American communities across the country, including in Milwaukee, Pittsburgh, and San Francisco (Bosch 2024; Rooney 2021; Sismaet 2022). Nonpartisan civic organizations serve as important touchpoints for Asian American community members and offer a space for civic learning. They also play an important role in expanding the political infrastructure of the Asian American community.

Despite the central role of local organizations in helping immigrants to navigate the political system, they are unlikely, and often unable, to provide strong partisan cues. While community organizations offer critical exposure to the American political system, they have limited resources and are typically only able to mobilize immigrants on one-off political issues (Ramakrishnan and Bloemraad 2008; Wong 2006). Additionally, many community organizations are nonpolitical, and others must take an explicitly nonpartisan stance to maintain nonprofit status (Wong 2006, 89–90). This suggests that community organizations are unlikely to provide immigrants with sufficient exposure to the political parties or candidates to initiate the process of partisan acquisition.

In sum, existing research suggests that immigrant families have less strongly held partisan views than nonimmigrant families. This may result in lower rates of the intergenerational transmission of partisan preferences within immigrant families. Recent studies also convey that mainstream political party organizations no longer take an active role in immigrant socialization, although local affiliated partisan groups and candidate-centered campaigns occasionally make efforts to appeal to immigrant groups. While community organizations offer exposure to targeted aspects of American politics, they are unlikely to offer clear partisan cues or incorporate immigrants into the political parties. To the extent that the partisan views of Asian American immigrants and their children cannot be explained by standard familial or institutional theories of political socialization, additional explanations must be considered.

Partisan Socialization within Local Contexts

Another strand of research focuses on the role of social ties in local contexts beyond the family in political socialization. Although this literature does not center immigrant constituencies, social ties may shape partisan acquisition in the Asian American community through similar processes. In *Citizens, Politics, and Social Communication: Information and Influence in an Electoral Campaign*, Robert Huckfeldt and John Sprague argue that "social communication is central to political life, and that the informal transmission of political information produces an interdependent electorate" (1995, 21). According to this theoretical perspective, interactions within local contexts like neighborhoods, schools, workplaces, and churches, influence Americans' political preferences. The literature on social context and political behavior includes research on the effects of structured neighborhood social contexts, and individual social networks consisting of small groups of people who regularly interact with each other.

The first line of research explores how neighborhood characteristics shape political participation and partisanship. Many studies show that neighborhood demographics, such as socioeconomic status and partisanship, have consequences for various political outcomes, including turnout, vote choice, and partisanship (Giles and Dantico 1982; Huckfeldt 1979; Huckfeldt and Sprague 1995; Leighley 1990). Recent work approaches the study of contextual political effects from a new perspective, focusing on partisanship and the racial demographics of local communities. For example, neighborhood-level racial demographics shaped Asian American turnout in the 2000 presidential election (Cho et al. 2006).

Other scholarship considers the potential influence of immediate discussion networks on political attitudes and participation. For example, Robert Huckfeldt and John Sprague (1987) contend that neighborhood partisan context conditions the effects of immediate discussion networks on vote choice. In addition, the characteristics of the social groups with which people discuss politics, including the partisan composition of these networks, have important consequences for their civic engagement and political attitudes (Carlson et al. 2020; Cramer 2004; Mutz 2002; 2006; Mutz and Mondak 2006; Sinclair 2012).

Taken together, this research indicates that social context may shape the political behavior of the individuals within them. Such theories are apt for explaining the partisan views of Asian Americans. As a predominantly immigrant constituency, Asian Americans are unlikely to enter the political process with strongly anchored partisan beliefs passed along through their families. Therefore, they may be particularly open to local partisan dynamics.

Partisan Influence Through Social Transmission from Peers: Evidence from Houston

Social transmission is a new theoretical account that aims to explain partisan acquisition in Asian American communities by centering social connections. It predicts that Asian Americans experience limited partisan exposure through the family during childhood and develop partisan preferences through social interactions with peers in local contexts. Once Asian Americans settle into local environments within the US, they participate in activities through social institutions, including neighborhoods, community organizations, informal social networks, workplaces, schools, and universities. Within these settings, Asian Americans interact with other members of their communities. These social experiences are politically formative because Asian Americans experience limited prior discussion of American politics during childhood. In turn, interactions with people within local communities lead to the development of political beliefs and partisan views.

The theory of social transmission predicts that Asian Americans develop partisan preferences through sustained exposure to the political views of peer groups, primarily in local contexts. By this account, peers in local contexts substitute for the family and political parties that are not focused on mobilizing new immigrant constituencies. However, the process of peer influence is not politically neutral. Peers provide Asian Americans with exposure to the political parties that is biased toward their own partisan preferences, especially when the peers who Asian Americans interact with hold strong, crystallized partisan views developed during childhood and young adulthood.

The theory predicts that Asian Americans learn about the political parties and develop partisan attachments through interactions with peers in local contexts. However, there are important differences in the composition of peer groups, nature of political interactions with peers, and role of transnational politics across generational and ethnic subgroups within the Asian American community. I discuss these sources of variation at length below.

In what follows, I detail each aspect of this argument, drawing on in-depth interviews with a diverse group of 22 Asian American residents of Houston to illustrate the mechanisms. This theoretical analysis builds general explanations from the personal accounts of these interview respondents. I use the findings from these interviews to offer inductive illustrations of social transmission in one local community, following other recent work on immigrant political behavior in political science (Anoll 2022).

Why Study Asian American Political Learning in Houston?

Houston's unusually large and varied Asian American population, along with its mixed partisan context, provide a distinctive opportunity for studying political socialization and partisan acquisition in this pan-ethnic community. As of 2021, the Houston–The Woodlands–Sugarland Metropolitan Area was home to the ninth largest US Asian American population of nearly 600,000 residents in the US, accounting for nearly 9% of the local population (Appendix Table A.1).[7] These statistics reflect remarkable growth in recent years, as the number of Asian Americans in the Houston metro area increased by over 200,000 residents between 2010 and 2020 (US Census Bureau 2020a).

The Asian American population in the greater Houston area is very diverse, reflecting nationwide trends. Appendix Table A.2 presents demographic characteristics of Asian Americans in the Houston metro area as of the latest five-year American Community Survey (2017–2021). The six largest national origin groups include Indian Americans (26.3% of Asian Americans locally), Vietnamese Americans (25.1%), Chinese Americans (16.8%), Filipino Americans (9.7%), Pakistani Americans (7.8%), and Korean Americans (3.3%) (US

---

[7] Appendix Table A.1 shows estimates drawn from the 2021 American Community Survey of Asian American population size in 15 metropolitan statistical areas with the largest Asian American populations (US Census Bureau 2024b).

Census Bureau 2024b; Appendix Table A.2). These are also some of the largest and fastest-growing Asian American subgroups nationwide (Budiman and Ruiz 2021b).

Turning to nativity and citizenship, about two-thirds of Houston-area Asian Americans are foreign-born and one-third are US-born. Nearly three-quarters are US citizens and one-quarter are noncitizens (Appendix Table A.2). Although there is variation in socioeconomic status across national origin groups, Asian Americans in Houston are relatively affluent, with a median household income of $96,947, compared to $72,551 for Houston residents overall (Appendix Table A.2).

Greater Houston also offers a useful case study for this research because of its partisan heterogeneity. Compared to other parts of the country with large Asian American populations, such as heavily Democratic metropolitan areas on the east and west coasts, Houston has a competitive partisan dynamic (Desilver 2014; Tausanovitch and Warshaw 2014). I focus on Harris County, which includes the city of Houston, and Fort Bend County, a suburban area southwest of the city where Asian Americans account for over 20% of the local population (US Census Bureau 2024b).

Republican candidates received most of the two-party vote share in every presidential election between 1968 and 2004 in Harris and Fort Bend counties (Amlani and Algara 2021).[8] Since then, Democratic presidential candidates have consistently received a larger number of votes than have Republicans in Harris County. In 2024, 52% of Harris County voters supported Kamala Harris and 46% supported Donald Trump (Bloch et al. 2024). In suburban Fort Bend County, a majority of voters supported Republican candidates as recently as 2012. Hillary Clinton won 53% of the two-party vote in Fort Bend County in 2016, representing the first time most voters supported a Democratic candidate since the racial realignment of the political parties (Amlani and Algara 2021). This pattern of close races with the Democratic candidate coming out ahead persisted through the 2024 presidential election, when Kamala Harris won just over 49% of the vote share and Trump won 48% (Bloch et al. 2024).

Although Houston is a left-leaning city in terms of voting trends, there is considerable variation in partisan attachments among local residents. Among respondents to the 2020 Kinder Houston Area Survey, a large-scale survey conducted by researchers at Rice University, approximately 29.1% of Houstonians identified as Democrats, 18.8% as Republicans, 23.5% as Independents, and 28.6% did not identify with any of these party labels (Kinder Institute for Urban

---

[8] These statistics are drawn from Sharif Amlani and Carlos Algara's (2021) database of county-level election returns (years: 1872–2020): https://dataverse.harvard.edu/dataset.xhtml?persistentId=doi:10.7910/DVN/DGUMFI.

Research 2021). This partisan composition reduces concerns that Asian American residents chose to live in Houston because it is a Democratic enclave, as might be the case in coastal cities.

Despite these partisan dynamics, Houston-area voters increasingly supported Democratic candidates as the Asian American population grew over the past 40 years. Figures 2.1 and 2.2 present changes in the Asian American population alongside partisan voting patterns in presidential elections between 1980 and 2020 for Harris and Fort Bend Counties.[9] Harris County has seen a steady increase in its Asian American population, which grew from fewer than 50,000 residents in 1980 to nearly 350,000 in 2020 ("Race/Ethnicity: 1980–2010 City of Houston" 2012; US Census Bureau 2020a). Fort Bend County, where Asian Americans are the fastest-growing demographic group, has seen an even sharper increase in its Asian American population (Bauman 2021). While just over 3,700 Asian Americans lived in Fort Bend County in 1980, the population grew to nearly 200,000 by 2020 (US Census Bureau 2020a).

This demographic shift occurred alongside a broader change in voting trends in both counties, although the partisan composition of Houston remains mixed. In both counties, Democrats have received an increasingly large proportion of the two-party vote share over the past four decades. In fact, Democratic presidential candidates narrowly received the support of a majority of voters from both urban Harris County and suburban Fort Bend County in 2016 and 2020. While Asian American population growth does not necessarily explain this shift, voting patterns in Houston have shifted as the city's population has become more racially diverse (Brust 2017).

Against the backdrop of these changing social and political dynamics, I conducted interviews with Houston-area Asian Americans during the summer of 2017 as part of an inductive case study that offers depth to the social transmission account. I recruited 22 Asian American residents of the Houston metro area to participate in in-depth individual interviews focused on their social experiences, immigration histories, and political perspectives. Interview participants were identified and recruited through a variety of sources, including local community leaders, Asian American community organizations, and student organizations at a local university. After an initial round of interviews, I recruited additional subjects through snowball sampling.

I intentionally selected a pool of survey respondents who reflect the diversity of the Houston-area Asian American population in terms of national origin, age,

---

[9] In Figures 2.1 and 2.2, the population data are drawn from decennial censuses conducted between 1980 and 2020 and the vote share data are drawn from Sharif Amlani and Carlos Algara's database of county-level election returns (Amlani and Algara 2021; US Census Bureau 2020a; US Census Bureau 2023b). I omit 2024 election results from these figures because decennial census population data was available through 2020 at the time of this research.

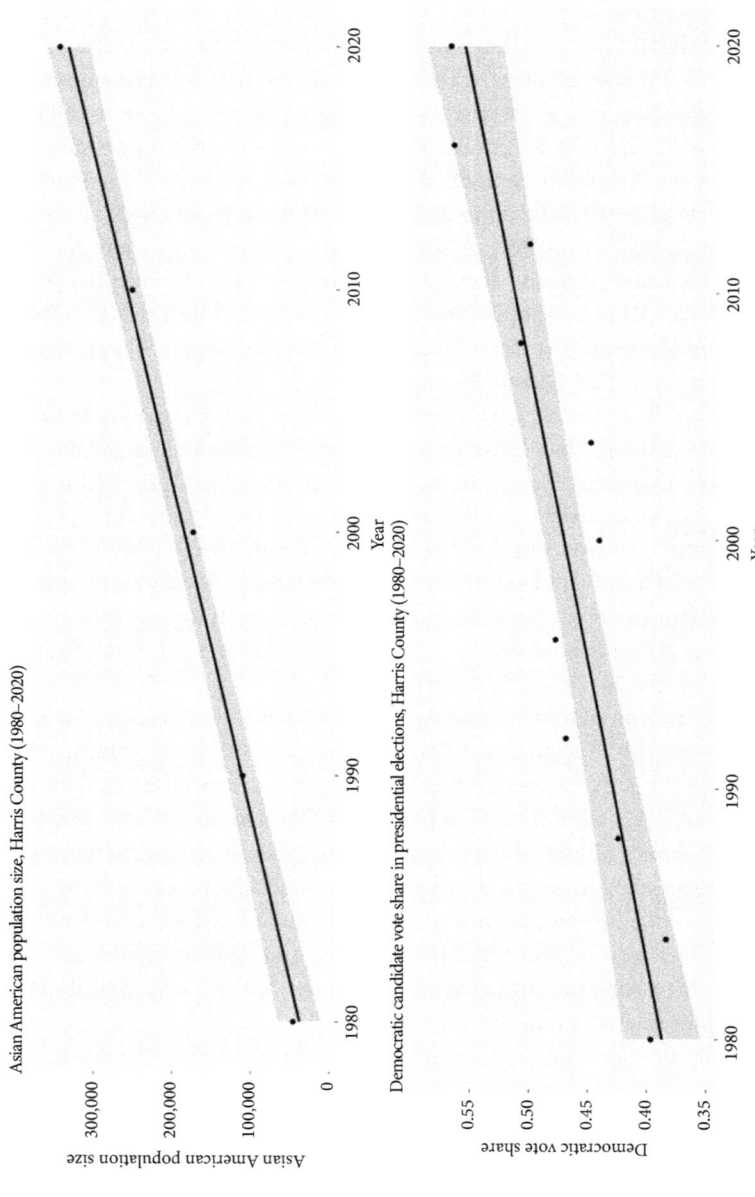

Figure 2.1 Asian American population and general voting trends in Harris County (1980–2020)

Source: The population data are drawn from decennial censuses conducted between 1980 and 2020 and the vote share data are drawn from Sharif Amlani and Carlos Algara's database of county-level election returns (Amlani and Algara 2021; US Census Bureau 2020a).

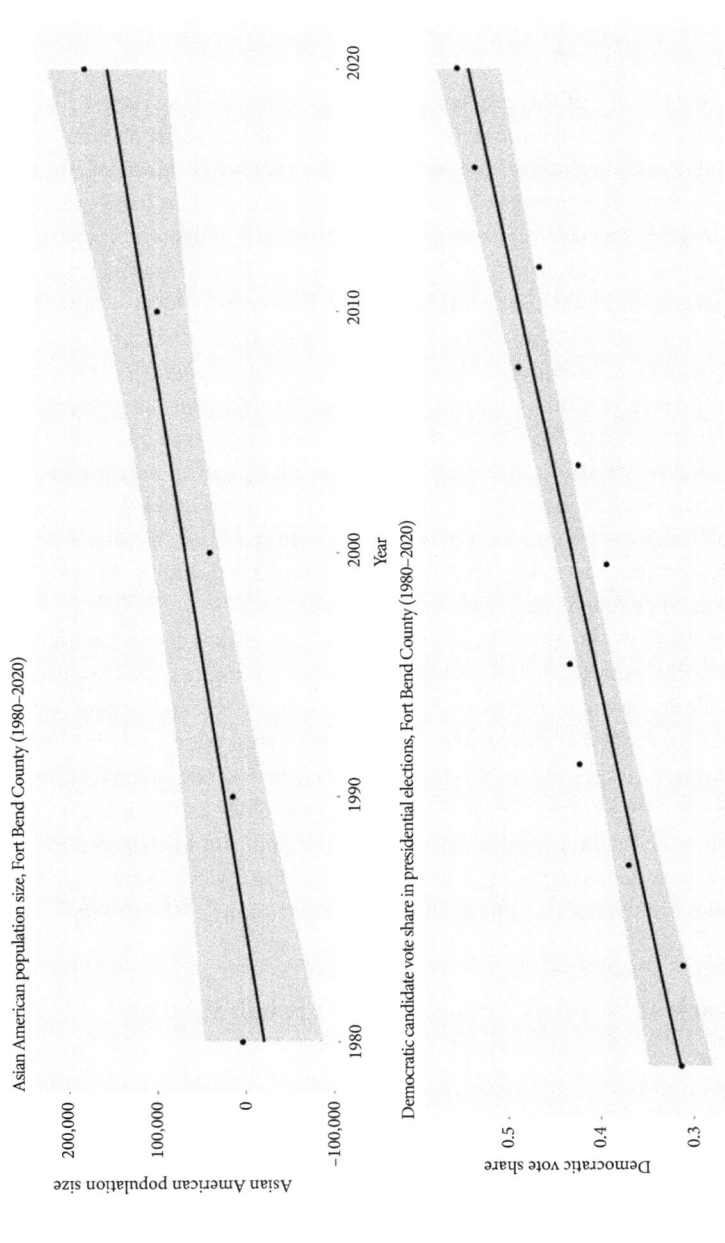

Figure 2.2 Asian American population and general voting trends in Fort Bend County (1980–2020)

Source: The population data are drawn from decennial censuses conducted between 1980 and 2020 and the vote share data are drawn from Sharif Amlani and Carlos Algara's database of county-level election returns (Amlani and Algara 2021; US Census Bureau 2020a).

socioeconomic status, nativity, and citizenship. Appendix Table A.2 presents the demographic characteristics of the interviewees and Asian American residents of the Houston metro area. This comparison highlights the diversity of the interview sample and the degree to which it reflects demographic patterns in the local community.

To offer a full picture of the process of political learning, I recruited a mix of recent immigrants who were not US citizens, naturalized citizens who had lived in the US for several decades, and second-generation children of immigrants. One interviewee represented the third generation of her family in the US. I also recruited interviewees from many national origin groups, including the largest subgroups in Houston (e.g., Indian American, Vietnamese American, Chinese American, and Pakistani American) as well as smaller local subgroups (e.g., Japanese American, Singaporean American, Taiwanese American).

The interviews were conducted between July 10 and August 2, 2017. The fieldwork and interview protocol were approved by the designated institutional review board prior to data collection. Most interviews occurred in person at various locations in Houston and Sugar Land, including coffee shops, restaurants, community organization offices, and conference rooms at a local university. Three interviews were conducted over video conferencing software based on interviewee preferences. The interviews were completed within 35 and 90 minutes. The average interview lasted for 60 minutes.

The interviews were semistructured and included questions about immigration and education history, social and professional experiences, and political perspectives. They were conducted in English by a single researcher and were recorded and transcribed with consent from interviewees. More details about subject recruitment, interview methods, and the full text of the interview protocol are included in Appendix A and the Chapter 2 Online Appendix ⊛. To analyze the interview data, I carefully read the transcripts and identified quotes and patterns across demographic groups using NVivo software. Excerpts from these interviews are included below as inductive illustrations of the theory.

A Lack of Political Socialization Through Parents During Childhood

The theory of social transmission contends that both Asian American immigrants and their children experience limited discussion of American politics, including conversations about the political parties, at home with their parents during childhood. Evidence from qualitative interviews with a diverse group of first-, transitional-, and second-generation Asian American residents of Houston illustrates this point.

First, Asian American immigrants rarely discuss American politics with family members while growing up in their countries of origin because their parents have limited knowledge of American politics. This point is supported among first-generation immigrants within the Houston interview sample, none of whom mentioned discussing American politics with their parents prior to immigrating. In fact, despite having relatively high levels of education, most Asian American immigrants interviewed said they knew veryAmerican political system prior to arriving in the US. For example, when asked if he understood how the American political system worked prior to immigrating to attend graduate school, a first-generation Indian American man in his late fifties stated, "Barely, I had a very vague sense." Another first-generation Indian American graduate student in his mid-twenties said that he "had a basic overview of it, but not the nooks and crannies . . . That I've learned over the years."

Second, I argue that transitional- and second-generation Asian Americans experience limited exposure to American politics at home during childhood, despite coming of age in the US. This is because many immigrant parents are reluctant to talk about American politics with their children. Immigrant parents may have several reasons for avoiding political discussion with their children, including a fear of controversy, time constraints, and language barriers.

Several interviews with respondents who grew up in US immigrant households illustrate this point. For example, a transitional-generation Korean American woman in her mid-fifties said, "We never discussed politics, the discussion was just 'don't get involved in politics because it's dirty and corrupt.'" A second-generation Chinese American woman in her late twenties made a similar point: "I never really talked about politics with my family . . . I've always had this impression that my family would not want to get involved in any civil movement or participate in politics." A transitional-generation Vietnamese American woman in her early twenties reported that her parents rarely discuss American politics because of busy work schedules and language barriers:

> My parents honestly don't really get involved with politics because they work a lot, and they don't really speak a lot of English. We do watch the news a lot. There's also a Vietnamese channel, which is easier for them to understand. We don't have that at home, only at their workplace; My parents and I are always at work and school and our conversation kind of revolves around family.

These accounts evince that many Asian American immigrants are reticent to discuss American politics with their children for a variety of reasons. This suggests that the process of political socialization may occur later in life and outside of the home in both generations.

A few US-born respondents reported occasional conversations about American politics with their parents during childhood, but they were limited in scope and frequency. For example, a second-generation Chinese American man in his mid-twenties remembered discussing politics with his parents ahead of elections. He stated, "It wasn't a common thing. We'd talk about it sometimes right around elections. I remember watching some debates with my dad. That was probably the biggest conversation in the family setting." A second-generation Indian American man in his late thirties indicated that he talked about American politics with his parents from time to time, "but they weren't nearly as political as I am."

In addition to avoiding controversial topics and language barriers, another explanation for a lack of discussion of American politics in immigrant households is that immigrants are more invested in politics in their country of origin than American politics. Excerpts from several interviews illustrate this claim. For example, a second-generation Filipina American woman in her early forties relayed:

> They [my parents] didn't want to be involved or have anything to do with it [politics]. They would never tell me if they voted, it was never a topic of conversation. Even though they are citizens, they are still thinking about things back there. Growing up, I heard more about Ferdinand Marcos than I did about George Bush, who was living down the street.

A second-generation Chinese American man in his late thirties echoed this point. He said the following about his parents' political views: "I think they follow homeland politics more. My mom definitely follows Taiwanese politics. She was more concerned about being able to go to Taiwan and vote in the election than she was about being able to vote in the presidential election here."

Although these respondents mentioned hearing their parents discuss politics in the Philippines and Taiwan, it is unlikely that discussions of transnational politics influence transitional- and second-generation Asian Americans' partisan views. This is because translating these views into the American context would require a detailed understanding of the political context in their country of origin and how it relates to the American political system. Few Asian Americans who were raised in the US reported deep engagement with politics in their country of origin. For example, a second-generation Vietnamese American man in his early twenties said that he does not follow politics in Vietnam at all, although he thinks that his parents might follow Vietnamese politics on Facebook. A transitional-generation Vietnamese American woman in her early twenties also reported a lack of interest in Vietnamese politics: "Probably not, because I moved to the US when I was very little. I don't really follow a lot of political things."

The few respondents who came of age in the US and reported following politics in their country of origin were also more civically engaged than the typical respondent. For example, a second-generation Indian American man in his late thirties stated, "I get *India Abroad*, it's a bizarre publication. I talk to my cousins, I talk to my dad, if there's something in the *New York Times* about India, I'll read that." However, this respondent was politically active and reported occasional discussion of American politics with his parents during childhood.

Although Asian Americans talk about American politics with their parents infrequently during childhood, it is possible that political discussion with parents occurs later in life. In these cases, children may influence the political views of parents, as "reversed" models of political socialization suggest (McDevitt and Chaffee 2002; Wong and Tseng 2008). For example, a second-generation Chinese American man in his late twenties reported some political conversations with his parents in recent years, but a reluctance to discuss politics with other adult family members. In describing political discussion with family members, he said, "More so now as an adult. I think it's because we can vote. With my parents it's ok, but usually with this uncle who is conservative, I still try not to, just because we have different opinions."

Another second-generation Chinese American man in his late thirties echoed the latter point: "I don't know if it's a stigma or anything, but whenever I'm around Asian adults, especially around my parents age, I don't know if they know a lot about politics, so it's hard for me to even bring it up." These accounts suggest that familial conversations about American politics may occur later in life after political views are established. In such cases, intergenerational influence can go in either direction. However, children of Asian American immigrants may also be hesitant to initiate political conversations with parents, even as adults, since they grew up without the habit of discussing politics with them (Fong 2021a; 2021b).

Social Transmission: The Partisan Influence of Peer Groups in Asian American Communities

Given a void of strong parental political socialization, the social transmission account argues that Asian Americans are open to political views expressed by the people around them in local social contexts. More specifically, I argue that Asian Americans develop partisan views through everyday interactions with peer groups in a diverse range of local social contexts. Merriam-Webster's dictionary definition of "peer" includes "one that is of equal standing with another, especially one belonging to the same societal group based on age, grade, or status" (Merriam-Webster 2023). Drawing on this definition, I describe peer groups as networks of people within local environments who are socially connected to each other. While peers are generally of equal status, peer groups may include people from different socioeconomic classes, racial backgrounds, and age groups. However, peers do not typically exert power over each other.

An individual's local peer network may include people who meet and interact in a range of different institutions and contexts, including schools, colleges, workplaces, neighborhoods, community organizations, places of worship, and informal friend networks. For young people, peers in educational settings consist of other students in their age group rather than faculty or administrators, who are of different professional rank. Among adults, workplace peer groups include colleagues of a similar rank. For example, high-level managers and executives are not typically embedded in the same social networks as ordinary workers. Peers in community organizations and places of worship may include organizational members and fellow parishioners. In some cases, organizational staff or spiritual leaders may be considered peers of congregation members if they are otherwise of equal status and are members of the same community. Neighbors, friends, and even extended family members are other important social connections in local environments.

Interactions with peers in these varied contexts are important sources of political information as Asian American immigrants and their children develop political orientations. Asian Americans may learn about politics from peer groups through a variety of active and passive mechanisms. For example, Asian Americans may engage in discussions of politics or ask questions about politics in daily interactions with peers. Alternatively, they could absorb political information shared by peers on social media or by listening to others engage in political conversations.

While there may occasionally be social conflicts or disagreements among members of peer groups, peers are rarely in positions where they can exert social control over each other. Some exceptions include friendships that develop between workers and managers, or parishioners and religious leaders. However, such instances are the exception rather than the rule. It is important to note that peers may differ in terms of the frequency with which they interact with each other, the levels of personal confidence they share, and the extent to which they share values. To that end, peers will not be equally persuasive when it comes to the development of political attitudes. The social transmission of partisan views is unlikely to occur when there are major conflicts in values and norms between Asian Americans and members of their peer groups.

Unlike political information presented by the mainstream media or civic education courses, political information shared by peer groups is not necessarily balanced or nonpartisan. Instead, most peers share political information or contextualize current events through the lens of their own political orientations and partisan identities. Therefore, once Asian Americans are consistently exposed to political messages from peers, partisan attitudes are likely to shift in the direction of the dominant views expressed in their social networks. An individual's peer groups can be influential as they develop political attitudes regardless of the strength of pre-existing political orientations reflected in the group. However, peers who have stable and crystallized partisan identities, especially when they are developed early in life through intergenerational transmission, are most likely to shape Asian Americans' partisan views.

While peer political influence is a universal mechanism that I argue applies across the Asian American community, the process of social transmission may be shaped by various dimensions of immigrant socialization. These include age and length of residency, reasons for migration, places of origin, transitional social and political ties, pre-migration socialization, access to mediated political information through the media, and generational status. I briefly discuss the implications of each of these dimensions for partisan acquisition and political learning through peer networks among Asian Americans as they navigate a new political system.

Although these factors all merit further consideration, in what follows I primarily focus on generational status, arguing it is a central facet that shapes the social connectedness of Asian Americans and the racial composition of peer groups. Later in the chapter, I focus on differences in the experience of peer socialization across immigrant generations within the Asian American community and elaborate on the implications of these differences, drawing on evidence from qualitative interviews.

Age and Length of Residence

Established studies of political learning argue that age is an important predictor of partisan stability because it is associated with political exposure and maturity (Campbell et al. 1960; Converse 1969). As a result, partisan attachments are deeply held and unlikely to change over the course of an individual's life (Sears and Funk 1999). Among Latino and Asian American immigrants, length of residence in the US is typically a better predictor of familiarity with American politics than age and is associated with the acquisition and the strength of partisan ties (Cain et al. 1991; Phan and Garcia 2009; Wong 2000; Wong et al. 2011).[10] However, age is also associated with partisanship among second-generation and third-generation Americans. For example, Roberto Carlos (2018) contends that

---

[10] Many of these studies find that time in the US is associated with the acquisition of Democratic partisanship, although Zheng (2019) finds that age and length of residence do not predict the direction of partisanship (e.g., Democratic vs. Republican).

the children of immigrants experience a "prolonged process of political socialization ... and come to find their partisan identity outside the home and later in life" (381).

Age and length of residence may also shape the acquisition of partisanship through social transmission. Immigrants are more likely to develop robust social networks and become integrated into local social contexts over time (Alba and Nee 2003). In turn, their exposure to political discussion in local peer networks may increase with their length of residency. Age may have a more complex relationship with exposure to political discussion in peer networks. While age is associated with political maturity, many Asian Americans who are raised in the US may be exposed to formative political discussion in the classroom or through informal interactions with friends during young adulthood.

Reason for Migration

Asian Americans immigrated to the US in the post-1965 era for a variety of reasons, including education, work, family reunification, and refugee status (Takaki 1998). The lived experiences of Asian Americans who immigrated for education or work are very different from those of Asian Americans who arrived as refugees or through family reunification (Chen et al. 2009; Wang et al. 2023). There are also regional differences in reasons for migration. For example, many contemporary East and South Asian immigrants are college educated and immigrated to the US based on a policy shift to attract highly educated migrants with professional skills (Wong et al. 2011, 11). In contrast, there is more variation in educational attainment among those who immigrated based on family reunification and refugee status.

Among first-generation Asian Americans, reasons for migration may have implications for several dimensions of the social transmission process, including peer group composition and the likelihood of exposure to political discussion through local social networks. For example, those who migrated for education or work are more likely to be exposed to racially diverse classmates and colleagues in educational and professional settings. In turn, they may be better connected with diverse and politically engaged local peer groups.

In contrast, those who immigrated as refugees or through family sponsorship are likely to settle in predominantly Asian ethnic enclaves (Li 2009). In turn, they may primarily build social connections with other immigrants from their own ethnic group. Many of these recent immigrants may not have strong partisan views as they navigate the American political system. However, the social transmission of political information will occur as they expand their social networks by working outside the home and make social connections with others in their communities.

Places of Origin

Given the diversity of the Asian American community, it is important to consider how national origin shapes political attitude formation. Although voters from most Asian national origin subgroups support Democrats at high rates, there are differences in partisan dynamics across ethnic groups. For example, Janelle Wong and her co-authors (2011) found that Japanese Americans, Indian Americans, and Korean Americans were most likely to identify as Democrats, while Vietnamese Americans were more likely to identify as Republicans (129). These differences in partisanship may be shaped by political systems in these countries of origin. In fact, those migrating from countries with a communist history, like Vietnam, are more likely to identify as Republican than those who immigrated from democratic countries (Cain et al. 1991; Lien et al. 2004). These differences may also have implications for civic engagement, which is higher among Asian Americans from countries with democratic systems of government (Lien 2008; Ramakrishnan 2005).

Differences in national origin may shape social transmission in several ways. First, political systems and cultures in Asian countries of origin may shape immigrants' interest in politics and civic inclinations. These differences could lead immigrants from Asian countries with democratic systems of government to be more interested in seeking out political information from local social networks than those from nondemocratic countries. Social transmission may also apply most directly to less acculturated Asian American groups that include many recent immigrants. For example, this account may be most applicable for Asian American subgroups with large immigrant populations that are open to political information from local peer networks, including Indian Americans and Chinese Americans. Members of these national origin groups are less likely to experience partisan influence through the family during childhood because many are recent immigrants. In contrast, peer groups may be less politically influential for more acculturated groups with few immigrants such as Japanese Americans, who have a longer family history in the US and may discuss American politics at home during early life.

Strength of Transnational Political and Social Ties

The strength of transnational ties may also influence Asian Americans' political engagement in the US context. Some scholars argue that strong connections to countries of origin lead to political disengagement (Jones-Correa 1998; 2016; Staton et al. 2007). For example, in *Between Two Nations: The Political Predicament of Latinos in New York City*, Michael Jones-Correa (1998) argues that many Latin American immigrants delay naturalization over fears of not being able to return to their country of origin. Others find that ties to countries of origin heighten immigrants' involvement in US politics by increasing social connectedness and political interest (Gershon and Pantoja 2014; Sui and Paul 2017; Wong et al. 2011).

Turning to political transnationalism, few Asian Americans actively take part in political activities in their country of origin (Lien et al. 2004; Wong et al. 2011). While 75% of respondents to the 2008 NAAS reportedly communicated with friends and family and 36% sent money back home, only about 4% reported that they were involved in politics in their country of origin (Wong et al. 2011, 78). This comports with low levels of transnational political activity reported among Latin American immigrants (Guarzino et al. 2003). However rare, a growing body of work shows that transnational political involvement predicts increased rather than decreased political engagement in the US among Asian American and Latino immigrants (Collet and Lien 2009; Gershon and Pantoja 2014; Sui and Paul 2017).

Transnational social and political ties may affect the process of social transmission by shaping the robustness of social networks and interest in political discussion. For example, having strong social ties with friends and family in countries of origin may lead people to also seek out social connections in the US. This may lead to increased social integration in American society and a more robust process of social transmission. Likewise, taking an interest in transnational politics may reflect an interest in politics more generally. This might lead immigrants to actively seek out information about American politics from social contacts in the host society after migrating.

Pre-Migration Socialization and Re-Socialization

For adult immigrants, pre-migration socialization in Asian countries of origin and resocialization in the US context may also influence partisan acquisition. Political socialization prior to migration may be especially important for those who were politically engaged in their countries of origin. In early research on this topic, Tom Rice and Jan Feldman (1997) argue that "civic culture" in countries of origin shape US political participation for European immigrants. In more recent work, Sergio Wals (2011; 2013) finds that Mexican immigrants who held attachments to political parties in Mexico or brought ideological perspectives with them to the US are politically active after migration. Other work shows that the ideologies of the government in countries of origin shape Latino partisanship (Irizarry 2024).

Despite the importance of political socialization in countries of origin, immigrants' pre-migration attitudes may be open to change (White et al. 2008). For example, European immigrants adopt the participatory culture in their host countries over time (Aleksynska 2011; Just and Anderson 2012). Social integration and interactions with other residents in their countries of settlement may play a role in this process (Dinesen and Andersen 2022). Listening to and engaging in political discussions with peer groups may help immigrants to learn about the political system in their country of settlement.

However, the effects of pre-migration socialization may also linger. For example, Mariya Aleksynska (2011) finds that Muslim immigrants to European counties are unlikely to engage in political activities in their host country regardless of their length of residence. In fact, some migrants continue to vote in the country of origin even after becoming active in politics in their country of settlement (Chaudhary 2017). Finally, immigrants from postcolonial commonwealth countries migrate to the UK with some familiarity with the British political system, which may lead to increased civic engagement (Heath et al. 2013).

Although pre-migration socialization may inform Asian American immigrants' political perspectives, it does not preclude the social transmission of political information in the US. Even for politically active immigrants, translating existing political beliefs to the American context, navigating the American policy space, and developing a working knowledge of the two-party system involves political learning. Moreover, developing partisan preferences requires understanding how their views fit with the policy goals and political agendas of the major parties. While immigrants may turn to various sources for information about the American political system, social ties may offer relevant political cues and information about the political parties, issues, and ideological debates.

Mediated Political Communication

Political information from media sources may also affect political learning among immigrants. Doris Graber (2004) claims that the media "functions as a tool for shared political socialization through which people learn basic values and political orientations to which their society subscribes" (549). The media landscape is rapidly evolving, and Asian Americans may receive political information through mainstream, ethnic, and social media. I briefly consider the messages immigrants receive from these varied media sources before discussing their impact on the process of social transmission.

Mainstream newspapers, radio, and television may facilitate political learning among immigrants by providing detailed coverage of political issues (Graber 2001; Iyengar and Kinder [1987] 2010). Although exposure to news coverage hinges on political interest, many viewers were inadvertently exposed to political news on T.V. during the broadcast era (Prior 2007). These days, few Americans regularly access news content since entertainment media options are readily available (Lipka and Shearer 2023; Prior 2007). The modern media environment is also becoming more ideologically diverse, and consumers may seek out news sources that align with their political perspectives (De Benedictis-Kessner et al. 2019; Tyler et al. 2022). This suggests that in the contemporary period, only avid news consumers who are not strong partisans have regular access to balanced political coverage.

Some immigrants consume ethnic media rather than the mainstream media. A report commissioned for New California Media estimated that nearly 13% of US adults consume ethnic news (Roy and Close 2007; *The Ethnic Media in America* 2005). Many Asian Americans read Asian-language newspapers, view ethnic news websites, and listen to Asian-language radio stations, especially in the Chinese, Filipino, and Vietnamese communities (*The Ethnic Media in America* 2005, 27). The number of Asian ethnic news media outlets is growing, especially in areas with large immigrant populations (Kaulessar 2023; Matsaganis et al. 2011). While little research focuses on the impact of ethnic media on political learning among Asian Americans, it is associated with lower turnout and conservative voting patterns (Masuoka et al. 2018; *The Ethnic Media in America* 2005).

Social media is another important source of mediated political information in the contemporary period. In contrast to mainstream and ethnic media, political information accessed on social media is often shared directly by peers. Many in the Asian American community, including young people and recent immigrants, are active on a variety of platforms, including Facebook, WhatsApp, Twitter, and Instagram (Mohsin et al. 2023; Lai 2022a). Asian Americans receive many different types of political messages from their peer networks on these websites, including mainstream political news stories, political misinformation, and calls to action on political issues (Lai 2022a; Nguyễn et al. 2023). Although many Asian Americans are exposed to political messages on social media, this experience may not increase civic engagement. For example, Asian Americans participate in online political activities at lower rates than whites (Chan 2021).

While many immigrants learn about American politics directly through media conduits, social connections may help them to contextualize this information. For example, conversations with peers could involve discussion of recent news stories. These interactions may help immigrants to develop perspectives on current events. When it comes to social media, peer groups also play a direct role in shaping the political content that people view. People are more likely to consume news stories posted on social media by friends and family, suggesting that peer cues could be particularly influential in shaping the political information that people view online (Anspach 2017). While there is some evidence that online social networks are polarized political "echo chambers" (e.g., Settle 2018), others find that many social networks are politically diverse (e.g., Bakshy et al. 2015; Barberá et al. 2015). Accordingly, immigrants may be exposed to a range of political opinions held by their peer groups, which could be influential as they develop political attitudes.

Generational Status

A final dimension of immigrant socialization that may shape the process of social transmission is generational status. The social transmission theoretical account centers the role of generational status because it shapes the racial composition of Asian American's peer groups. While there are many ways that the process of social transmission may vary (some of which are described above), the racial composition of peer groups is an important aspect of this theoretical account that merits further attention. This is because it may affect the composition of peer groups, the nature of political discussion, and type of political information that Asian Americans are exposed to.

The composition of Asian Americans' peer groups varies across immigrant generations. Many recent immigrants have racially homogeneous social networks, largely composed of other immigrants from their national origin group. Outside of professional and educational settings, Asian American immigrants primarily interact with other members of their ethnic group in informal social networks, neighborhoods, and community organizations (Mok et al. 2007; Qian et al. 2001; Zhou and Xiong 2005). In contrast, Asian Americans raised in the US have more diverse peer groups. For example, a 2013 Pew survey found that nearly half of first-generation but less than a fifth of second-generation Asian Americans report that most of their friends are from their ethnic group (*Second-Generation Americans* 2013). Responses to questions about intergroup contact in the 2016 National Asian American Post-Election Survey reflect a similar pattern. Among US-born Asian Americans, 31% report having a lot of contact with whites, 19% with Latinos, and 15% with African Americans. In contrast, only 16% of Asian American immigrants report frequent contact with whites, 9% with Latinos, and 6% with African Americans (Ramakrishnan et al. 2016). This suggests that Asian American immigrants are not fully included into nonimmigrant American social networks which their children have greater access to.

In fact, Asian Americans raised in the United States are more likely to interact with members of other racial groups than similarly positioned whites, Latinos, and African Americans. Compared to their non-Asian peers, Asian American young people are more likely to marry someone from another ethnic group. According to another survey, 29% of Asian American, 27% of Latino,

18% of African American, and 11% of white newlyweds married someone of another race (Livingston and Brown 2017). Asian Americans are also the least likely to attend schools where most students are from their own racial group or live in localities with a large co-ethnic population (Anoll et al. 2024; Orfield et al. 2019).

Drawing on these social patterns, I argue that variation in the racial composition of peer groups has implications for political learning. First-generation Asian Americans, who primarily socialize with other Asian immigrants, develop partisan attitudes through conversations with Asian peers, including adult immigrants from their own national origin group. In contrast, transitional- and second-generation Asian Americans, who interact with more diverse peers than their parents' generation, develop partisan attitudes through conversations with Asian and non-Asian peers. These interactions often occur during young adulthood, in schools and universities.

In the next two sections, I draw on interviews with Houston-area residents to offer insight into the dynamics of peer networks and the nature of interactions that shape the partisan views of Asian Americans. These quotes also offer insight into the role that several dimensions of immigrant socialization discussed within this section, such as generational status, continuing ties to countries of origin, political transnationalism, and reasons for migration, play in the process of political learning.

Peer Influence Among Immigrants: Adult Family Members and Immigrant Social Networks

The theory of social transmission predicts that first-generation Asian American immigrants arrive in the US with limited knowledge of American politics and develop partisan attitudes through interactions with adult family members and friends from their ethnic group. Interactions with colleagues may also shape partisan views among those who work, but to a lesser degree because people are reluctant to discuss controversial topics at work.

To offer an example, a first-generation Indian man in his mid-twenties who was not a US citizen at the time of the interview said, "It's about learning through conversations with people who have lived here for a long time. Through friends and their family." A first-generation Vietnamese American woman reported that she discussed American politics with adult relatives, including with her husband, a fellow Vietnamese immigrant. She characterized these political conversations as engaging and divisive: "In my family, I don't know how, but they all get into fights about politics when they get together, so I hear a lot of discussion there." In contrast, occasionally discussed politics with "some of my colleagues through the election, but not much because at work we tend to respect different opinions." Her political attitudes were mixed—she had positive views about some aspects of Republican ideology but supported Democratic candidates in recent presidential elections. When asked about her vote choice in the 2016 presidential election, she indicated that "even though I like to vote for Republicans, I couldn't vote for Trump."

These quotes also emphasize the fact that political learning is a long-term process that unfolds over the course of an individual's life. As such, familial influence is not restricted to childhood and may play an important role in political learning alongside peer influence. In fact, both these first-generation respondents indicated that conversations with adult family members, including spouses, siblings, and other relatives exposed them to information about American politics after immigrating to the US. Adult family members may be particularly influential for Asian Americans who immigrate to the US through family reunification policies. Although these experiences suggest that familial ties still are relevant to Asian American political socialization, this account differs from the standard intergenerational transmission model, which focuses on parents and children during early life (e.g., Jennings and Niemi 1968).

Several other interview respondents reported similar experiences. For example, a first-generation Indian graduate student in his late twenties explained that he learned about American politics through interactions with fellow Indian immigrants. Regarding discussing American politics, he said, "It was all my roommates ... They were all other Indian students ... When there are six people in a room, and you don't know anything, you can just start a conversation, and you get to know what they know." Although he did not have strong partisan views, he learned about American politics through his interactions with other recent immigrants from his national origin group.

To offer another example, a first-generation Indian American man in his mid-fifties identified friends and colleagues, to a lesser degree, as his primary political conversation partners: "Primarily it's friends ... There's a handful of colleagues who I occasionally discuss politics with. One thing to keep in mind is that my friends and contacts tend to be overwhelmingly liberal. Although I have a few who are, at least in the traditional sense, conservative." This respondent identified as a Democrat and voted for Hillary Clinton in the 2016 presidential election.

To offer a point of contrast, a first-generation Singaporean American man in his late forties, related that "when I moved to this country, I didn't have any family, so my closest colleagues became my closest friends. They were very kind and very open minded to help me to understand." However, at the time of the interview, he discussed politics with members of his national origin group (he was of Indian origin), mainly his wife and friends: "Indians, you know, what happens when we get together. It is heavy political debate, shared views, agree to disagree." However, he rarely discussed politics at his place of work, "just in wanting to be sensitive and respectful, we don't do it too much. We do at times have some form of event that makes us talk about these issues . . . but I think everyone is very respectful here." At the time of the interview, he identified as a Democrat and planned to vote once he became a citizen.

Peer Influence Among Children of Immigrants: Diverse Peer Groups in Educational Settings

In contrast, the social transmission account predicts that transitional- and second-generation Asian Americans develop partisan preferences through interactions with racially diverse peer groups in educational settings. Asian Americans raised in the US are particularly open to the partisan views expressed by their peers because they experience limited prior exposure to American politics through their families. Conversations with peers who have well-developed political views may be particularly formative. Peer influence may also occur earlier in life for Asian Americans who come of age in the US and interact with American peers during childhood and adolescence. Such experiences may be particularly formative during college, when young adults are influenced by peers on a variety of topics and, in many cases, live away from home for the first time.

These expectations are reflected in the experiences of several interview respondents who grew up in the US. For example, a transitional-generation Vietnamese American college student in her early twenties discussed politics with friends on social media. She said, "Some of my friends are not fans of Trump. Especially with the election, all over Facebook, all my friends were posting about how he's not the candidate that we want." This respondent identified as a Democrat and was a first-time voter who supported Clinton in the 2016 presidential election.

A second-generation Vietnamese American college student, also in her early twenties, described discussions of politics with a close college friend, a liberal white woman who is very interested in politics. She characterized those conversations as follows: "During the election season, we talked about politics maybe once a week. It would come up in conversation. She talked more; I never argue with her because I just assume that she knows what she's talking about. I'd say she's very interested in politics." Although this respondent did not think of herself in partisan terms, she voted for Clinton in the 2016 presidential election. Both respondents did not discuss politics at home with their parents during childhood, which might have made them open to listening to their peers.

A transitional-generation Pakistani American man in his late forties learned about American politics through diffusion from the people he interacted with when he first arrived in the US as a teenager to attend boarding school. He initially developed conservative views, reflecting the norms in his local environment. However, his attitudes changed during college:

> It was not talking with people but hearing other people converse [about politics]. Through osmosis, you kind of pick it up. It's funny because my host family when I first moved here was a little on the conservative side. Until the second year of college, I grew up loving Rush Limbaugh ... I didn't even realize that I was on the conservative end of the spectrum, then I found my wings a little bit after.

Several others who came of age in the US identified discussion with peers in educational settings as an important source of political information. For example, a second-generation Chinese American woman in her late twenties claimed that her first exposure to American politics occurred through interactions with peers in her college's economics honor society: "I think I got very involved in politics personally when I was in college because that was the election of 2008. I talked a lot about it with my peers from my organization and with my friends." She went on to become interested in politics, identify as a Democrat, and voted for Clinton in 2016. These experiences suggest that college may be a particularly important social environment in which peer interactions shape the partisan views of transitional- and second-generation Asian Americans.

Yet other transitional- and second-generation interviewees indicated the centrality of social and academic experiences in college to their partisan attitudes. For example, a second-generation Vietnamese American student in his early twenties attended college at a large university he felt was right leaning. Although he did not vote in 2016, his experience suggests that social diffusion in college can also lead to Republican preferences in conservative social contexts:

> I was trying to be in the middle and just observing the people around me, like my classmates and my professors ... Basically, everyone was saying that if Hillary won, it would be the end of the oil industry. Especially, after the election, all my professors were extremely happy, so I thought I should be happy too.

Reflecting on her experiences in college, a transitional-generation Korean American woman in her early fifties who identified as a Democrat and voted for Clinton in 2016 expressed a similar sentiment:

> Until age 18, my influence was my family. With my parents being first-generation immigrants, they hold certain political beliefs, very conservative. Then once I went to [Liberal Arts College], that opened a whole world that

I've never been exposed to. I think because I went away from home and I was relatively young, I was like a sponge.

Although it is possible that interactions with colleagues shape the political views of transitional- and second-generation Asian Americans later in life, most interview respondents entered the workplace with established partisan views and limited their political discussions to like-minded co-workers. For example, a second-generation Filipina American woman in her early forties who identified as a Democrat and worked for a large oil company avoided political discussion with colleagues, many of whom she thought were Republicans. She said, "I don't really engage. I've noticed that a lot of white coworkers tend to talk about politics . . . Just like you have to keep the peace with your neighbors, you have to keep the peace with your coworkers."

A second-generation Pakistani American woman in her mid-twenties who identified as a Democrat and worked in a creative field offered the following thoughts about political discussion at work: "I think it depends from person to person. There are very few people in the office who are conservative. I would say where I work now, it's mostly just commiserating and shared views, like reinforcing what we already believe."

These excerpts provide a glimpse into the experiences of political socialization of transitional- and second-generation Asian Americans in Houston. While each experience is unique, some commonalities emerge. First, few transitional- and second-generation respondents discussed politics at home during childhood. Given a lack of political exposure through the family, they were receptive to the partisan views expressed by friends and acquaintances in educational settings.

Second, these excerpts point to the centrality of colleges and universities as settings for social transmission among Asian Americans who come of age in the United States. More specifically, many interview respondents centered interactions with peers in college in their process of partisan acquisition. In contrast, few Asian Americans who came of age in the United States discussed politics openly with their colleagues. By the time they entered the workplace, they had already developed their partisan leanings.

Accordingly, social experiences in college may be a driver of partisan preferences among transitional- and second-generation Asian Americans. This explanation is plausible because over 53% of Asian Americans have at least a bachelor's degree (Ryan and Bauman 2016). Furthermore, about 63% of recent Asian American high school graduates were actively enrolled in a four-year college or university in 2022, compared to 48% of white, 48% of African American, and 33% of Latino recent graduates (Digest of Education Statistics 2023).

Interactions with peers in college may lead to the development of Democratic rather than Republican preferences because colleges and universities are historically liberal political environments. Several studies find that attending college shifts political views in a liberal direction, especially on social issues (Astin 1977; Pascarella and Terenzini 1991). Second, college educated Americans are becoming more politically liberal than they were several decades ago, leading to a growing partisan divide across lines of college attendance (Cohn 2021; Grossman and Hopkins 2024;) For example, about 60% of college educated white Americans voted for Biden in 2020 while approximately 45% voted for Gore in 2000 (Cohn 2021). College educated Americans are also more ideologically consistent in their positions than those with low levels of education ("Ideological Gap Widens" 2016).

Why Does Social Transmission Predict Democratic Views Among Asian Americans?

Turning to recent partisan trends, this theoretical account predicts that most Asian Americans develop Democratic rather than Republican preferences through peer interactions due to their settlement patterns. Most Asian Americans live in left-leaning local environments (Gelman 2012). In a report on Asian American settlement patterns, Logan and Zhang (2013) offer evidence that "Asian nationalities are spread very unequally around the country," with the vast majority living in the following nine states: California, New York, Texas, New Jersey, Hawaii, Illinois, Washington, Florida, and Virginia (5–6). Within these states, Asian Americans also settle in left-leaning metropolitan areas. For example, most Asian Americans live in the following metropolitan areas: Los Angeles/Long Beach, New York/New Jersey/Long Island, Oakland, San Jose, Santa Ana/Anaheim/Irvine, Honolulu, Chicago, San Francisco, Washington, Houston, San Diego, and Seattle (Logan and Zhang 2013, 7).

Asian Americans who settle in liberal areas are more likely to interact with peers who hold Democratic than Republican views because relatively few Republicans live in these local environments. This experience may shape their political socialization, providing pro-Democratic and anti-Republican cues when they are still relatively unfamiliar with the political parties. While Asian Americans may occasionally be exposed to Republican views within their peer groups, these experiences are likely few and far between. In an era of increasing partisan polarization, the exact opposite pattern is likely to occur when Asian Americans settle in conservative areas.

The theory of social transmission is also contingent on the social integration of Asian Americans into local communities. Asian Americans who do not have frequent contact with other community members are unlikely to pick up the partisan norms of their local environments (Huckfeldt and Sprague 1995, 110).

In other words, living in a very Democratic community is not sufficient for the social diffusion of Democratic partisan views. Asian Americans need to interact with people in these communities to receive these partisan cues. This suggests that the theory of social transmission is most applicable to Asian Americans who work outside of the home, are active in local community organizations, or attend school and college in the United States. These experiences reflect a degree of sustained interaction with other community members that allows for the social diffusion of partisan views.

While it is possible that Asian Americans select where to live based on existing partisan preferences (e.g., Gimpel and Hui 2015), this is unlikely for several reasons. First, recent research in political behavior suggests that partisans do not sort into politically congenial local environments. Using a conjoint experiment, Jonathan Mummolo and Clayton Nall (2016) show that Democrats express preferences to live in more populous and racially diverse places than Republicans. However, when it comes to actual moving behavior, both Democrats and Republicans move to moderate but Republican-leaning zip codes, which tend to be better resourced (56). Data from the 2008 NAAS suggests that a similar process occurs among Asian American immigrants who moved (Ramakrishnan et al. 2008). On average, immigrants relocated to a county that was more Republican leaning than their initial county of settlement. This may reflect the trajectory of Asian American immigrants from urban ethnic enclaves to the more affluent suburbs of metropolitan areas (Lai 2011; Li 2009).

Political Influence from Asian American and Non-Asian Peers

The social transmission account also considers how variation in the racial composition of Asian American peer groups impacts partisan acquisition. As mentioned in the previous section, the diffusion of partisan preferences is particularly likely when Asian Americans interact with peers who have strong partisan views. In general, African Americans, Latinos, and whites are more likely to develop deep and stable partisan views through family than Asian Americans. Therefore, all else equal, non-Asian peers are more likely to express consistent partisan views in social interactions and be more effective messengers of partisan cues than Asian peers.

However, this expectation is contingent on the assumption that Asian Americans are frequently exposed to partisan cues from non-Asian peers, which may not be the case. As detailed above, the racial composition of peer networks differs substantially across immigrant generations. Asian American immigrants and their children may react differently to messages from Asian and non-Asian peers. Immigrants primarily interact with other members of their ethnic group.

Therefore, they may be more likely to develop partisan views through social transmission from Asian than non-Asian peers. In contrast, Asian Americans who are raised in the US have more diverse peer groups. They may develop partisan views through social transmission from both Asian and non-Asian peers who they encounter in educational settings.

Do Peers Influence Policy Views in Addition to Partisanship?

A final point to consider is whether these predictions about social transmission extend to other political outcomes. There is disagreement within the discipline of political science about whether attitudes about specific policies underlie partisan views. The Downsian school of thought argues that partisan views are developed in a rational process based on the aggregation of policy preferences (Downs 1957). In contrast, the Michigan and Columbia schools argue that partisan views are stable social and psychological connections, developed during childhood and young adulthood (Berelson et al. 1954; Campbell et al. 1960; Green et al. 2004). While I do not attempt to adjudicate between these explanations, the social transmission account aligns more clearly with social theories of political attitude formation that center group-based identities than theories of rational voter behavior rooted in sophisticated policy preferences. While Asian Americans may display some level of political sophistication when making decisions about politics, I argue that they primarily develop partisan attitudes through social connections.

Nevertheless, partisan cues from peer groups likely include substantive justifications for supporting one party over another and center policy issues.[11] Therefore, it is important to explore whether Asian Americans develop policy views through social transmission from peers. It is possible that Asian Americans' policy views develop in tandem with partisan attitudes, as individuals gain exposure to the American political system. Existing research offers some evidence supporting this possibility. For example, the policy views of Asian Americans Evangelicals align with their political ideology (Wong 2015). On the one hand, they are more ideologically liberal than their white Evangelical counterparts, but on the other hand, they are more conservative than the non-Evangelical Asian American counterparts on a wide range of policy issues, including abortion, same-sex marriage, the war in Iraq, universal healthcare, tax increases for the

---

[11] Theories of information processing could provide insight on how Asian Americans respond to cues from peer groups and develop political attitudes at the individual-level (McGraw and Lodge 1996; Taber 2003). While Asian Americans may be genuinely open to information from across the partisan spectrum early in the process of political learning, motivated reasoning may factor into how receptive they are to messages in support of the out-party once they begin to form partisan attitudes (Taber and Lodge 2006).

wealthy, and in-state tuition for undocumented immigrants (Wong 2015, 164). Other research reveals a similar alignment between political ideology and policy views about immigration among Asian Americans (Masuoka and Junn 2013).

Conclusion

This book explores partisan acquisition among Asian Americans, the fastest growing racial and immigrant group in the US, focusing on the role of peers in the process of political socialization. This chapter presents the central argument and offers illustrations of its key predictions, drawing on excerpts from in-depth interviews with Asian Americans in the Houston area. The social transmission account of partisan acquisition argues that peer interactions within local environments explain contemporary partisan trends within this diverse, pan-ethnic community. In exploring these patterns, the book also provides insight into how political socialization works among Asian Americans, a pan-ethnic immigrant constituency.

Is social transmission from peer groups distinctive to the Asian American community? This is an important question for scholars to consider in future research, as the role of peer groups in the process of political learning has not been thoroughly investigated for members of various identity groups in the US. Although it is beyond the scope of this book, I argue that the social transmission account may apply more broadly to people who receive little partisan information during childhood from their parents, distance themselves from their families during young adulthood, or experience little outreach from the political parties. Some examples might include immigrants from other parts of the world, such as Latin America, the Middle East, Africa, and the Caribbean; LGBTQ youth; people who move far from home; and people whose parents had no interest in politics.

Another open question is whether the process of social transmission will evolve as parties and candidates increasingly turn their attention to the Asian American community. Peer groups play a particularly important role in political learning in the absence of consistent political cues from parents and political parties. However, political candidates and parties are starting to invest in efforts to mobilize Asian American immigrant communities ahead of close elections in places like Atlanta, Georgia and Orange County, California (Barrón-López 2020; Lai 2022b). In these environments, peer groups may work alongside parties to engage Asian Americans in the political process. In some cases, peers may even participate in focused mobilization efforts such as multilingual canvassing and phone banking (Yoo and Ung 2022).

Nevertheless, both parties still have a long way to go before they successfully incorporate Asian Americans in their recruitment efforts nationwide. In fact, Asian American voters in cities across the country, including Dallas, Houston, and New York City, have expressed frustrations at the lack of attention their communities have received from political parties and candidates (McDonough 2023; Nguyen 2022). For example, in an interview with the *Texas Tribune* on the eve of the 2022 midterm elections, a Chinese American resident of Texas said, "Specific Asian outreach, I've seen very little to none on either side. I really hope we get more of a voice in politics" (Nguyen 2022). This suggests that peer groups may continue to play a central role in exposing Asian Americans to the political system in places where the parties are reticent to acknowledge them.

In the remaining chapters of Part I, I test this theoretical account using data from national surveys of Asian Americans. I turn to this empirical evidence in Chapter 3, combining analyses of the vote choices of Asian Americans as a pan-ethnic group and the six largest national origin subgroups within this diverse community in presidential elections. In doing so, I test the core contextual expectation of the social transmission—that local partisan norms shape Asian Americans' partisan preferences.

3
Local Partisan Context and Vote Choice in Asian American Communities

An article published in *The Atlantic* ahead of the 2020 presidential election illustrates the link between local partisan norms and the vote choices of contemporary Asian American voters. The story profiled a dozen Asian American voters in cities, suburbs, and towns across Pennsylvania (Huang and Lee 2020). The voters interviewed were diverse in terms of national origin, generation, age, gender, occupation, education, and socioeconomic status. Although several supported Republicans in previous elections, all but one planned to vote for Biden in 2020.

The lone Trump voter profiled was a 46-year-old Filipina American immigrant who voted for the first time in 2020. In explaining her vote choice, she claimed that she liked Trump's "approach to taxes, immigration, and abortion," but added that "he needs to do better on people and race." Another thing that stood out was her county of residence. She lived in Carbon County, a rural area where residents voted overwhelmingly in favor of Republican candidates in four of the past six presidential elections. In the 2020 presidential election, about 65.4% of Carbon County residents voted for Trump (Vestal et al. 2021).

In contrast, most of the Biden supporters featured in the article lived in liberal urban and suburban areas of Pennsylvania. They included a recent college graduate in left-leaning Harrisburg, a doctor in the liberal suburbs of Philadelphia, a young education administrator, and small business owners in the heavily Democratic city of Philadelphia, as well as an ex-State Department official and a public high school student in Pittsburgh. In fact, only two of the 11 Biden supporters lived in counties where a majority of voters supported Trump in 2020.[1]

While the article features only a handful of voters in a single state, the partisan characteristics of their local environments aligned neatly with their vote choices. Do these trends extend beyond a dozen Pennsylvania voters to Asian Americans nationwide? How, if at all, does local partisan context shape the vote choices of Asian Americans? Are Asian Americans who settle in politically liberal areas more likely to support Democrats than those who live in conservative areas?

---

[1] One was a senior at Indiana University, a liberal arts college in rural Indiana County, and the other a retiree in Republican Schuylkill County.

The Social Roots of Asian American Partisanship. Tanika Raychaudhuri, Oxford University Press.
© Oxford University Press (2025). DOI: 10.1093/9780197826560.003.0003

On the other side of the coin, are Asian Americans who live in conservative environments more likely to support Republicans than their counterparts who live in liberal enclaves?

In Chapter 2, I argued that Asian Americans develop partisan preferences through a process of social transmission, which centers interactions with peers in local contexts. While social interactions with localized peer groups are the primary mechanisms driving political socialization in this theory, the characteristics of an individual's broader political context shape the partisan direction of political learning. By this account, social interactions in local contexts often push Asian Americans' views in a Democratic direction because they tend to settle in liberal areas where they receive more liberal than conservative cues from local peer groups. However, social interactions should lead to Republican views among Asian Americans who settle in conservative areas. Before delving into the role of social interactions and political discussion with peer groups in later chapters, I consider the extent to which Asian Americans' political preferences reflect partisan norms in the local environments they live in.

This chapter considers the relationship between local partisan norms and vote choice among Asian Americans as a pan-ethnic group and across major ethnic subgroups within the Asian American community.[2] I explore whether local partisan context shapes vote choice independently and alongside several other explanations for how Asian Americans make voting decisions, including socioeconomic status, religion, national origin, discrimination, and group consciousness. Where possible, I consider these explanations separately among the six largest national origin subgroups within this community: Chinese Americans, Indian Americans, Filipino Americans, Vietnamese Americans, Korean Americans, and Japanese Americans. Taken together, this chapter presents a breadth of evidence indicating that local partisan context shapes voting decisions across diverse subgroups of Asian Americans.

The primary focus of this chapter is understanding how differences in local partisan context relate to vote choice in the Asian American community. To that end, I compare the voting preferences of Asian Americans who live in majority Democratic local environments to those who live in predominantly Republican environments. The voting preferences of the Pennsylvania voters featured in the *Atlantic* article suggest that local partisan dynamics shape Asian American vote choice. I test this expectation more systematically using data collected from over 2,000 Asian American likely voters nationwide in the 2008 National Asian American Survey (NAAS), one of the first large-scale nationally representative political surveys focused on Asian Americans (Ramakrishnan et al. 2008).

---

[2] This chapter is derived in part from my article in *Electoral Studies* (Raychaudhuri 2020).

The NAAS was a multilingual telephone survey conducted in the fall of 2008 on a diverse sample of Asian American respondents from a wide range of national origin subgroups ahead of the 2008 presidential election. In addition to offering a glimpse at the political attitudes of many Asian Americans, including recent immigrants, naturalized citizens, and US-born citizens, it includes respondents from many national origin subgroups. These data offer insight into the process of social transmission during a period when Democratic vote choice was steadily increasing within the Asian American community.

Are Asian Americans who settle in liberal environments more likely to vote for Democrats than those who settle in conservative environments? Answering this question is at the crux of the analyses presented in this chapter. I explore this possibility by analyzing the relationship between local partisan context and intended vote choice in the 2008 presidential election. Where possible, I test whether these patterns hold across varied ethnic groups in the Asian American community. This provides a perspective on the applicability of the social transmission account for immigrants from diverse regions of Asia, who have different reasons for migration, pre-migration experiences of political socialization, and patterns of migration.

To briefly preview the results, Asian Americans who live in majority-Democratic counties are more likely to vote for the Democratic candidate than those who live in majority-Republican counties. This relationship holds after accounting for many other factors that may shape vote choices, including demographic characteristics, socioeconomic status, religious identification, national origin, experiences of discrimination in the US, and generational status. This pattern also applies across many national origin groups within the Asian American community and is strongest among Chinese Americans, Indian Americans, and Korean Americans, some of the fastest-growing subgroups in recent years (see Figure 1.1).

Theory and Hypotheses: Do Local Partisan Context and Other Factors Shape Vote Choice?

As discussed in further detail in the previous chapter, the theory of social transmission argues that Asian Americans raised in the US and abroad experience limited political exposure through the family and develop partisan attitudes through the diffusion of partisan preferences from peers in local contexts. By this account, most Asian Americans vote for Democrats because they settle in Democratic areas and absorb local political norms. Within liberal political environments, Asian Americans are more likely to receive pro-Democratic than pro-Republican cues from local peer groups. Conversely, Asian Americans are more likely to receive pro-Republican than pro-Democratic cues from peers in conservative political environments, which should lead them to prefer the Republican Party. Asian Americans are generally open to the influence of local political norms because they often enter these contexts without strong pre-existing partisan views passed down through their families (Carlos 2018; Hajnal and Lee 2011).

This theory is apt for explaining contemporary trends in Asian American vote choice because many Asian Americans settle in liberal metropolitan areas within mixed partisan or Democratic-leaning states (Budiman and Ruiz 2021b; Gebeloff et al. 2021; Logan and Zhang 2013). For example, the typical Asian American respondent to the Cooperative Election Study (CES) surveys conducted in 2016 and 2020 lived in a county with 63% Democratic vote share in the two most recent presidential elections (Ansolabahere and Schaffner 2017; Schaffner et al. 2021). In contrast, the typical white respondent lived in a county with 49% Democratic vote share in the two election cycles combined. Drawing on these observations, the *local partisan context hypothesis* predicts that Asian Americans who live in majority-Democratic counties are more likely to vote for Democrats than those who live in majority-Republican counties. Conversely, Asian Americans who live in majority-Republican counties are more likely to vote for Republicans than those who live in majority-Democratic counties.

As noted in earlier chapters, there may be variation in the extent to which the social transmission account applies across Asian American ethnic subgroups. The *subgroup variation hypothesis* predict that local partisan context will have a strong association with vote choice for Asian Americans from rapidly growing immigrant subgroups, including Chinese Americans, Korean Americans, and Indian Americans. In turn, local partisan norms may be less reflective of the vote choices of Asian Americans who belong to more established subgroups, such as Japanese Americans, who may develop partisan views through familial transmission.

I test these hypotheses alongside several alternative explanations rooted in prior research. Existing studies offer several potential explanations for Asian Americans' vote choices and partisan preferences, which I discuss at length in previous work (Raychaudhuri 2020). These include standard theories of partisan preferences, such as *socioeconomic status* (Bartels 2008; Gelman 2009) and *religion* (Wong 2018), and theories that may apply particularly well to immigrants, like *discrimination* (Kuo et al. 2017), *linked fate* (Lien et al. 2004), and *national origin* (Cain et al. 1991; Wong et al. 2011).

Prior research finds strong support for some of these theories and weaker support for others. For example, age, gender, income, religious identification, and citizenship status emerged as significant predictors of partisanship among Asian Americans in previous studies (Wong 2018; Wong et al. 2011). Socioeconomic theories of vote choice predict that people with higher levels of socioeconomic status are more likely to vote for Republicans than people of lower socioeconomic status (Bartels 2008; Gelman 2009). However, socioeconomic theories do not fully explain civic engagement in the Asian American community, a pattern that may extend to partisanship (Junn 1999; Lien et al. 2001; Zheng 2019). Other research finds that Evangelical Asian Americans are more likely to support conservative social policies than their non-Evangelical counterparts (Wong 2018). Since many Asian Americans identify with conservative Christian religious denominations, religion may play a role in shaping their vote choices.

Yet other work finds that linked fate—a concept developed in research on African American political behavior—may also shape Asian American's partisan views (Dawson 1995; Lien et al. 2004). According to theories of linked fate, an individual Asian American voter's belief that their life chances are linked to those of members of their own national origin group, other Asian Americans, and other racial minorities in the US may increase their likelihood of voting for Democrats (Lien et al. 2004; Zheng 2019).

Theories of national origin focus on how differences in systems of government in countries of origin may shape vote choice. For example, Asian Americans who migrated from countries with a communist or authoritarian system of government, including Vietnam, Korea, and China, were less likely to support Democrats than those who migrated from Asian countries with democratic systems of government (Cain et al. 1991; Lien et al. 2004; Wong et al. 2011). Finally, recent research tests whether experiences of racial discrimination drive Asian Americans to support Democrats, who they perceive as more racially inclusive than Republicans (Chan et al. 2021; Kuo et al. 2017). Drawing on this wide-ranging discussion, Table 3.1 summarizes the full set of hypotheses tested in this chapter.

Local Partisan Context and Vote Choice: Evidence from the 2008 NAAS

I explore these explanations for vote choice among Asian Americans as a panethnic group and across national origin subgroups using data from 2008 NAAS, the first nationally representative political survey of Asian Americans.[3] This multilingual survey was conducted by phone in English, Cantonese, Hindi, Hmong, Korean, Mandarin, Tagalog, and Vietnamese. Data were collected in the summer and fall before the 2008 presidential election. The sample used in this analysis

---

[3] A second NAAS survey was conducted in 2016 (Ramakrishnan et al. 2016). It was not used in this analysis because it does not include county-level geographic indicators.

Table 3.1 Summary of Hypotheses

Hypothesis	
Local partisan context hypotheses	
Local partisan context hypothesis	Asian Americans who live in predominantly Democratic/Republican counties are more likely to vote for Democrats/Republicans than those in predominantly Republican/Democratic counties.
Subgroup variation hypothesis	Local partisan context more strongly predicts vote choice for Asian Americans from rapidly growing immigrant subgroups, such as Chinese Americans and Indian Americans, than those from more acculturated subgroups like Japanese Americans.
Alternative hypotheses	
Religion hypothesis	Asian Americans who identify with conservative Christian religions, like Evangelicalism and Catholicism, are less likely to vote for Democrats than those who do not identify with these religious groups.
Socioeconomic status hypothesis	Asian Americans of high socioeconomic status are less likely to vote for Democrats than those of lower socioeconomic status.
Discrimination hypothesis	Asian Americans who report experiencing racial discrimination are more likely to vote for Democrats than those who have not experienced discrimination.
Linked fate hypothesis	Asian Americans with high levels of linked fate with other Asian Americans, their national origin group, or other racial minorities are more likely to vote for Democrats than those with low levels linked fate with members of these groups.
National origin hypothesis	Asian Americans from countries with democratic systems of government are more likely to vote for Democrats than those from countries with communist or authoritarian histories.

includes responses from 2,206 Asian Americans who indicated they were US citizens and very likely to vote for a major party candidate in the 2008 presidential election.

This sample of likely voters consisted of 18.4% Chinese American, 23.6% Indian American, 11.0% Filipino American, 17.4% Vietnamese American, 11.4%

Korean American, and 18.1% Asian American respondents who did not specify their country of origin or traced their origin to other countries, including Bangladesh, Bhutan, Cambodia, Malaysia, Pakistan, Singapore, and Thailand. Approximately 56.3% of respondents identified as male and 43.7% as female. The ages of the survey participants ranged between the ages of 19 and 97. The average respondent was 55 years old.

Turning to generational status, approximately 84.3% of respondents were first-generation immigrants, 10% were second-generation children of immigrants, and 5.7% represented the third generation of their families in the US. The average immigrant respondent had lived in the US for 24 years at the time of the survey. However, the number of years immigrants had spent in the US ranged from less than one year to over 75 years.

Although the sample used in this analysis is diverse in terms of national origin, age, gender, immigrant generation, and length of residence, it is restricted to more acculturated Asian Americans who were eligible to vote in the 2008 election. Nevertheless, many respondents were immigrants and there is a great deal of variation in terms of their length of residence in the US. Future chapters test the social transmission account using surveys that include Asian American noncitizens and those who are less civically engaged.

Although several cross-sectional national surveys focus on Asian American political behavior, I use data from the 2008 NAAS because it is a high-quality, diverse, and representative political survey of Asian Americans. Moreover, it includes local geographical indicators on a level more granular than states. The 2008 NAAS includes county-level geographic indicators for each respondent, a level of geographic specificity necessary for testing the social transmission hypotheses. This allows for analysis of local partisan context and voting trends among the pan-ethnic Asian American community and the six largest national origin groups within it. Although the data is drawn from a single election cycle, it occurred when the trend of Democratic support solidified among Asian Americans at that national level. Therefore, it offers insight into the factors that shape Asian American vote choice in the contemporary period.

The main outcome is a binary measure of intended vote choice in the 2008 presidential election. I refer to this outcome as "intended vote choice" and "vote choice" interchangeably. Vote choice in presidential elections is a useful measure of partisan preferences for Asian Americans. Although partisanship is a stable and lasting political attachment, it is an incomplete measure of partisan views for many Asian American immigrants, who vote in elections but do not identify with a political party (Hajnal and Lee 2011; Phan and Garcia 2009). This reluctance to identify with either party also extends to second-generation Asian Americans who come of age in the United States (Carlos 2018).

For example, nearly a third of 2008 NAAS respondents did not identify with any partisan label (Democrat, Independent, or Republican). In contrast, 27% did not intend to vote for either major party candidate. Among registered voters, 26% did not identify with any partisan label and 17% did not intend to vote for a major party candidate. In other research, Natalie Masuoka and her co-authors (2018, 206) find that 44% of Asian Americans who are registered to vote do not identify as Democrats or Republicans. These gaps between vote choice and party identification among registered Asian American voters suggest that focusing on partisanship may underestimate their partisan preferences.

Three variables capture various dimensions of an individual's local environments. Local partisan context, the key predictor, is a measure of the vote share won by the Democratic candidate in respondent's county of residence in the 2008 presidential election.[4] This measure reflects partisan norms in the respondents' local environment at the time they made their voting decisions. The county-level vote share data were merged with the NAAS survey responses and coded as a categorical measure with a theoretically relevant baseline for comparison: "Majority Republican" (baseline) and "Majority Democratic." Length of residence is a categorical control variable with the following categories: "Less than one year," "one to four years," and "five years or more." Finally, local Asian American context is a continuous measure of the percentage of the population that was Asian American in the respondent's county of residence in 2008, drawn from US Census estimates (US Census n.d.). It is included as a control to account for Asian American population size, an important factor that may shape vote choice and be associated with living in liberal metropolitan areas. See the Online Appendix for further details about the variables included in this chapter (Online Appendix Table 3.1A ⊚).

I use these data and measures to evaluate the relationship between local partisan context and vote choice in several ways. In the first half of the chapter, I present detailed descriptive information, exploring variation in vote choices, local partisan context, and local Asian American population context among Asian American respondents to the NAAS. I also conduct simple descriptive tests to explore the relationships between these key variables. I end this section by modeling the effects of local partisan context on vote choice. I present these results for all Asian Americans and separately for the six largest national origin subgroups. The second half of the chapter extends these analyses to account for alternative explanations and the possibility that Asian Americans select to live in left-leaning political environments.

---

[4] The county-level presidential vote share data are drawn from David Leip's (2024) Atlas of US presidential elections.

Does Local Partisan Context Shape Asian American Vote Choice?

In line with exit poll results from the 2008 election cycle, most Asian American NAAS respondents supported the Democratic presidential candidate. Figure 3.1 presents the percentage of likely voters who intended to vote for Barack Obama among all Asian Americans and the six largest national origin groups. Approximately 63% of Asian Americans who planned to vote for a major-party candidate reported an intention to vote for Obama and 37% for John McCain.

These patterns are largely reflected across national origin groups with some notable exceptions. A diverse range of national origin groups within the Asian American community supported Democratic candidates in 2008. However, in line with prior findings, some Southeast Asian ethnic groups supported Republicans at high rates (Lien et al. 2004; Wong et al. 2011; but see Le and Su 2017). About 82% of Indian American, 73% of Chinese American, 77% of Japanese American, and 61% of Korean American likely voters intended to vote for Obama. In contrast, just under half of Filipino American and only a quarter of Vietnamese American likely voters intended to vote for Obama.

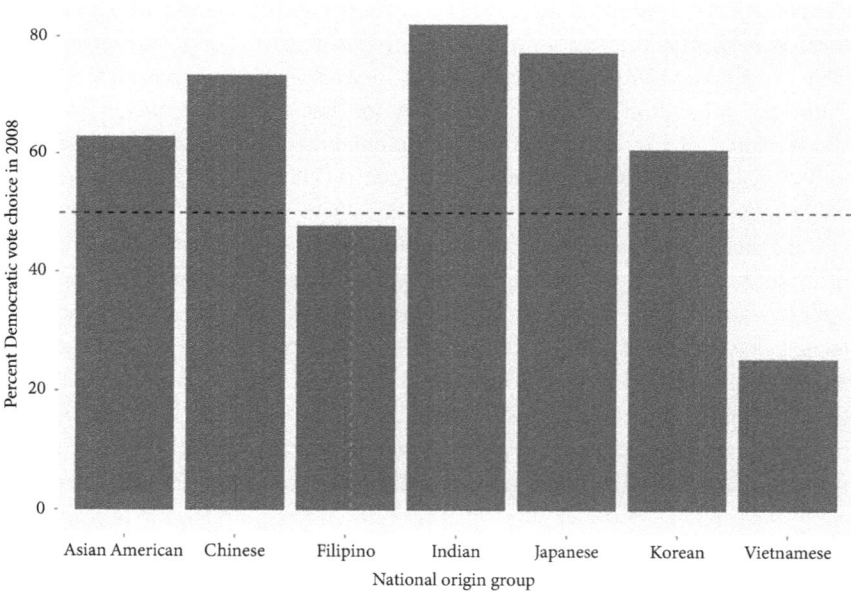

Figure 3.1 Intended Democratic vote choice among likely Asian American voters

Source: The data are drawn from the 2008 National Asian American Survey (Ramakrishnan et al. 2008).

In what follows, I explore what explains these voting patterns. Most centrally, I test the local partisan context hypothesis, which predicts that local partisan norms shape vote choice among Asian Americans. To that end, Figure 3.2 presents the distribution of Democratic vote share in the 2008 presidential election in counties where Asian American NAAS respondents lived when the survey was conducted.[5] While most Asian Americans settled in predominantly Democratic environments, there is variation in partisan norms across counties of residence.

The typical NAAS respondent lived in a liberal county where approximately 65% of voters supported Obama (Figure 3.2). However, at the extremes, Asian American likely voters lived in counties where as few as 37% and as many as 86% of voters supported the Democratic candidate. While nearly a fifth of the sample lived in majority-Republican areas, few resided in strongly Republican areas. This aligns with previous findings that many Asian Americans settle in politically liberal environments (Gebeloff et al. 2021; Logan and Zhang 2013; Li et al. 2016). When the survey was administered, over 75% of respondents

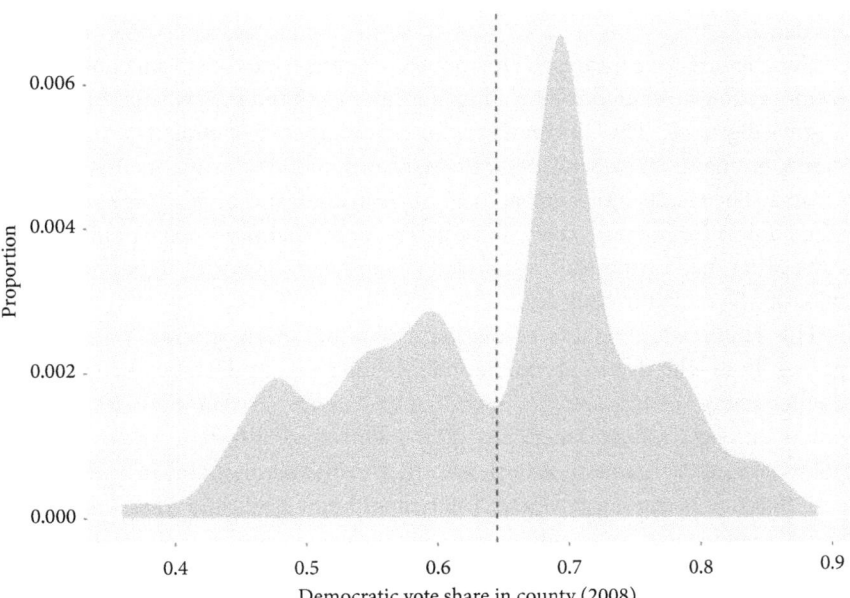

Figure 3.2 Democratic vote share in counties of residence

Source: The data are drawn from the 2008 National Asian American Survey (Ramakrishnan et al. 2008).

---

[5] About 16.8% of respondents did not report their county of residence.

had lived in their counties of residence for at least five years, which suggests that they had time to pick up on local partisan norms.

Next, Figure 3.3 shows the distribution of Democratic vote share in the 2008 presidential election in NAAS respondents' counties of origin, separately for the six largest Asian American national origin groups. The top three panels present these distributions for Chinese Americans, Indian Americans, and Filipino Americans. The bottom three panels present the distributions for Vietnamese Americans, Korean Americans, and Japanese Americans. Across national origin groups, patterns in partisan local context largely reflect the distribution for Asian Americans as a whole (Figure 3.3). Most members of all six ethnic groups lived in majority-Democratic counties, although Democratic vote share was highest in the counties where Japanese Americans and Chinese Americans resided and lowest in counties where Vietnamese Americans resided. Moreover, sizable minorities of Vietnamese American and Filipino American respondents lived in predominantly Republican counties, which aligns with higher rates of Republican vote choice in these groups. The distribution of local partisan context for Japanese Americans is clustered around the average because many lived in highly Democratic counties and 15.4% did not report their county of residence.[6]

Next, Figure 3.4 explores the relationship between local partisan context and Democratic vote choice among all Asian Americans and the six largest national origin subgroups.[7] The bars represent the percentage of respondents who resided in predominantly Democratic and Republican counties who intended to vote for Obama. The results indicate that local partisan context is highly correlated with vote choice. Democratic vote choice increases by 13.4 percentage points when comparing Asian American respondents who live in majority-Republican and majority-Democratic counties.

This relationship persists across many national origin groups. When comparing those who live in predominantly Republican and Democratic counties, the percentage of respondents intending to vote for Obama increases by 13.9 points among Chinese Americans, 17.8 points among Indian Americans, 3.6 points among Vietnamese Americans, 18.9 points among Korean Americans, and 20.8 points among Japanese Americans. Among Filipino Americans, vote choice does not vary substantially across partisan environments. Taken together, these patterns indicate that Asian Americans' voting choices reflect local partisan norms in the aggregate and across many national origin groups. However, this

---

[6] For example, 25% of Japanese American respondents lived in Los Angeles County, California; 11.4% lived in Honolulu County, Hawaii; and 9.3% lived in Santa Clara County, California.

[7] Appendix B includes a full cross-table of intended vote choice among likely voters by local partisan context (Appendix Table B.1).

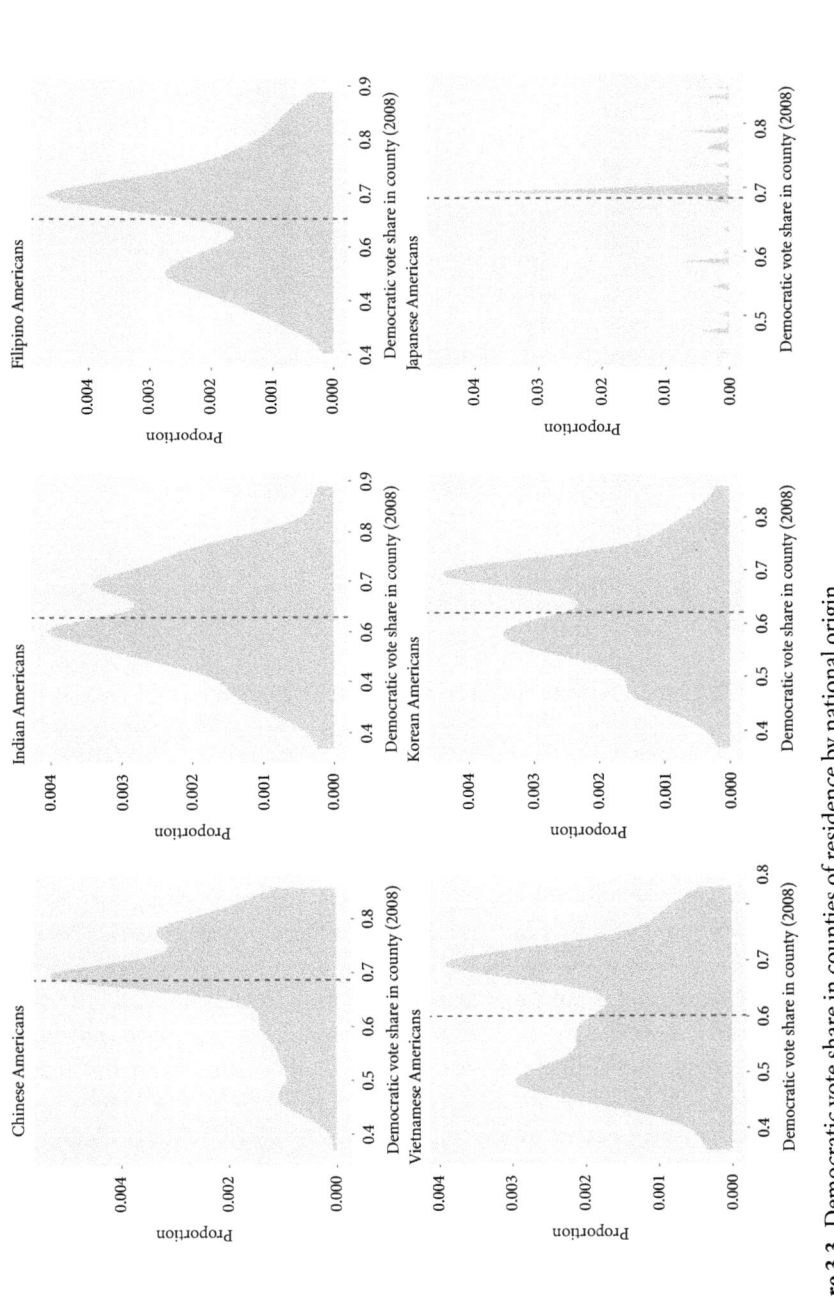

Figure 3.3 Democratic vote share in counties of residence by national origin
Source: The data are drawn from the 2008 National Asian American Survey (Ramakrishnan et al. 2008).

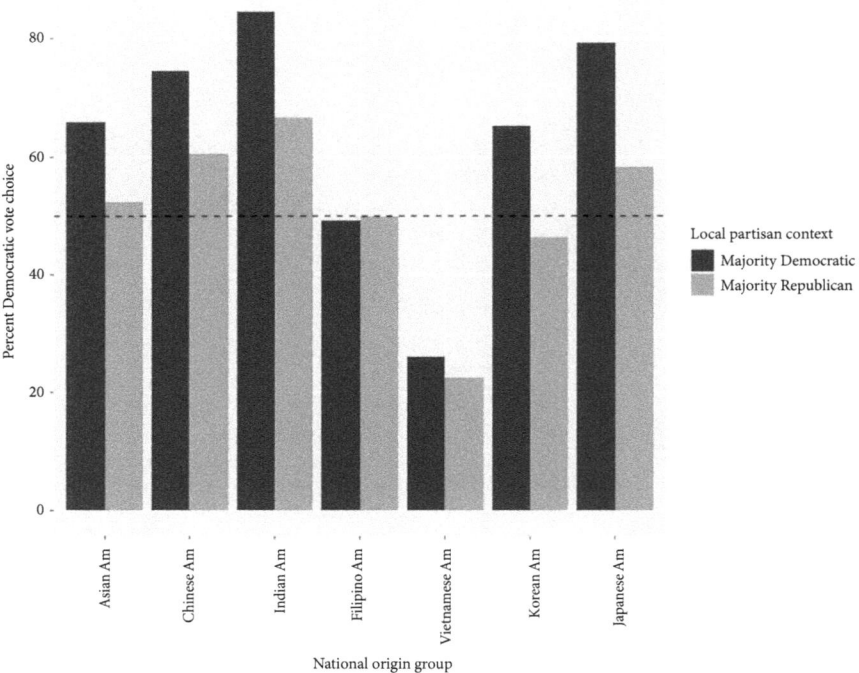

Figure 3.4 Asian American vote choice by local partisan context

Source: The data are drawn from the 2008 National Asian American Survey (Ramakrishnan et al. 2008).

relationship is weaker among Vietnamese Americans and Filipino Americans, in keeping with the prior findings.

These findings support the local partisan context hypothesis but offer mixed support for the subgroup variation hypothesis. Recall that the latter hypothesis predicts that the social transmission account applies most readily to recent immigrant groups and least readily to more acculturated groups. Local partisan context aligns well with vote choice among rapidly growing immigrant groups like Chinese Americans and Indian Americans, but may also shape vote choice for more established groups like Japanese Americans. Instead, local partisan context is less aligned with the vote choices of Filipino Americans and Vietnamese Americans, whose partisan preferences may be shaped by a history of migration from nondemocratic countries (Lien et al. 2004; Wong et al. 2011).

Does Local Asian American Population Context Shape Asian American Vote Choice?

Since many Asian Americans settle in similar environments, it is important to consider whether local Asian American population share rather than partisan context drives their voting choices. I address this possibility by analyzing the relationship between local Asian American population context and vote choice among Asian Americans as a pan-ethnic community and the six-largest national origin subgroups.

It is important to note that few Asian Americans live in counties with large Asian American populations. Figures 3.5 and 3.6 present the distribution of the Asian American population in respondent's counties of residence for all Asian American respondents and separately by national origin group. As Figure 3.5 shows, the typical Asian American likely voter lived in a county where about 16.6% of residents identified as Asian American in 2008. In fact, most respondents resided in counties where fewer than 30% of residents were Asian American.

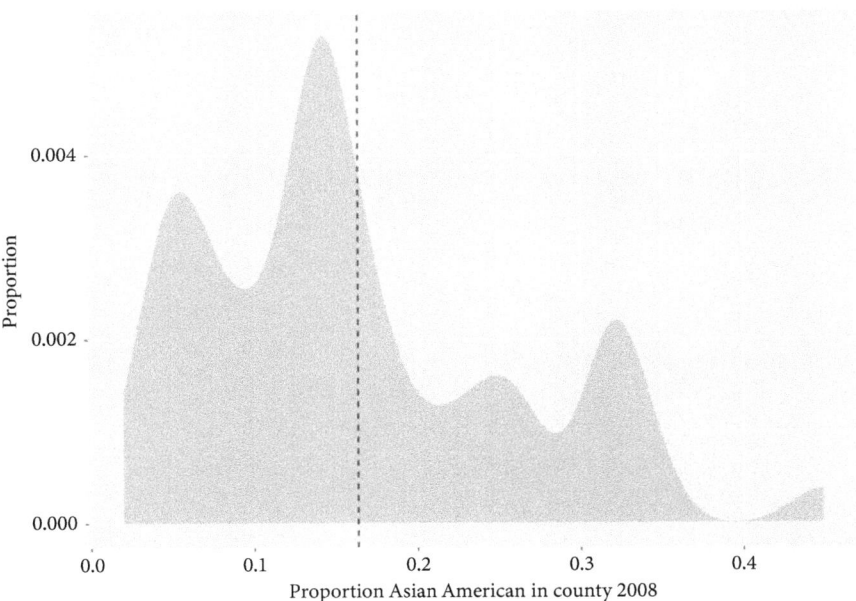

Figure 3.5 Asian American population percentage in counties of residence

Source: The data are drawn from the 2008 National Asian American Survey (Ramakrishnan et al. 2008).

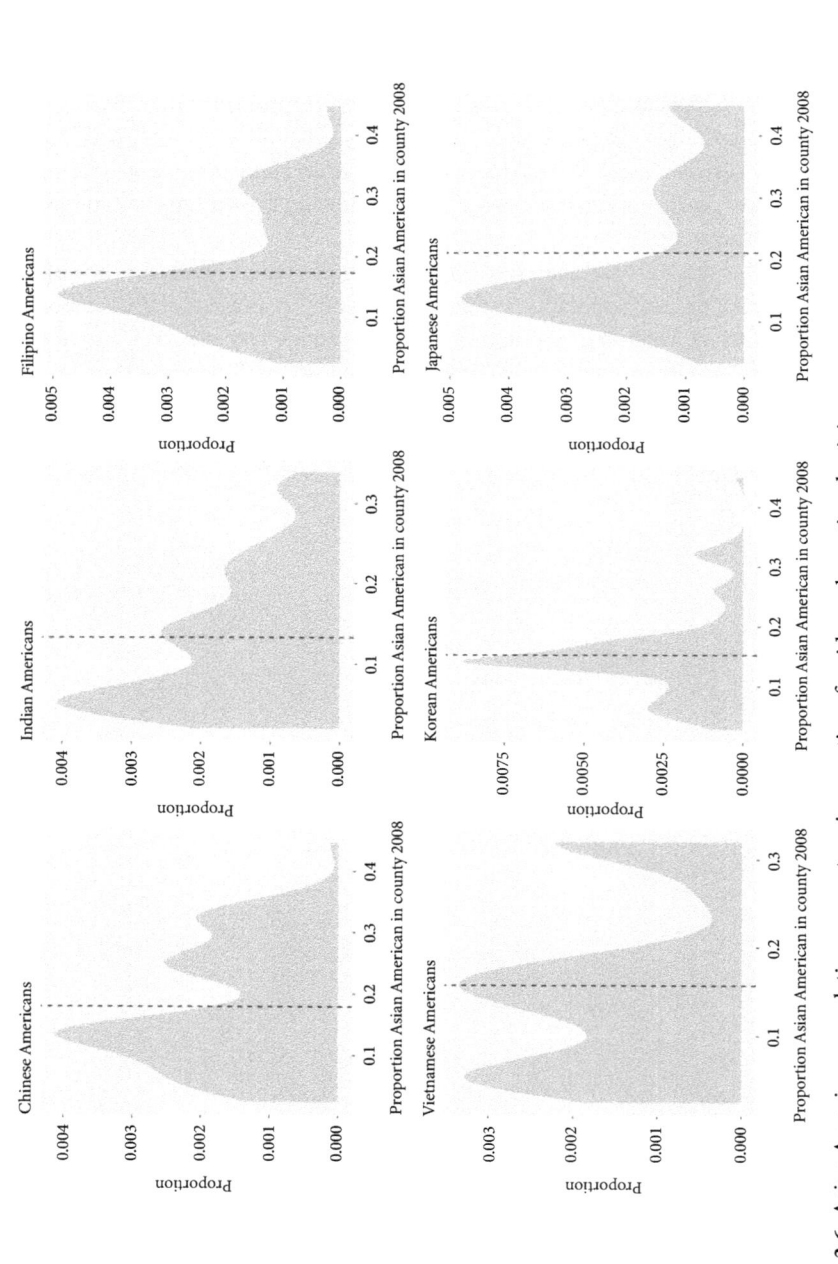

Figure 3.6 Asian American population percentage in counties of residence by national origin
Source: The data are drawn from the 2008 National Asian American Survey (Ramakrishnan et al. 2008).

There is some variation in local Asian American population context across national origin groups, but most follow a similar pattern. Figure 3.6 shows that most Chinese Americans, Indian Americans, Filipino Americans, Vietnamese Americans, and Korean Americans live in counties with less than 20% of the population is Asian American. The average percentage of Asian Americans in counties of residence is highest for Japanese Americans at 21.1%. This reflects the fact that many Japanese Americans live in California and Hawaii, states with large Asian American populations. Although many Asian Americans may live in towns and neighborhoods with larger Asian American populations, these analyses indicate that relatively few Asian Americans live in counties where their racial group makes up a plurality or majority of residents.

To what extent does variation in local Asian American population context explain Asian Americans' vote choices in 2008? Figure 3.7 illustrates the relationship between county-level Asian American population share and vote choice in 2008.[8] These data show a weak correlation between Asian American population size and vote choice for all but Filipino Americans. Starting with

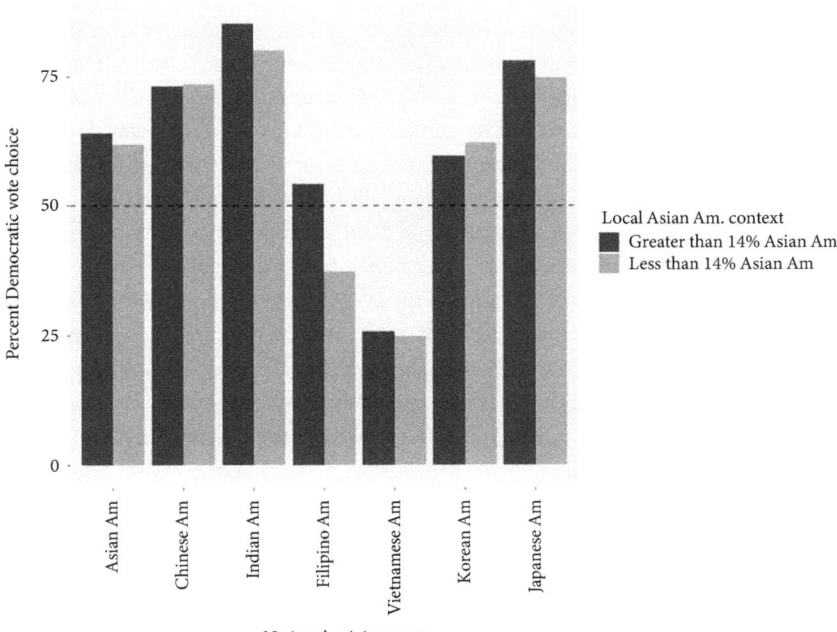

Figure 3.7 Asian American vote choice by local Asian American population context

Source: The data are drawn from the 2008 National Asian American Survey (Ramakrishnan et al. 2008).

---

[8] Appendix B includes a full cross-table of intended vote choice by local Asian American population context (Appendix Table B.2).

Asian Americans as a pan-ethnic group, the percentage of respondents voting for the Democratic candidate increases by just 2 percentage points when comparing those who reside in counties with small and large Asian American populations. These differences are also minimal for most national origin subgroups, including Chinese Americans (−0.5 percentage points), Indian Americans (5.3 points), Vietnamese Americans (0.9 points), Korean Americans (−2.5 points), and Japanese Americans (3.2 points). In contrast, local Asian American context has a strong correlation with vote choice among Filipino Americans. In fact, Democratic vote choice increases by 16.9 percentage points when comparing Filipino Americans who reside in counties with many and few Asian American residents.

Exploring the Relationship Between Local Context and Asian American Vote Choice

Next, I test the local partisan context hypothesis while also accounting for local Asian American population context. Do local partisan norms still have a strong relationship with vote choice after accounting for the size of the local Asian American population? In this analysis, I regress vote choice onto local partisan context, Asian American population context, and length of residence for all Asian Americans and the six largest national origin groups using standard OLS regression models. Figure 3.8 presents the regression coefficients, which quantify the effects of local partisan context (e.g., living in a predominantly Democratic county) and Asian American population context (e.g., the percentage of residents in county who are Asian American) on vote choice.[9]

I find that the partisan dynamics of a respondent's county of residence have a large and statistically significant association with vote choice for Asian Americans as a pan-ethnic group and several ethnic subgroups. Focusing first on all Asian American respondents, those who live in majority-Democratic counties were over 16 percentage points more likely to vote for Obama than those who lived in majority-republican counties (Figure 3.8). This regression coefficient is large and statistically significant at the $p < 0.01$ level. In contrast, the effect of local Asian American context on vote choice is not statistically significant among Asian Americans as a pan-ethnic group. This indicates that local partisan norms rather than racial context shape Asian Americans' voting decisions.

Turning to the six ethnic subgroups, living in a majority-Democratic partisan context increases Democratic vote choice by about 19 percentage points among Chinese Americans ($p < 0.05$), 13 points Indian Americans ($p < 0.05$), and 17 points among Korean Americans ($p < 0.10$). The association is similar

[9] The full regression results are included in Appendix B (Appendix Table B.3).

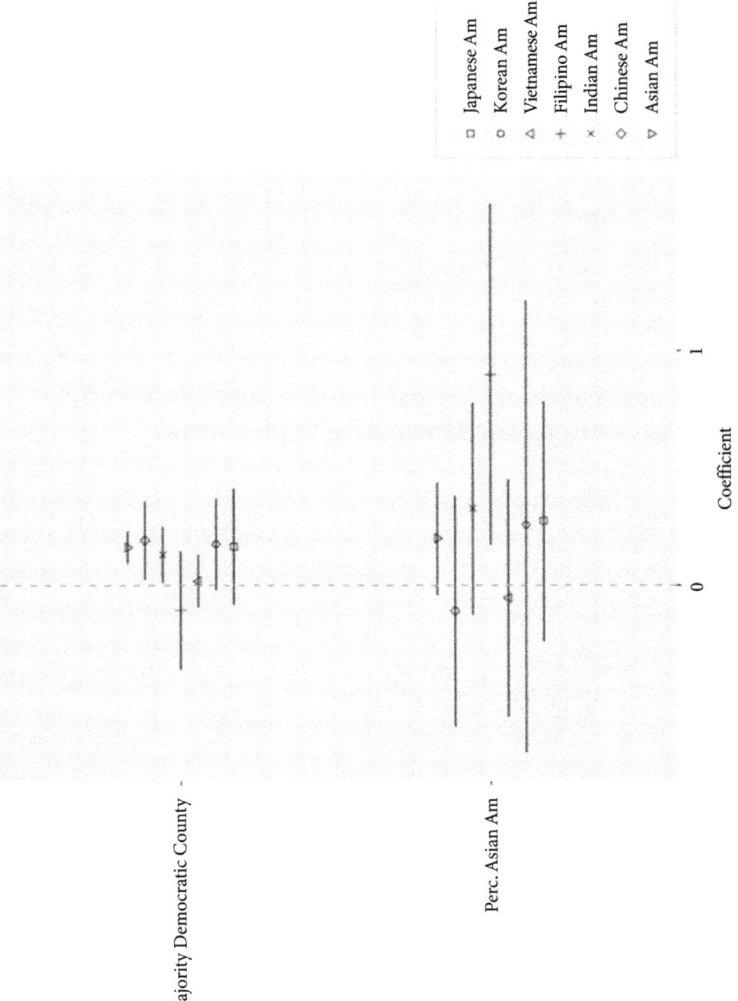

Figure 3.8 Associations between local context measures and vote choice
Source: The data are drawn from the 2008 National Asian American Survey (Ramakrishnan et al. 2008).

in magnitude for Japanese Americans at 16 points but does not approach standard thresholds for statistical significance. In contrast, the association between partisan context and vote choice is weaker and statistically insignificant for Vietnamese Americans (0.18 points) and negative but statistically insignificant for Filipino Americans (−10.6 points).

In line with the descriptive results presented earlier in the chapter, the only subgroup for which local Asian American context does not predict vote choice is Filipino Americans. Instead, living in a county with a large Asian American population increases Democratic vote choice by nearly 90 percentage points for Filipino Americans. This does not mean that social transmission does not apply to this subgroup. Perhaps this contextual analysis does not tap into the dynamics of the peer groups that Filipino Americans interact with. Instead, it is possible that the political attitudes reflected in the social networks of Southeast Asian Americans are embedded into do not reflect broader partisan norms in their counties of residence.

Does Local Partisan Context Explain Vote Choice after Accounting for Alternative Explanations?

The results presented in the previous two sections show that local partisan context shapes the vote choices of Asian Americans from a diverse range of national origin groups. This relationship holds when accounting for local Asian American population context and length of residence. Next, I explore whether local partisan context predicts Asian Americans' vote choices after accounting for other established predictors of voting behavior. This section only focuses on Asian Americans as a pan-ethnic group due to sample size limitations.

To test the local partisan context hypothesis alongside alternative explanations, I regress vote choice onto different sets of variables using logistic regression models.[10] I call these the "naive model," the "main model," and the "full model." The naive model only contains characteristics of an individual's local environment: local partisan context, local Asian American context, and length of residence. The main model adds demographic (e.g., age, gender, marital status, employment status, homeownership, parent of child under 18, resides in Southern state), religious (e.g., Evangelical, Catholic, no religion, church attendance, and church social engagement), and socioeconomic (e.g., education and income) predictors to the naive model. The full model adds national origin, discrimination, and linked fate (with other minorities, with Asian Americans,

---

[10] I use logistic models because the vote choice outcome is binary. Vote choice equals 1 if the respondent intended to vote for the Democratic candidate and 0 if they intended to vote for the Republican candidate. Since coefficients from logistic regression models are difficult to interpret, I contextualize the results using substantively meaningful concepts like the predicted probability of voting for Obama, expressed as a percentage.

with national origin group) predictors to the main model.[11] These models do not control for Democratic partisanship, because it may be a downstream consequence of vote choice.

Figure 3.9 depicts how likely Asian Americans who lived in majority-Democratic and majority-Republican counties were to vote for Obama in 2008 based on the model results. This evidence offers strong support for the local partisan context hypothesis, indicating that the partisan norms expressed in local environments shape Asian Americans' vote choices. Living in a majority-Democratic (vs. majority-Republican) county increases the likelihood of Democratic vote choice by over 16 percentage points in the naive model, 14 percentage

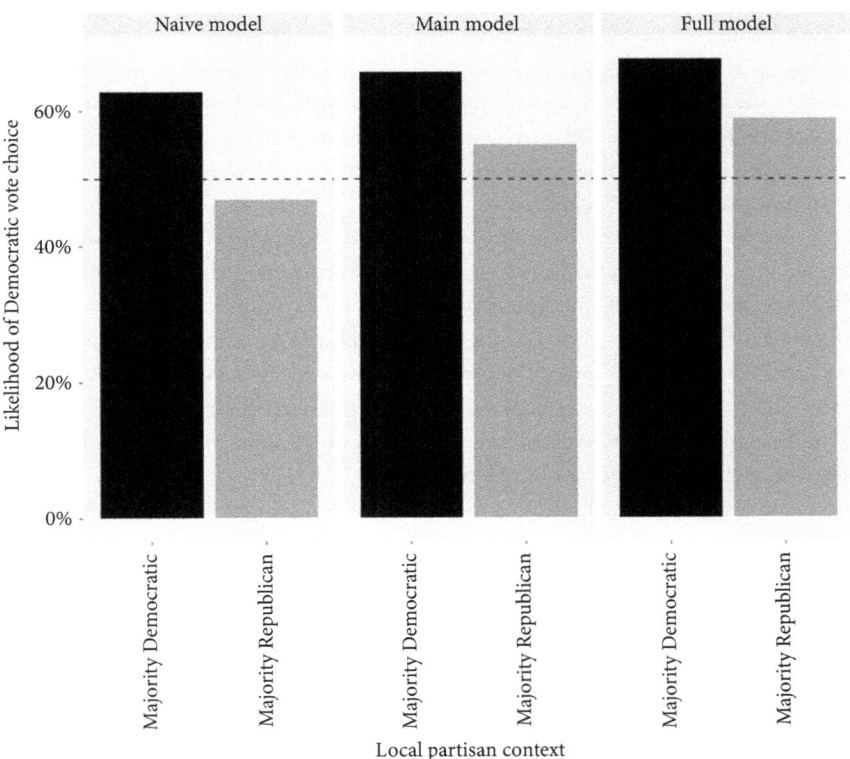

Figure 3.9 Likelihood of Democratic vote choice across local partisan contexts

All models control for local Asian American context, and length of residence. The main and full models also control for demographic, religious, and socioeconomic factors. The full model controls for national origin, discrimination and linked fate.

Source: The data are drawn from the 2008 National Asian American Survey (Ramakrishnan et al. 2008).

[11] The models also include indicators for predictors with more than 15% missing data. The complete regression results are included in Table 3.2A, in the Online Appendix.

points in the main model, and 8 percentage points in the full model. These coefficients are all statistically significant at the $p < 0.05$ level. These results largely comport with the descriptive trends presented in the previous section. Local partisan context is a large and statistically significant predictor of vote choice after accounting for several other factors, including age, religion, national origin, and linked fate.

How does local partisan context compare to established predictors of vote choice? I contextualize the effects of local partisan context on the likelihood of voting for Obama alongside other significant predictors of vote choice from the full model. Starting with local partisan context, recall that those who live in predominantly Republican counties were over 8 points less likely to vote for Obama than those who lived in predominantly Democratic counties. Turning to alternative explanations, most notably religious denomination, age, region, national origin, and interminority, linked fate emerge as other important predictors of vote choice. For example, identifying as an Evangelical Christian decreased the likelihood of voting for Obama by nearly 19 points. Age was another important dimension. Young people were more likely to vote for Obama than the elderly by a margin of over 15 points.

There were also major differences by national origin group. Those who immigrated from countries with authoritarian or communist histories were more likely to vote for McCain. Identifying as Korean, Filipino, and Vietnamese decreased the likelihood of Democratic vote choice by a margin of about 11, 32, and 52 percentage points respectively. These results point to the important role that national origin plays in shaping Asian Americans' vote choice. Finally, exhibiting high levels of linked fate with other racial minorities increased Democratic vote choice by over 19 points.

Taken together, these findings provide several key insights about Asian American vote choice in the contemporary period and support for the social transmission account. Local partisan dynamics are an important predictor of vote choice when tested independently and alongside alternative explanations. This suggests that Asian Americans may absorb the partisan norms of their local contexts.

Do Asian Americans Choose to Live in Liberal Contexts for Political Reasons?

Finally, I explore the possibility that the association between local partisan context and vote choice is driven by residential selection. Rather than picking up on local norms after settling in localities, it is possible that Asian Americans choose to live in environments because residents have a clear preference for Democrats or Republicans. Readers who are less interested in this technical analysis may skip ahead to the next section, which considers the implications of the findings presented in this chapter.

First, I test for the possibility that the effects of local partisan context are driven by politically engaged Asian Americans selecting where to live based on partisan preferences. In this analysis, I re-estimate the main logistic model separately across levels of political interest (Table 3.2). If residential selection is at play, then the largest effects should be observed among those with are very interested in politics. In contrast, social transmission predicts that local partisan norms have the strongest effects on vote choice among those who have limited prior political exposure and little political interest.

The results indicate that residential selection is unlikely. As Table 3.2 shows, the effects of local partisan context on vote choice are largest among those who are not too interested in politics, increasing the likelihood of Democratic vote choice by about 20 percentage points. This finding provides strong evidence against self-selection and in support of social transmission. People with low political interest are particularly unlikely to select where to live based on partisan preferences because they do not care too much about politics. Compared to their counterparts with high and medium levels of political interest, those with low political interest are also the most likely to absorb local partisan norms.

Second, I consider whether differences in the demographic characteristics of people who live in majority Democratic and Republican areas drive the effects of local partisan context. To do so, I run weighted regressions that match similar respondents who live in Democratic or Republican partisan environments. This method conceptualizes local partisan context as a binary treatment: each respondent either lives in a county that is predominantly Democratic or

Table 3.2 Effects of Social Transmission Predictors on Vote Choice, by Levels of Political Interest

	Dependent variable: Voted for Democrat in 2008 election		
Level of political interest:	Low	Medium	High
County partisan context: Majority Democratic	0.777*** (0.242)	0.366 (0.312)	0.450* (0.232)
Intercept	1.230* (0.717)	2.229* (1.166)	2.335** (0.977)
Observations	762	456	842

Note: ***p < 0.001; **p < 0.01; *p < 0.05.
Omitted county partisan context category: Majority Republican.
Controls included in models: length of residence, percentage Asian American in county, Evangelical, Catholic, no religion, church attendance, church social, income, education, age, gender, married, employed, homeowner, parent, South.
Source: The data are drawn from the 2008 National Asian American Survey (Ramakrishnan et al. 2008).

Republican.[12] The effects of local partisan context on vote choice hold in analysis (Table 3.3). Living in a predominantly Democratic county has a statistically significant relationship with vote choice across the three models. The continued explanatory power of local partisan context after accounting for demographics is another indication that residential selection is unlikely.

A final analysis focuses on Asian American immigrants because it would be more difficult for immigrants to select politically congenial environments than their US-born counterparts. I also test whether the partisan context in immigrants' first county of residence influences vote choice for those who moved between counties. This is important because immigrants have some degree of choice in where to settle once they establish themselves in the US, but they are particularly constrained when they first arrive in the country. In this analysis, I substitute local partisan context in the respondent's current county with their initial county of residence.[13] The length of residence variable also measures residence in the initial county. Figure 3.10 presents the likelihood of Democratic

Table 3.3 Effects of Social Transmission Predictors on Vote Choice, Weighted Model

	Dependent variable: Voted for Democrat in 2008 election		
	Naive model	Main model	Full model
Treatment: Majority Democratic county	0.715*** (0.164)	0.680*** (0.167)	0.533*** (0.194)
Intercept	0.690 (0.453)	0.974 (0.701)	0.952 (0.955)
Observations	1,669	1,623	1,473

Note: ***$p < 0.001$; **$p < 0.01$; *$p < 0.05$.
Omitted county partisan context category: Majority Republican County.
Controls included in naive model: length of residence, percentage Asian American in county.
Additional controls included in main model: Evangelical, Catholic, no religion, church attendance, church social, income, education, age, gender, married, employed, homeowner, parent, South.
Additional controls included in full model: national origin, discrimination, and linked fate (1) with other minorities, (2) with Asian Americans, and (3) with national origin group.
Source: The data are drawn from the 2008 National Asian American Survey (Ramakrishnan et al. 2008).

[12] I calculate propensity score weights by regressing this treatment onto demographic and socioeconomic predictors that may influence both residential selection and vote choice (Online Appendix Table 3.3A). The results of a balance test show that these covariates are statistically indistinguishable across treated and control units (Online Appendix Table 3.4A).
[13] This variable was binned at 70% to ensure sufficient variation between the two categories. The 2008 NAAS included a question about initial cities of residence. I extrapolated counties of residence from this information.

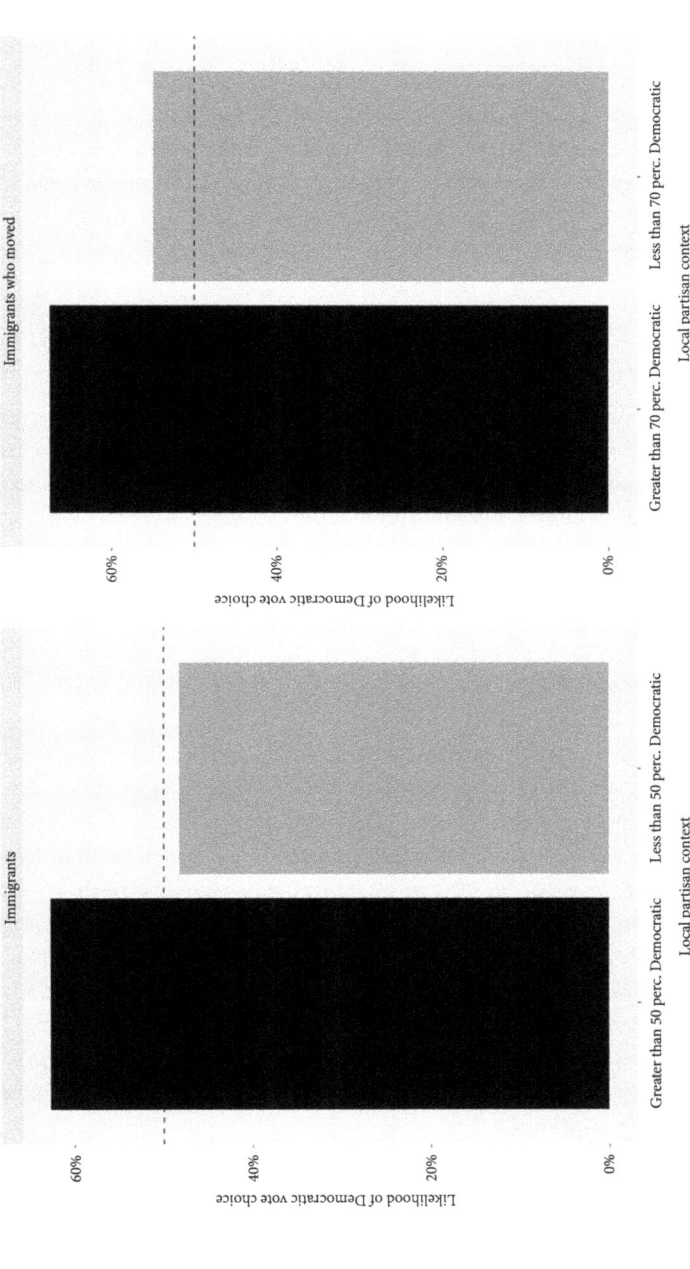

Figure 3.10 Likelihood of Democratic vote choice among immigrants across local partisan contexts
Source: The data are drawn from the 2008 National Asian American Survey (Ramakrishnan et al. 2008).

vote choice across partisan contexts for immigrants and those who moved from their initial city of residence.

Local partisan context has a statistically significant effect on vote choice for both groups. As Figure 3.10 shows, living in a Democratic county increases the probability of Democratic vote choice among immigrants by over 14 percentage points. Among immigrants who moved from the first county where they settled in the US, the effects of their initial county of residence on vote choice are similar in magnitude. These findings suggest that the association between local partisan context and vote choice holds among Asian American immigrants, who are constrained in making decisions about where to live.

Conclusion

This chapter provides evidence supporting the social transmission account by showing that settling in liberal local contexts contributes to Democratic vote choice among Asian Americans. More specifically, living in predominantly Democratic partisan contexts has important consequences for Asian Americans' vote choices, increasing the likelihood of Democratic voting by as much as 16 points. By the same logic, residing in more conservative local contexts contributes to Republican vote choice, which has increased among Asian Americans over the past few years. This suggests that local partisan context may be an important factor that contributes to partisan socialization in the Asian American community.

Taken together, the analyses presented in this chapter offer a comprehensive test of the relationship between local partisan context and vote choice. By exploring vote choice in presidential elections among Asian Americans as a whole and the six largest national origin groups, this chapter provides added insight into the explanatory power of social transmission. The results indicate that local partisan context explains variation in vote choice among Asian Americans in the aggregate and across diverse national origin subgroups, including Chinese Americans, Indian Americans, Japanese Americans, and Korean Americans. While the patterns are less clear for Filipino Americans and Vietnamese Americans, they suggest that the partisan characteristics of the local environments that Asian Americans settle in shape partisan preferences for diverse segments of the community.

Among the accounts tested in this analysis, social transmission offers a compelling explanation for the contemporary trend in Democratic support among Asian Americans given their settlement patterns in left-leaning metropolitan areas. However, one weakness is that the observational nature of the survey data limits the ability to draw causal claims about the effects of local partisan context on vote choice. This suggests that there may be other factors driving the relationship between local context and vote choice among Asian Americans. The most concerning alternative explanation is residential selection, or the possibility that Asian Americans select where to live based on existing partisan preferences. I end the chapter with multiple analyses that address this concern.

More broadly, this chapter offers several important contributions to the literature on political learning and partisan socialization in diverse Asian American communities. First, these analyses uncover evidence of social transmission while accounting for other possible explanations for vote choice in the Asian American community. Although several previous studies investigate the partisan dynamics of the Asian American community using survey data, this racial group is growing and their partisan behavior changed rapidly between the 1990s and 2000s. The results indicate that local partisan norms played a role in this process. Second, this chapter offers insight into the extent to which the social transmission account applies across diverse Asian American ethnic groups that have markedly different experiences in the US but often settle in similar left-leaning local environments. Third, the results generalize to the national population of Asian American likely voters. Given the challenges of studying the political behavior of small minority groups empirically, nationally representative surveys offer valuable insights and have wide-ranging implications.

Despite these strengths, this chapter offers little evidence about the nature of social interactions with peer groups within local environments that shape Asian Americans' partisan preferences. After all, these analyses do not explore whether and how social interactions with peers within local social environments shape Asian Americans' partisan preferences. Chapter 4 addresses these important points, exploring whether Asian Americans develop partisan views by discussing American politics with peers, the primary mechanism underlying social transmission, or through similar political discussions with family, as standard accounts in American politics predict.

4
The Relative Partisan Influence of Peers and Family

Does discussing American politics with family members and peer networks shape Asian Americans' partisan attitudes? Chapter 4 begins to explore whether and, if so, how social connections drive partisan acquisition among Asian Americans. In a two-part reflection piece entitled "How to Talk to Your Parents about Politics," journalist Dominque Fong (2021a and 2021b) chronicles the difficulties that many second-generation Asian Americans face when discussing American politics with their immigrant parents. The author draws on her personal experiences as a second-generation Chinese American and those of other Asian American adult children of immigrants. Fong (2021a) argues that generational divides often lead to fraught conversations because "we don't have the tools to navigate political discussions." Further probing the reasons behind her reticence to speak openly about politics with her parents, she claims:

> Growing up in a Chinese American family in the Bay Area, my siblings and I didn't speak about politics. We were taught that it wasn't a polite dinner table subject, so we never learned the skills of how to debate civics or share differing opinions. (Fong 2021a)

The lack of civic guidance Dominique experienced in early life comports with the experiences of other Asian American children of immigrants she spoke with. For example, Jamie, a Chinese American who participated in Black Lives Matter protests in Oakland, California, claimed she "had voted since she was 18 . . . but up until the 2020 presidential elections, she didn't talk openly about politics with anyone, especially not close family" (Fong 2021a). Katherine, an Indonesian American in her early forties who lives in Philadelphia, cited a lack of understanding of the "traumas of my mother's past" prior to immigration as a reason "she keeps politics out of their talks and sticks to safer topics like food and cooking" (Fong 2021b). The author also offers several tips to young Asian Americans hoping to discuss politics with their immigrant parents, including understanding how their parents learned about American politics and realizing their perspectives may be rooted in "traumas of the past," like migrating to the US as refugees escaping authoritarian regimes (Fong 2021b).

The Social Roots of Asian American Partisanship. Tanika Raychaudhuri, Oxford University Press.
© Oxford University Press (2025). DOI: 10.1093/9780197826560.003.0004

Collectively, these examples align with the expectation that Asian Americans experience little in the way of political discussion growing up in immigrant households and must develop political perspectives and civic skills elsewhere. Moreover, while many Asian Americans support Democrats, these anecdotes reflect a generational divide in political views within some families, such that some immigrant parents are more politically conservative than their children. This pattern may apply more broadly, especially in Southeast Asian communities (Abdelkader and Liu 2020; Le and Su 2017). This investigation also indicates that the sources of political information that immigrants and their children have access to may differ.

How do Asian Americans learn about American politics across diverse national origin and generational groups? To what extent do social forces, including family members and peer groups, play a role in shaping their political attitudes? The previous chapter shows that Asian Americans who live in predominantly Democratic areas vote for Democrats at higher rates than those who live in Republican environments after accounting for other factors that contribute to their voting decisions. However, the evidence presented so far offers little insight into the social experiences that inform Asian Americans' political views at the individual level. The rest of the book turns to exploring the social interactions that shape Asian Americans' vote choices, partisan views, and political identities. This chapter focuses on the role of political discussion with family during childhood and peers during adulthood.

Before delving into the details, I offer another motivating example, drawing from in-depth interviews conducted with Asian Americans nationwide in 2021. These interviews provide a useful complement to the Houston area case study because they are not geographically bounded to a particular city or part of the country. According to the social transmission account of partisan acquisition, Asian Americans experience limited exposure to American politics and the party system through the family during childhood, which makes them open to the political influence of peers outside the home. In-depth interviews with diverse Asian American residents of Houston illustrate this point in Chapter 2. Several respondents reported occasional discussion of American politics with peers, suggesting that equal-status peer groups and social connections outside of the home play a larger role in partisan acquisition than the nuclear family. Conversations with peers about American politics may contribute to Democratic voting because many Asian Americans settle in Democratic-leaning political environments where they are more likely to interact with Democratic than Republican peers.

Additional interviews with Asian Americans who live in various regions of the US largely reflect the experiences of respondents in the Houston case study.

These interviews were conducted between February and June of 2021 as part of another study focused on the role of interactions in the workplace in political learning. To that end, we interviewed 39 self-identified Asian American[1] immigrants and children of immigrants who worked in white-collar roles in the technology sector about their experiences discussing politics at work.[2] These respondents were diverse in terms of national origin, age, generational status, and regions of residence. Although partisan acquisition was not the primary focus of this research project, these interviews included questions about political discussion with family members and peer groups. The interviewees are also geographically unbounded and offer insight on whether parents, other family members, and peer groups outside the home shape the political perspectives of Asian Americans living in various parts of the country. I draw on these responses to offer two examples below, which highlight the role of family members and of peer groups in the process of political learning.

For example, an Indian American immigrant in his mid-thirties who lived in Atlanta, Georgia at the time of the interview reported that he rarely had conversations about American politics at home when he was growing up in India. When asked if he ever discussed American politics with his parents, he said they would occasionally engage in a surface level conversation, but his parents did not have enough knowledge of US politics for extended discussion:

> Whatever we heard from media gave us bias and then we'd say, "Oh, what are they doing? What is this?" And I would ask my dad about it. Even then, [my parents] were limited in their ideas ... they could answer, but it was never an extended Q&A session.

The recollections of a transitional-generation Indian American woman in her early twenties who grew up in a liberal northern California suburb suggest a similar experience may extend to Asian Americans brought up in the US. When asked if she discussed American politics with her parents during her childhood, she said it began when she was a teenager, when she started to learn about the topic in high school. In line with accounts of "reversed" intergenerational political learning in immigrant families, she initiated these conversations and provided her parents with political information (McDevitt and Chaffee 2002; Wong and Tseng 2008).

---

[1] In total, 17 interviewees identified as East Asian, 18 as South Asian, and 3 as East Asian. One respondent identified as both East and Southeast Asian.
[2] The interviews were conducted online over Zoom and took between 30 and 90 minutes to complete. We recruited respondents by advertising the study on Asian American professional networking groups on LinkedIn and Facebook. The project was approved by the designated institutional review board prior to conducting the interviews.

Not until I reached high school . . . We started learning more about like American government and politics in AP Gov . . . And then once I got to college, you became aware of like, different issues. And so, a lot of it would be like just relaying what was going on back to my parents.

Despite a lack of parental influence, she was exposed to discussions about American politics from her friends in school as a teenager. When asked if she ever talked about American politics with peers, she recalled:

We started discussing it more in high school . . . one of my friends used to read the newspaper before going to school every morning. She was the one who was more politically aware than all of us. And she'd be like, "Hey, do you guys know what's going on in the world today?" And we'd be like, "No, tell us," And we would like, start discussing things from there.

Her experiences suggest that conversations in peer groups and educational settings may provide the children of Asian American immigrants with information about American politics. Both respondents had developed partisan views at the time of the interview, expressing a preference for Democrats over Republicans, and voted for Biden in the 2020 presidential election.

While the experiences of the Asian Americans profiled in Dominque Fong's article and these two interview respondents indicate that peers may play a central role in the political socialization of Asian Americans, it is unclear whether these experiences apply more broadly. Do Asian Americans discuss American politics more frequently with peers than family? If so, what is the racial composition of the peer groups that influence their political attitudes? To what extent do conversations about American politics with family members and peer groups shape Asian Americans' partisan preferences? Do these conversations contribute to how Asian Americans make their partisan decisions in communities across the United States?

Using evidence from the Omnibus Asian American Survey (OAAS), a national survey of over 1,500 Asian Americans from varied national origin groups and immigrant generations, this chapter explores these questions, directly comparing peer influence, the book's hypothesized mechanism of partisan socialization, to theories of familial influence. The results point to the political influence of peers across immigrant generations and national origin groups.

In this chapter I show that most Asian Americans discuss American politics more frequently with peers during adulthood than they did with their family during childhood. In turn, frequent political discussion with peer groups is associated with identification with a major party. In terms of the direction of partisanship, discussion with peers often leads to Democratic rather than

Republican partisan views because most Asian Americans settle in liberal areas where their peer groups are more likely to hold Democratic views. In contrast, frequent political discussion with family during childhood is not strongly related to Asian Americans' partisan preferences or identities. These patterns largely hold across the six largest Asian American national origin groups and the first, second, and third immigrant generations.

There are also some notable differences in the racial composition of political peer groups that Asian Americans discuss politics with across immigrant generations. Asian American immigrants report more frequent discussion of American politics with Asian peers than transitional-, second-, and third-generation Asian Americans do. In contrast, Asian Americans who were born or raised in the US report more frequent political discussion with non-Asian peers than first-generation immigrants do. I present these findings in detail in the rest of the chapter, after discussing the socializing role of family members and peer groups in American politics.

Evaluating the Role of the Family and Peer Groups in Partisan Acquisition

There are several potential explanations for the development of partisan preferences among Asian Americans, including direct mobilization by political parties, community organizations, experiences of discrimination or social exclusion, and political exposure through the family.[3] For example, historical research on the role of institutions in immigrant political socialization centers political parties. In the nineteenth and twentieth centuries, the major political parties directly engaged with immigrants at the local level and encouraged them to join their ranks (Archdeacon 1983; Cornwell 1960; Erie 1990). While both major parties participated in these efforts, Democrats were particularly focused on attracting naturalized immigrants between the 1930s and 1960s (Andersen 1979).

However, both Democrats and Republicans lost the organizational capacity and political desire to recruit contemporary immigrant voters after 1965, when large numbers of Asian American and Latino immigrants began migrating to the US (Hajnal and Lee 2011; Wong 2006). In the absence of local party recruitment efforts, advocacy and community organizations help immigrants to navigate the American political system in communities across the US (de Graauw 2016; Ramakrishnan and Bloemraad 2008; Wong 2006). While these organizations aid in the process of political learning, they are often nonpartisan and unlikely to

---

[3] I discuss these explanations at length in Chapter 2.

provide strong partisan cues as immigrants learn about the American political system.

Since political institutions play a limited role in partisan socialization among most contemporary immigrants, research on the acquisition of partisanship among Asian Americans has largely focused on social and behavioral factors. For example, some research highlights differences in partisan preferences based on country of origin (Cain et al. 1991; Wong et al. 2011). Recent work explores whether experiencing racial discrimination leads Asian Americans to prefer Democrats over Republicans, but support for this theoretical perspective is mixed across studies (Chan et al. 2022; Hopkins et al. 2020; Kuo et al. 2017).

While these explanations are all worthy of further investigation, this chapter considers a new explanation, comparing the role of political discussion with peer groups to the family in the development of Asian Americans' partisan identities. Longstanding accounts of American political socialization center parental influence in early life. For example, many scholars argue that Americans inherit partisan preferences from their families through social exposure during childhood and young adulthood (Davies 1965; Greenstein 1965; Hyman 1959; Jennings and Niemi 1968; Jennings et al. 2009).

Since the early days of behavioral research in political science, scholars have argued that parents are the primary "socializing agents" who expose their children to the political world (Davies 1965; Greenstein 1965; Hyman 1959). Some claimed that parental influence is bounded to exposure to the American system of government rather than the development of political perspectives (Hess and Torney 1967). However, the disproportionate influence of parents in the process of political socialization is cited as a central reason for the stability of partisan views over the course of an individual's life in foundational political science texts (Berelson et al. 1954; Campbell et al. 1960).

Research on familial political influence focused on the role parents and other family members play in the development of a range of political perspectives, including political interest, policy views, and partisan identification. In a landmark study of the role of parents in shaping the political views of their children, M. Kent Jennings and Richard Niemi (1968) evaluated this intergenerational transmission perspective using then-contemporary data. The authors argued that the narrow focus on the role of parents in classic research on political socialization was driven by striking commonalities in the political preferences of parents and children (Jennings and Niemi 1968, 169).

At that time, most parents and children held similar political views, which implied that they were developed through discussions at home. The study defined "political values" broadly and analyzed the convergence of the attitudes of parents and children on a variety of themes, including "party identification, opinions on specific issues, political cynicism, and evaluations of socio-political groupings" (Jennings and Niemi 1968, 173–79). While the authors found modest correlations between the views of parents and children on many political outcomes, there was a high degree of similarity in partisanship, which supported the intergenerational transmission account of partisan acquisition.

Decades later, a research team that included one of the original authors revisited the political perspectives of parent-child pairs, as well as the views of the next generation of children (Jennings et al. 2009). The results reflected those of the original study and showed commonalities in the partisan views of a new generation of parents and children, especially in families that frequently discussed politics (Jennings et al. 2009). Outside of a handful of studies (e.g., Tyler and Iyengar 2023), research on political socialization and the role of the family in the process became out of vogue by the 1970s. In fact, several articles have been published encouraging scholars to revisit these questions with titles like "The Rebirth of Political Socialization" and "Not Your Parent's Political Socialization: Introduction for a New Generation" (Niemi and Hepburn 1995; Sapiro 2004).

While a large body of empirical research offers evidence of intergenerational partisan transmission within families, much of this work is dated and worthy of investigation in a new era characterized by increasing political polarization and racial diversity. First, contemporary social networks are becoming more clearly divided across racial and partisan lines (Carlson et al. 2020; Settle 2018). This suggests that peer groups may play a larger role in shaping partisan perspectives than they did 50 years ago but raises concerns about self-selection into congenial networks.

Another major limitation of existing work is that it relies on survey data that does not reflect the racial diversity of the modern American electorate. For example, several well-known studies find strong correlations between the partisan views of parents and children across generational cohorts (Jennings and Neimi 1968; 1974; 1981; Jennings et al. 2009). Much of this research draws on a single longitudinal survey called the "Youth Parent Political Socialization Study." The four-wave survey was conducted over several decades with a national sample of American high school seniors from the class of 1965 and their parents ("Youth Study Series" 2021). Where possible, children of the original 1965 seniors were also interviewed in the final survey wave, which was used in recent research (Jennings et al. 2009). The youth-parent study represents a rare high quality longitudinal political survey of family units. This research offers evidence of intergenerational familial partisan transmission among the cohort of Americans who came of age in the 1960s, their parents, and their children. However, immigrants and their children from Asia, Africa, Latin America, and the Caribbean who have joined the American polity over the past 50 years are not represented among the respondents.

As discussed in further detail in Chapter 2, familial explanations for political socialization may not apply well to these new groups of immigrants and their descendants who represent the first few generations of their families in the United States. Several scholars argue that the family plays a smaller role in partisan acquisition and more broadly, in the process of political learning, for immigrants than nonimmigrants (Carlos 2018; Hajnal and Lee 2011). For example, Zoltan Hajnal and Taeku Lee (2011) attribute high rates of nonidentification with any of the mainstream partisan categories among Asian Americans and Latinos to a lack of exposure to the American political system through the family or political parties. Roberto Carlos (2018) builds on this work, finding that a consequence of limited exposure to the party system in early life in immigrant families is that many second-generation Asian Americans and Latinos develop partisan identities well after entering adulthood.

While both studies argue that little discussion of American politics occurs between immigrant parents and their children (or the parents of immigrants and immigrants themselves), this claim has not been directly tested with contemporary data among members of the Asian American community. Moreover, existing research has not directly explored whether peers play a role in immigrant political socialization in the absence of political discussion with parents during childhood.

Despite the enduring focus on parental political influence, research in American politics has also considered the possibility that social and educational sources outside of the home shape political learning and partisan acquisition. Dating back to research from the 1960s, a major conclusion from Robert Hess and JV Torney's (1967) book was that public schools play an important role in the development of children's political perspectives. Many other scholars focus on curricular initiatives in exploring how educational environments shape political attitudes and engagement (Campbell 2006; Campbell 2019; Willeck and Mendelberg 2022). In fact, recent research indicates that civic education programs may be particularly formative for the children of immigrants who attend American schools but receive limited political exposure at home (Callahan and Muller 2013; Campbell and Niemi 2016; Junn 2004).

Others narrow in on the social influence of peer groups in the development of political attitudes. Although this research is not primarily focused on racial minorities or immigrants, studies focused on peer effects among high school seniors offer modest support for the theory that peers influence the political perspectives of young adults (Campbell 1980; Tedin 1980). Another line of work argues that daily social interactions are central to the political attitudes and choices of ordinary Americans (Carlson et al. 2020; Cramer 2004; Sinclair 2012). For example, in *Talking about Politics: Informal Groups and Social Identity in American Life*, Katherine Cramer (2004) argues that quotidian political conversations that occur in various social environments are politically consequential. She argues that people "make sense" of politics through the lens of their social identities and the perspectives shared in their local communities (Cramer 2004, 2).

Building on these ideas, in *The Social Citizen: Peer Networks and Political Behavior*, Betsy Sinclair (2012) finds that "people's social networks are not merely sources of political information but have a direct and immediate influence on their political behavior," which includes vote choice and partisan identification (xii). Finally, in *Talking Politics: Political Discussion Networks and the New American Electorate*, Taylor Carlson, Marisa Abrajano, and Lisa García Bedolla (2020) extend these accounts to an increasingly racially diverse American public. These studies indicate that many Americans discuss politics with their social networks, which has implications for their political decisions and behavior.

Hypotheses: Discussing American Politics with Family Members and Peer Groups

I build on these theoretical perspectives and extend these arguments to partisan acquisition in the Asian American community. To that end, I develop several hypotheses about the nature and consequences of political discussion with family and peers for the partisan choices of Asian Americans from varied national origin groups and immigrant generations. The hypotheses are discussed below and summarized in Table 4.1.

First, I explore the extent to which Asian Americans discuss American politics with their parents during childhood and peer networks later in life. The *political discussion hypothesis* compares the frequency of discussing American politics with peer groups to similar discussion with parents and other family members. It predicts Asian Americans are more likely to discuss American politics with adult peers later in life than with family members during childhood. It builds on prior arguments that Asian Americans experience limited political exposure from parents and other family members during childhood (Carlos 2018; Hajnal and Lee 2011).

Next, the *peer partisan influence hypothesis* considers whether these political discussions shape Asian Americans' political perspectives. Building on the prior expectation, this hypothesis predicts that Asian Americans who discuss American politics frequently with peers are more likely to identify with one of the two major parties than those who rarely have political conversations with peer groups. In contrast, discussing American politics with family during childhood should not be associated with Asian Americas' partisan attitudes. Even in instances where Asian Americans discuss American politics with parents during childhood, it will not have a strong association with partisan attitudes because their parents do not have strongly held partisan views to ground these discussions.

Does frequent discussion of American politics with peer groups lead Asian Americans to support Democrats or Republicans? In terms of the direction of peer partisan influence, I hypothesize that discussing American politics with peers is associated with a preference for Democrats over Republicans among most Asian Americans because they live in liberal environments. In turn, their partisan views will shift in the direction of the preferences expressed by the people around them. However, the direction of partisan acquisition should be conditioned by local partisan context. As such, I explore whether political discussion with peers is more likely to lead to Democratic preferences in liberal than conservative states in the Chapter 4 Online Appendix ⊚.[4]

After exploring whether peers play a larger role in the political socialization of Asian Americans than family members, I then consider whether the racial composition of Asian Americans' peer groups varies by generational status.[5] Recall that the social transmission account of political learning argues that the racial composition of peer groups differs across immigrant generations. I argue that Asian Americans who immigrated as adults primarily interact with other Asian immigrants, while those who were born or raised in the United States have comparatively diverse peer groups (Mok et al. 2007; "Second-Generation Americans" 2013; Qian et al. 2001; Zhou and Xiong 2005). In line with these expectations, the *racial composition hypothesis* predicts that first-generation immigrants are more likely to discuss American politics with Asian peers than their US-born counterparts. In contrast, transitional-, second-, and third-generation Asian Americans are more likely to discuss American politics with non-Asian peers than first-generation immigrants.

Finally, the *racial group influence hypothesis* predicts that differences in peer group racial composition have implications for how Asian Americans acquire partisan identities. Asian American immigrants are more likely to develop partisan views through political discussion with Asian (than non-Asian) peers. In contrast, political discussion with both Asian and non-Asian

---

[4] Although this is an imperfect test of the moderating effects of local partisan norms, the state is the most granular level of geographical data available in the OAAS.

[5] Peer group demographics may vary across a range of characteristics, including race, age, gender, and socioeconomic status. I focus on race because it is a central force that structures patterns of social grouping in the United States.

peers may inform the partisan views of transitional-, second-, and third-generation Asian Americans who are embedded into racially diverse peer groups.

Once again, the direction of partisan socialization is shaped by the partisan composition of the community where Asian Americans live. On average, discussing American politics with peers, regardless of the race of those peers, typically leads to Democratic preferences because most Asian Americans settle in liberal areas. However, if Asian Americans settled in predominantly Republican areas or happen to engage with more conservative peer groups, discussing American politics with peers will lead to Republican preferences.

Table 4.1 Summary of Hypotheses

Hypothesis	Description
Comparing the frequency of discussing American politics with peers and family	
Political discussion hypothesis	Asian Americans are more likely to discuss American politics with peers during adulthood than family during childhood.
The partisan consequences of discussing American politics with peers and family	
Peer partisan influence hypothesis	Discussing American politics with peers (but not with family) shapes Asian Americans' partisan views.
	Discussing American politics with peers typically leads to preferences for Democrats over Republicans.
Generational differences in the racial composition of peer groups	
Racial composition hypothesis	Compared to their counterparts born or raised in the US, Asian American immigrants are more likely to discuss American politics with Asian peers.
	Compared to their immigrant counterparts, Asian Americans born or raised in the US are more likely to discuss American politics with non-Asian peers.
Racial group influence hypothesis	Asian American immigrants are more likely to develop partisan views through political discussion with Asian than through discussion with non-Asian peers.
	Political discussion with both Asian and non-Asian peers inform the partisan views of transitional-, second-, and third-generation Asian Americans.

Comparing the Partisan Influence of Peers and Family: Evidence from the 2020 OAAS

I test these hypotheses using data from the 2020 OAAS, a national survey of Asian Americans conducted with Vivien Leung and several other collaborators in late February and early March of 2020, just before the onset of the COVID-19 pandemic (Leung et al. 2020). Respondents included 1,558 self-identified Asian American members of Forthright, a proprietary Internet panel recruited by the survey firm Bovitz. Although respondents choose whether to participate in the panel, Bovitz is a reputable survey research firm offering high quality data from respondents who take only a few surveys per month. The survey firm directly recruits panel members using a variety of methods, including online contact and address-based sampling methods ("Proprietary Panel" 2025). Eligible panel members are randomly selected and invited to participate in surveys over email.[6]

The survey was administered in English online between February 27 and March 3, 2020, through the Bovitz Forthright platform. The use of an English-only survey restricts the generalizability of the findings to more acculturated Asian Americans. However, it is important to note that the sample includes both US citizens and foreign citizens. Eligible respondents included self-identified Asian American adults who live in the United States. We targeted an approximately even balance of foreign-born and US-born Asian Americans to allow for comparisons across immigrant generations.

The survey took between 10 and 15 minutes to complete and contained a range of demographic, social, and political questions. Respondents began by providing informed consent and answered questions about demographic characteristics (e.g., age, education, state of residence, income) and their immigrant generation (e.g., place of birth, length of residence in the United States). Next, they answered questions about political participation, vote choices, and partisan preferences, as well as questions about experiences of discrimination and the frequency of political discussion with peers and family members. The survey also included embedded experiments about workplace discrimination and political candidates.

The sample of 1,558 OAAS respondents includes a diverse cross-section of Asian Americans from many national origin and generational groups. Starting with national origin, about 31.3% of the respondents identified as Chinese American, 16.2% as Indian American, 12.8% as Filipino American, 6.4% as Vietnamese American, 7.1% Korean American, and 14.1% as Japanese

---

[6] Bovitz's Forthright panel has been used in several political science studies published in reputable peer-reviewed journals (Bakker et al. 2020; Bankert et al. 2023).

American.[7] About 54.4% were born in the US and 45.6% were born in another country. Most respondents were US citizens at the time of the survey. The average survey participant was 46 years old, just three years older than the median age of the Asian American adult population at large (Ruiz et al. 2023a). About 57.1% identified as female and 42.9% as male. Only one respondent identified with another gender category.

Turning to generational status, OAAS participants represent a diverse range of immigrant generations. Approximately 28.3% were first-generation immigrants who arrived in the US as adults, 17.3% were transitional-generation immigrants who migrated to the US as children about 31.3% were second-generation US-born children of immigrants, and 23% represented at least the third generation of their families in the US. These demographics reflect the fact that the survey oversampled US-born Asian Americans. Nationwide, about 68% of Asian American adults are first-generation immigrants (Ruiz et al. 2023a). This unusual variation in generational status makes these data useful for testing whether the social transmission account applies among Asian Americans who are both closer to and further removed from the immigrant experience.

The analyses presented in this chapter focus on two measures of partisan preferences: partisan identification and feeling thermometer ratings of the Democratic Party. Partisan identification is measured on the standard seven-point scale. In some descriptive tests, I use a categorical measure of partisanship which captures the percentage of respondents who identify as Democrats or Independents who lean toward the Democratic Party (e.g., "leaners"). Since partisan identification not a perfect measure of partisan preferences among Asian Americans, who often do not have strong attachments to either party (e.g., Hajnal and Lee 2011; Phan and Garcia 2009), I follow other studies that use feeling thermometer ratings as an alternative measure that does not require deeply held personal attachments (Hopkins et al. 2020; Kuo et al. 2017). These ratings are measured from 0 (very cold ratings) to 100 (very warm ratings). Both outcomes are continuous and re-scaled from 0 to 1, with higher values reflecting greater support for Democrats.

These measures capture the strength and direction of partisanship because social transmission predicts that political discussion with local peer groups leads Asian Americans to partisan views depending on the partisan norms where they settle. However, it is also important to consider the role peer groups play in shaping whether Asian Americans identify with any of the standard partisan labels in the American context. This measure of any partisan identification is

---

[7] The remaining 12.1% of respondents identified with multiple categories or other national origin groups. The OAAS sample reflects the diversity of the Asian American community nationwide at the time, which was approximately 21.3% Chinese American, 19.5% Indian American, 18% Filipino American, 9.3% Vietnamese American, and 6.7% Japanese American (US Census Bureau 2021).

a binary indicator, where 0 represents identification with neither political party and 1 represents leaning toward or identifying with either the Democratic or Republican Party.

This chapter also uses measures of the frequency with which Asian Americans recall discussing American politics with peers and family. Respondents were asked how often they "discuss American politics in their daily lives with friends, colleagues, neighbors, or acquaintances" from the four major racial groups in the US (e.g., African Americans, Asian Americans, Latinos, and whites). Responses were measured on five-point scales with values ranging from "never" to "very frequently." The frequency of discussing American politics with peers is a scaled index of discussion with peers from different racial groups.

In addition to the general measure of peer discussion, I created separate measures of the frequency of discussing American politics with Asian peers and non-Asian peers (e.g., African American, Latino, and white peers). To measure the frequency of discussing American politics with family during childhood, respondents were asked, "when you were growing up, how frequently did you discuss American politics at home with your parents and other family members?" Responses were measured on the same five-point scale. I also created a difference score by subtracting the frequency of discussing American politics with family during childhood from peers during adulthood.

Finally, I include the following demographic characteristics as control variables: gender, age, education, income, homeownership, marriage, and generational status in some analyses. Additional descriptive information is included in Table 4.1A in the Chapter 4 Online Appendix ⊕.

Partisan Preferences and Identities Among Diverse Asian American Survey Participants

Next, I present descriptive analyses of the key partisan outcomes and political discussion measures. Most Asian Americans who participated in the 2020 OAAS rated the Democratic Party favorably, identified with some partisan label, and identified as Democratic partisans or leaners if they identified with a major party. Figure 4.1 presents these values for all Asian Americans and the six largest national origin groups. Figure 4.2 presents these same outcomes across immigrant generations. Several patterns emerge in partisan choice.

First, most survey participants rated the Democratic Party favorably. The average rating of the Democratic Party was 58.7 among all Asian Americans, 55.0 among Chinese Americans, 67.4 among Indian Americans, 55.4 among Filipino Americans, 57.2 among Vietnamese Americans, and 57.4 among both Korean Americans and Japanese Americans (Figure 4.1). These favorable ratings

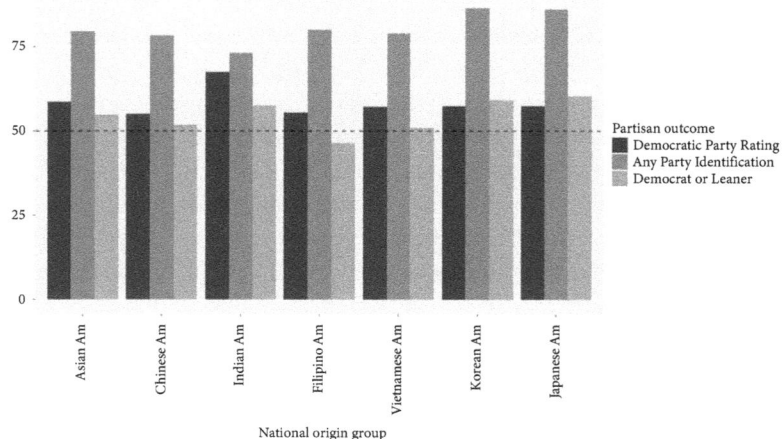

Figure 4.1 Partisan preferences among Asian Americans by national origin
Source: The data are drawn from the 2020 Omnibus Asian American Survey (Leung et al. 2020).

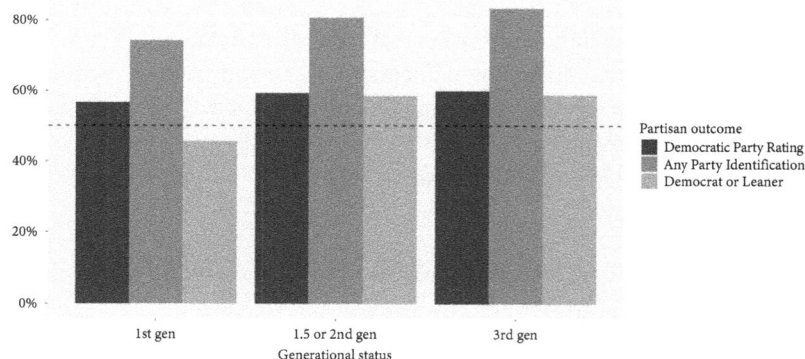

Figure 4.2 Partisan preferences among Asian Americans by generational status
Source: The data are drawn from the 2020 Omnibus Asian American Survey (Leung et al. 2020).

of the Democratic Party are particularly notable among groups like Vietnamese and Filipino Americans who historically supported Democrats at lower rates than other Asian American ethnic subgroups. They may reflect the generational balance of the OAAS sample, which includes many US-born respondents (Le and Su 2017). Nevertheless, the breakdown across generational subgroups reveals high ratings for Democrats, even among first-generation immigrants. The average rating of the Democratic Party was 56.6 among first-generation

Asian Americans, 59.4 among the transitional and second generations, and 60 among third-generation Asian Americans (Figure 4.2).

To what extent are these preferences for Democrats reflected in Asian Americans' partisan identities? Well over 70% of OAAS respondents identified with a mainstream partisan category, across national origin and generational subgroups (Figures 4.1 and 4.2). These low rates of nonidentification in the OAAS sample may reflect the fact that respondents were acculturated and fluent in English.

Most respondents also identified as Democratic partisans or leaners, although there was considerable variation across national origin groups. As Figure 4.1 shows, while 54.9% of all Asian American respondents identified as Democrats or leaners, these rates were highest among Japanese Americans (60.5%), Korean Americans (59.1%), and Indian Americans (57.4%). Rates of Democratic identification were lowest among Vietnamese Americans (51%) and Filipino Americans (46.5%). This aligns with analyses of the 2008 National Asian American Survey in Chapter 3, which showed that a majority of Filipino American and Vietnamese American voters supported John McCain in the 2008 presidential election. When comparing generational subgroups, 45.6% of first-generation, 58.4% of transitional- and second-generation, and 58.8% of third-generation respondents identified as Democrats or leaners, indicating that identification with the Democratic Party increases as Asian Americans become more acculturated (Figure 4.2).

The Frequency of Discussing American Politics with Peers and Family

What explains these partisan preferences across a diverse range of national origin and generational subgroups in the Asian American community? This chapter focuses on one potential set of explanations: political discussion with peer groups and family members. Before delving into the connection between these two factors, I report the extent to which Asian Americans discussed American politics with family members and peer groups.

Are there differences in how often Asian Americans discussed American politics with family members during childhood and with adult peer groups consisting of friends, colleagues, neighbors, and acquaintances? Figure 4.3 presents average self-reported levels of political discussion[8] with family during childhood and peers during adulthood for all Asian American OAAS respondents and the

---

[8] In this chapter, I use the term "political discussion" to refer to discussing US rather than transnational politics. It is used interchangeably with the term "discussion of American politics."

110 SOCIAL ROOTS OF ASIAN AMERICAN PARTISANSHIP

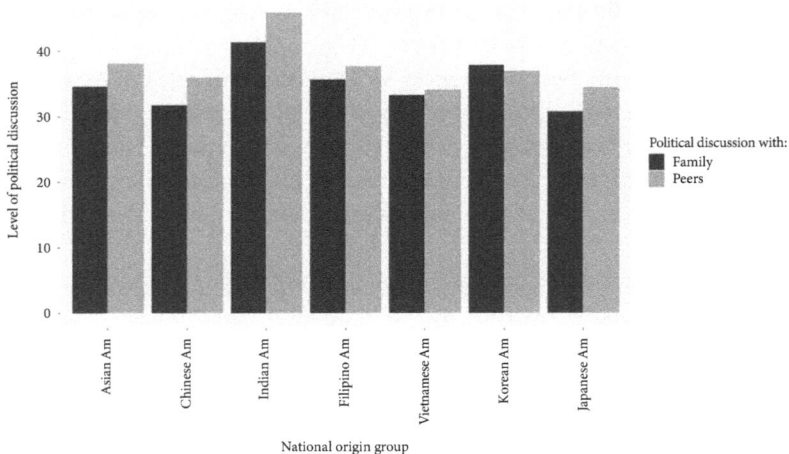

Figure 4.3 Frequency of political discussion with family and peers by national origin
Source: The data are drawn from the 2020 Omnibus Asian American Survey (Leung et al. 2020).

six largest national origin groups represented in the survey.[9] These values range from 0 ("never") to 1 ("very frequently"). I convert them to percentage point values for ease of interpretation. This descriptive analysis also offers initial insight into the viability of the political discussion hypothesis, which predicts that most Asian Americans experience more political discussion with peers than family members.

Figure 4.3 indicates that across national origin groups, most Asian American discuss American politics in their peer networks as adults more frequently than they did with parents and other family members during childhood. For example, the average level of political discussion with peer groups was 34.6% with family during childhood and 38.1% with adult peers for all Asian American respondents. This pattern of discussing American politics more often with peers than family members is reflected across all national origin subgroups except for Korean Americans, who reported similar levels of political discussion with peers and family. The largest differences are among Indian Americans, Chinese Americans, and Japanese Americans, who reported discussing American politics with adult peers at rates that were between 4 and 5 percentage points higher than similar conversations with family during childhood.

---

[9] This section focuses on variation across national origin groups. I also break down the sample by generational status later in the chapter.

Surprisingly, Japanese Americans, the most acculturated national origin subgroup in terms of generational status, reported the lowest levels of reported political discussion with family during childhood at 30.7%. This indicates that discussions of American politics between Asian American parents and children may not become more common as they become more incorporated into American society. To the contrary, growing up without much political discussion at home may hamper the development of civic skills necessary to initiate political conversations with family later in life. This finding may also reflect legacies of ethnic targeting and discrimination, as recent work finds that Japanese Americans with family members who were incarcerated in internment camps during World War II are less politically engaged than those who do not have a direct connection to the internment (Komisarchik et al. 2022).

Next, I test the political discussion hypothesis more formally, directly comparing reported levels of political discussion with peers and family. This analysis is restricted to all Asian American respondents. Figure 4.4 presents average levels of discussing American politics with family during childhood and peers (e.g., friends, colleagues, neighbors, and acquaintances) during adulthood. It also presents the racial composition of peers who Asian Americans reported engaging in political discussion with. Here, I plot average levels of political discussion as points (rather than bars) with 83.4% confidence intervals to illustrate the

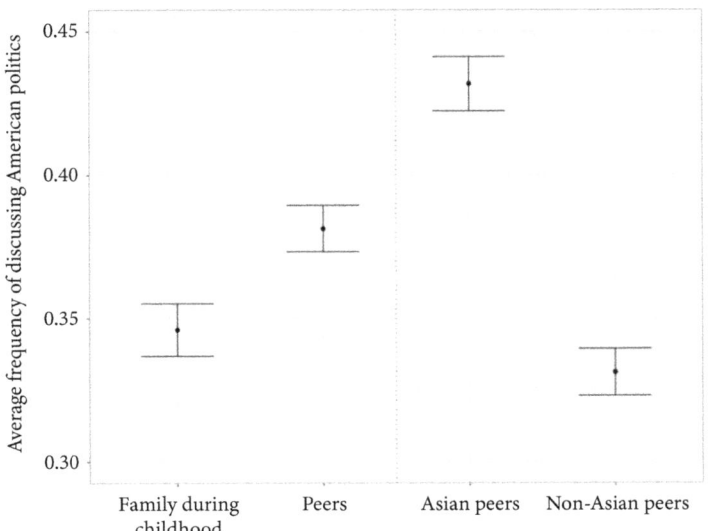

Figure 4.4 Comparing the frequency of political discussion with family and peers (83.4% CIs)

Source: The data are drawn from the 2020 Omnibus Asian American Survey (Leung et al. 2020).

range of plausible values each measure could take on. If the confidence intervals for two values do not overlap, this indicates a statistically significant difference at the $p < 0.05$ level (Frost 2019; Goldstein and Healy 1995).

This analysis offers additional evidence that supports the political discussion hypothesis. As predicted, Asian American OAAS respondents report significantly higher levels of political discussion with peers during adulthood than with family during childhood. The average self-reported level of political discussion with family during childhood is 0.346 on a scale from 0 to 1, which corresponds to a value halfway between "rarely" and "occasionally." In contrast, the mean self-reported level of discussing American politics with peers during adulthood is 0.381, which corresponds to a value closer to "occasionally." The difference in reported discussion is sizable and statistically significant, at 3.5 percentage points ($p < 0.01$). This indicates that on average, Asian American OAAS respondents experienced significantly more discussion of American politics with peer groups than with family members.

Although these data indicate that Asian Americans experience some discussion of American politics at home, the frequency of these conversations is relatively low. At best, these conversations were occasional, occurring less frequently than similar conversations about politics with weaker social ties, including neighbors and acquaintances. This comports with the expectation that Asian Americans are reticent to discuss politics in general but are particularly unlikely to talk about this topic with their close family members. For example, Jamie, a second-generation Chinese American quoted in Dominique Fong's (2021a) article, indicated that "she didn't talk openly about politics with anyone, *especially not close family.*"

Figure 4.4 also offers insight into how frequently Asian Americans have conversations about American politics with peers who are of Asian American and non-Asian descent (e.g., African American, Latino, or white peers). Most OAAS respondents were much more likely to discuss American politics with other Asian American peers than peers from other racial groups. This difference is substantively and statistically significant at 10 percentage points ($p < 0.001$). In fact, average reported levels of political discussion with Asian peers (0.43) are about 9 percentage points higher than levels of discussion with family during childhood (0.35) ($p < 0.001$). In contrast, average levels of political discussion with non-Asian peers are comparatively low (0.33) and are not significantly different from discussion with family during childhood (0.35).

These patterns reveal that many Asian Americans primarily interact with other Asian American peers, regardless of their generational status. Even still, Asian Americans are just about as likely to discuss American politics with peers from different racial groups, who may represent weak social ties with, than with family members. Later in the chapter, I explore how these trends vary across generational subgroups.

These descriptive results offer systematic descriptive evidence that across a diverse set of national origin groups, Asian Americans experience infrequent discussion of American politics with family members during childhood. In contrast, political discussion with peers—a wide-ranging term that includes close friends as well as weaker social connections, like colleagues, neighbors, and acquaintances—is more common. Finally, most respondents discussed American politics more frequently with Asian than non-Asian peers. I explore the implications of political discussion with peers across generational subgroups later in the chapter.

Does Discussing American Politics with Family and Peers Shape Partisan Choices?

Next, I consider whether discussing American politics with family or peers is associated with Asian Americans' partisan views. These analyses test the peer partisan influence hypothesis. First, I explore the relationship between political discussion and the partisan outcomes using simple cross-tabulations. To create these charts, I separate levels of political discussion with family members and peers into three categories (e.g., "low," "medium," and "high" levels of discussion).

First, there are major differences in evaluations of the Democratic Party and Democratic partisanship among OAAS respondents who discussed American politics with adult peers rarely and frequently. Table 4.2 shows that the average rating of the Democratic Party increased by 8.2 points when comparing Asian Americans who reported "low" and "high" levels of political conversation in peer groups. This pattern holds across all major national origin groups. Ratings of Democrats increased by 6.2 points among Chinese Americans, 11.1

Table 4.2 Average Ratings of Democratic Party Across Levels of Political Discussion with Peers

Feeling thermometer ratings of Democratic Party	Level of political discussion with peers		
	Low (0–25)	Medium (26–49)	High (50–100)
Mean rating of Democratic Party	54.9	57.4	63.1

Source: The data are drawn from the 2020 Omnibus Asian American Survey (Leung et al. 2020).

Table 4.3 Cross-Tabulation of Political Discussion with Peers and Identification as a Democrat or Leaner

Democrat or Leaner	Level of political discussion with peers		
	Low (0–25)	Medium (26–49)	High (50–100)
Yes	49.0%	54.5%	60.6%
No	51.0%	45.5%	39.4%
Total	100.0 %	100.0%	100.0%

Source: The data are drawn from the 2020 Omnibus Asian American Survey (Leung et al. 2020).

points among Indian Americans, 11.6 points among Filipino Americans, 4.1 points among Vietnamese Americans, 4.7 points among Korean Americans, and 7.2 points among Japanese Americans, when comparing those who engaged in frequent and infrequent discussion of American politics with peers (Appendix Table C.1).

These differences extend to partisan identification, indicating that political discussion with peers is associated with developing long-term attachments to the political parties. Table 4.3 shows that Asian Americans who frequently discussed politics with peers were 11.6 percentage points more likely to identify as Democratic partisans or leaners than their counterparts who experienced little political conversation in peer groups. This pattern also holds across diverse subgroups. For example, respondents who reported high levels of political discussion with peers were more likely to identify with or lean toward Democrats by 7.9 points among Chinese Americans, 20.6 points among Indian Americans, 26.2 points among Filipino Americans, 8.1 points among Vietnamese Americans, and 7.7 points among Japanese Americans (Appendix Table C.2). Finally, political discussion with peers has a similar relationship with identifying with any partisan label, increasing identification by 11.7 points between those who experienced low and high levels of political discussion, from 72.8% to 84.5% (Appendix Table C.3).

In contrast, there is less evidence that differences in the frequency of political discussion with family members during childhood are associated with evaluations of the Democratic Party. Table 4.4 shows that ratings of Democrats increased slightly with the frequency of political discussion with family. The average rating of the Democratic Party increased by 5.3 points when comparing respondents who reported low and high levels of political discussion with family during childhood. While this difference is notable, it is smaller than the corresponding 8.2 point difference that emerges when comparing respondents who report high and low levels of political discussion with peers (Table 4.2). Moreover, when breaking down the sample by national origin, ratings of the Democratic Party are more favorable among those who experienced more

Table 4.4 Average Ratings of Democratic Party Across Levels of Political Discussion with Family

	Level of political discussion with family		
	Low (0–24)	Medium (25–49)	High (50–100)
Mean rating of Democratic Party	55.2	58.7	60.5

Source: The data are drawn from the 2020 Omnibus Asian American Survey (Leung et al. 2020).

Table 4.5 Cross-Tabulation of Political Discussion with Family and Identification as a Democrat or Leaner

Democrat or Leaner	Level of political discussion with family		
	Low (0–24)	Medium (25–49)	High (50–100)
Yes	54.0%	55.3%	55.0%
No	46.0%	44.7%	45.0%
Total	100.0%	100.0%	100.0%

Source: The data are drawn from the 2020 Omnibus Asian American Survey (Leung et al. 2020).

frequent political discussion with parents among Indian Americans, Filipino Americans, and Japanese Americans, but do not differ substantially among other ethnic subgroups (Appendix Table C.1).

These differences in evaluations of Democrats based on levels of political discussion with family do not translate into differences in partisan identification. Table 4.5 shows that 54% of OAAS respondents who reported low levels of political discussion with family and 55% of those who reported frequent political discussion identified with or leaned toward Democrats. Moreover, these differences are not consistent across national origin groups (Appendix Table C.2). For example, the percentage of Chinese Americans and Vietnamese Americans who identified as Democrats is higher among those who experienced low levels of political discussion with family. However, the reverse pattern holds among Indian Americans, Filipino Americans, Korean Americans, and Japanese Americans. Finally, rates of identification with any partisan label do not vary across levels of political discussion with family (Appendix Table C.4).

Taken together, these descriptive results support the peer political influence hypothesis, indicating that partisan preferences and identities vary substantially with levels of political discussion with peer groups and less so with discussion with family. Do these relationships hold when accounting for other characteristics that may affect Asian Americans' partisan choices? I answer this question by modeling the relationship between these measures and the partisan outcomes. I use standard OLS regression models that include the demographic controls described above. I also estimate weighted versions of these models to account for differences in observed demographics among respondents who discussed American politics with peers frequently and infrequently.[10]

The results offer stronger evidence in support of the peer political influence hypothesis. Figure 4.5 presents the regression coefficients representing the association between political discussion with family and peers, extracted from the standard and weighted models with demographic controls. The coefficients are plotted as points with 95% confidence intervals to illustrate the plausible set of values each estimate could take on. The first panel presents the effects of political discussion on Democratic Party feeling thermometer ratings and the second presents the effects on partisanship. The full regression results are included in Appendix Table C.5.

As Figure 4.5 shows, the results support the peer partisan influence hypothesis. Accounting for political discussion with family during childhood, discussing American politics with adult peers is associated with an 18.1 percentage point increase in ratings of the Democratic Party ($p < 0.001$) and a 10.8 percentage point increase in Democratic partisanship ($p < 0.01$) in the standard models. The partisan effects are just as large in the weighted models, which offer more precise estimates of the partisan effects of discussing American politics with peers. It is important to note that discussing American politics with family during childhood does not have statistically significant associations with partisan choices in either model.

As mentioned earlier in the chapter, the social transmission account predicts that the partisan direction of peer influence is explained by Asian American settlement patterns. Discussing American politics with peer groups should lead to Democratic views in liberal environments and Republican views in conservative environments. The OAAS does not include local geographical markers, which would allow for a fine-grained analysis of whether local partisan norms condition the direction of partisan choices. However, I explore whether state-level partisan context conditions the relationship between political discussion and partisan outcomes. I find that respondents who live in mixed partisan and Democratic states are more likely to develop Democratic views when they discuss politics with peers than their counterparts who live in Republican states (Online Appendix Figure 4.1A ⊛).

---

[10] This weighting method models political discussion with peers as a binary treatment, regressing it onto the following predictors, which may influence both political discussion with peers and partisan preferences: education, age, income, and foreign-born.

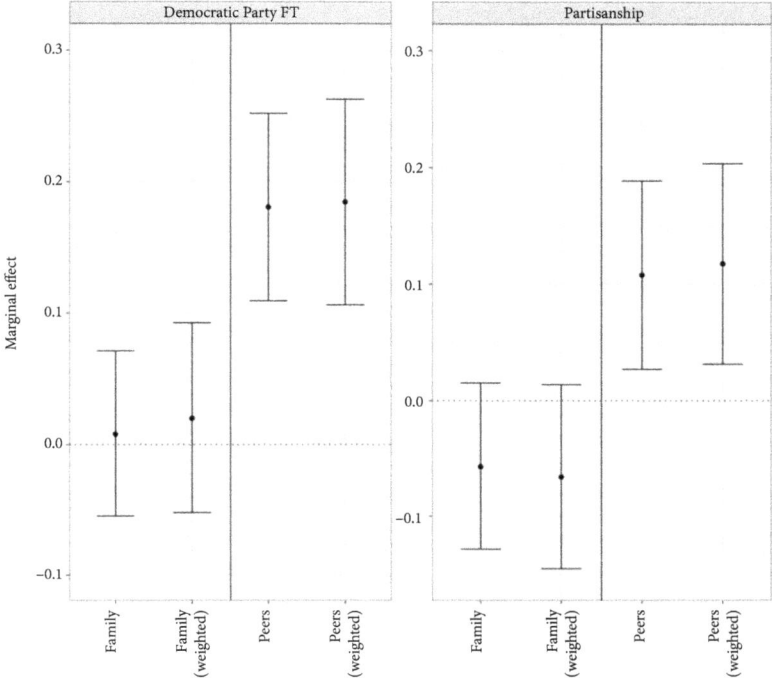

Figure 4.5 Association between political discussion measures and partisan outcomes (95% CIs)

Source: The data are drawn from the 2020 Omnibus Asian American Survey (Leung et al. 2020).

Discussing American Politics with Peers More Frequently Than Family

Does discussing American politics more frequently with peers than family predict partisan preferences among Asian Americans? To test this possibility, I re-estimate these models, substituting the two separate political discussion measures with a single difference score that subtracts the frequency of discussing American politics with family from the corresponding measure for discussion with peers. This analysis helps to identify whether peers or family are more politically influential. Figure 4.6 presents the regression coefficient for the difference measure for each partisan outcome.[11]

---

[11] The full regression results are included in Chapter 4 Online Appendix Table 4.3A ⊙.

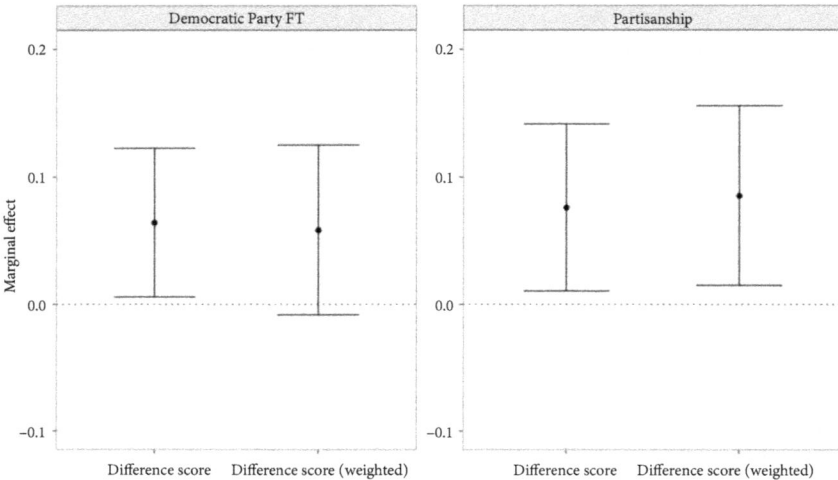

Figure 4.6 Association between discussing American politics more frequently with peers than family and partisan outcomes (95% CIs)
Source: The data are drawn from the 2020 Omnibus Asian American Survey (Leung et al. 2020).

The results presented in Figure 4.6 offer further evidence supporting the peer partisan influence hypothesis. In the standard models, discussing American politics with peers more often than family members is associated with about a 6 percentage point increase in feeling thermometer ratings of the Democratic Party and nearly an 8 percentage point increase in Democratic partisan identification (Figure 4.6). These associations are statistically significant ($p < 0.05$). Both associations are similar in magnitude in the weighted model, although the former is marginally significant ($p < 0.10$).

Does Political Discussion with Peers and Family Affect Identification with Any Party?

It is possible that the previous analyses do not offer a fair test of intergenerational transmission. Perhaps parental influence leads to Democratic support among some respondents and Republican support among others, depending on the partisan preferences of their parents. If this is the case, the effect of political discussion with family during childhood may wash out in models with directional partisanship as the outcome. Likewise, it is possible that political discussion with conservative peer groups leads to Republican partisan identification. To consider these possibilities, I re-estimate these models, replacing

Table 4.6 Association Between Discussing American Politics with Family or Peers and Any Partisan Identification

Outcome:	Any Partisan identification	
	Logistic model	Weighted logistic model
Political discussion with peers during adulthood	1.546***	1.675***
	(0.340)	(0.364)
Political discussion with family during childhood	−0.290	−0.259
	(0.298)	(0.300)
Constant	0.712*	0.946**
	(0.316)	(0.331)
Observations	1,535	1,535

Note: ***p < 0.001; **p < 0.01; *p < 0.05.
Controls included in models: Female, age, education, income, homeowner, married, and foreign-born.
Source: The data are drawn from the 2020 Omnibus Asian American Survey (Leung et al. 2020).

the directional measure of partisanship with an indicator for leaning toward or identifying with either party (Hajnal and Lee 2011). These analyses use logistic regression techniques because the outcome is binary. The shortened regression results are presented in Table 4.6.

Table 4.6 shows that discussing American politics with peers during adulthood has a large and statistically significant association with identifying with either major party ($p < 0.001$). In contrast, discussing American politics with family during childhood is not associated with identifying with either major party after accounting for political discussion with peers and standard demographic controls. This analysis offers further evidence that political discussion with family during childhood does not shape partisan choices among Asian Americans, whether they identify as Democrats or Republicans.

Taken together, these analyses show that the frequency with which Asian Americans discuss American politics with peers and family members differs. In turn, these political discussions have consequences for partisan choices. Political discussion with adult peers during adulthood is associated with developing partisan attachments and specifically, with Democratic partisan views. In contrast, political discussion with family during childhood is not associated with partisan views. Moreover, when the two are put in a head-to-head test, discussing American politics with peers more often than family is also associated with Democratic partisan views.

Generational Differences in the Racial Composition of Peer Groups

The final section of this chapter considers whether there are differences in the racial composition of peer groups across immigrant generations. Do Asian American immigrants discuss American politics with Asian peers more frequently than Asian Americans who were raised in the US? Conversely, do Asian Americans who were raised in the US discuss American politics with non-Asian peers more frequently than Asian American immigrants?

To test the racial composition hypothesis, I compare self-reported rates of discussing American politics with peers across immigrant generations. I compare first-generation immigrants to transitional- or second-generation children of immigrants and third-generation grandchildren of immigrants. Figure 4.7 presents the average levels of discussing American politics with family (panel 1), peers from all racial groups (panel 2), Asian peers (panel 3), and non-Asian peers (panel 4) across immigrant generations. These mean values are plotted as points with 83.4% confidence intervals to illustrate statistically significant differences across generations.

As the first panels of Figure 4.7 show, there are no meaningful differences in the frequency of political discussion with family when comparing immigrants to the transitional- or second-generation children of immigrants and even third-generation Asian Americans. A similar pattern persists when comparing levels of political discussion with peer groups in general, without accounting for their racial composition (Figure 4.7, panel 2). These findings align with the core expectations of social transmission. Asian Americans experience little partisan socialization at home during childhood regardless of their generational status. Given a void of political discussion with their family, many Asian Americans discuss American politics with peer groups in local contexts.

However, as the racial composition hypothesis predicts, several generational differences emerge in the frequency of political discussion with peers from different racial groups. The third panel of Figure 4.7 shows that first-generation immigrants discuss American politics with Asian peers more frequently than transitional- and second-generation or even third-generation respondents. This aligns with prior findings that many Asian American immigrants primarily interact with other members of their ethnic group (Mok et al. 2007; Qiang et al. 2001). Although first-generation Asian Americans rarely discuss American politics with their children at home, they occasionally discuss American politics with Asian peers. In fact, they engage in political discussion with Asian peers more frequently than their children's and grandchildren's generations.

These patterns are reversed when it comes to discussion with non-Asian peers. The fourth panel of Figure 4.7 shows that Asian American children and

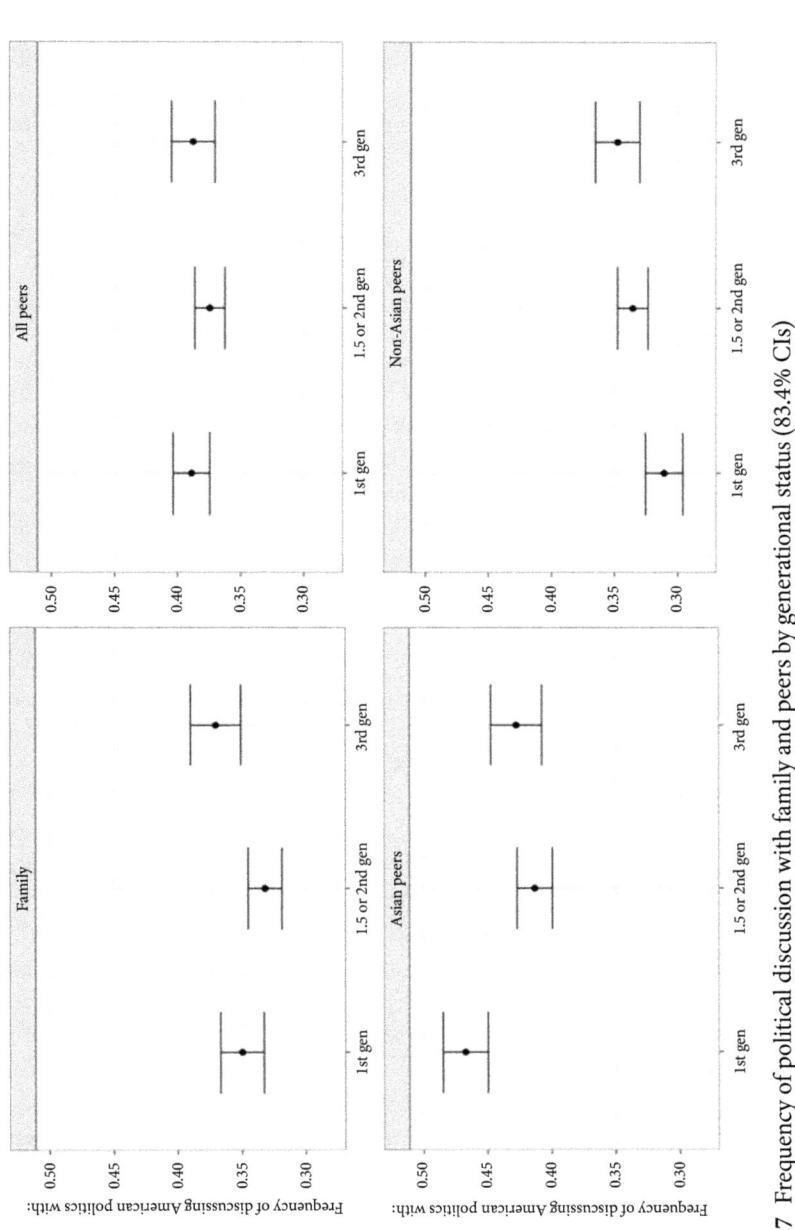

Figure 4.7 Frequency of political discussion with family and peers by generational status (83.4% CIs)

Source: The data are drawn from the 2020 Omnibus Asian American Survey (Leung et al. 2020).

grandchildren of immigrants are more likely to discuss American politics with African American, Latino, or Asian (e.g., non-Asian) peers than their immigrant counterparts. It is important to note that even transitional-, second-, and third-generation Asian Americans are more likely to discuss American politics with Asian peers than non-Asian peers. However, they are more likely to engage in political discussion with peers from other racial groups than first-generation Asian Americans.

How Does Political Discussion with Asian and Non-Asian Peers Shape Partisan Choices?

Finally, I explore whether discussing American politics with Asian and non-Asian peers shapes the political choices of Asian Americans across immigrant generations. Recall that the racial group influence hypothesis predicts that first-generation Asian Americans are more likely to develop partisan views through political discussion with Asian than non-Asian peers. However, Asian Americans raised in the US may develop partisan views through discussion with peers from all racial groups.

To explore these possibilities, I regress the partisan outcomes onto political discussion with Asian and non-Asian peers across three generations. Figure 4.8 plots the associations between discussing American politics with Asian and non-Asian peers and the partisan outcomes, separately for first-, transitional- or second-, and third-generation Asian Americans. Panel 1 presents the results for Democratic Party feeling thermometer ratings and panel 2 presents the results for partisanship (see Appendix Table C.6 for regression results).

The results offer mixed evidence about the racial group influence hypothesis. As predicted, discussing American politics with Asian peers is associated with a 12.3 percentage point increase in ratings of the Democratic Party among first-generation immigrants (Figure 4.8 panel 1; $p < 0.10$). Although only marginally significant, this association aligns with the expectation that discussion with other Asian Americans plays a central role in the political socialization of Asian American immigrants. In comparison, discussing American politics with Asian peers does not have statistically significant associations with partisan outcomes for transitional-, second-, or third-generation respondents.

Figure 4.8 also shows that discussing American politics with non-Asian peers is associated with a 14.4 point increase in ratings of the Democratic Party among transitional- and second-generation Asian Americans ($p < 0.05$) and a 19.6 point increase among third-generation Asian Americans ($p < 0.10$). In contrast, discussion with non-Asian peers does not have a significant association with either partisan outcome among first-generation respondents. These patterns are

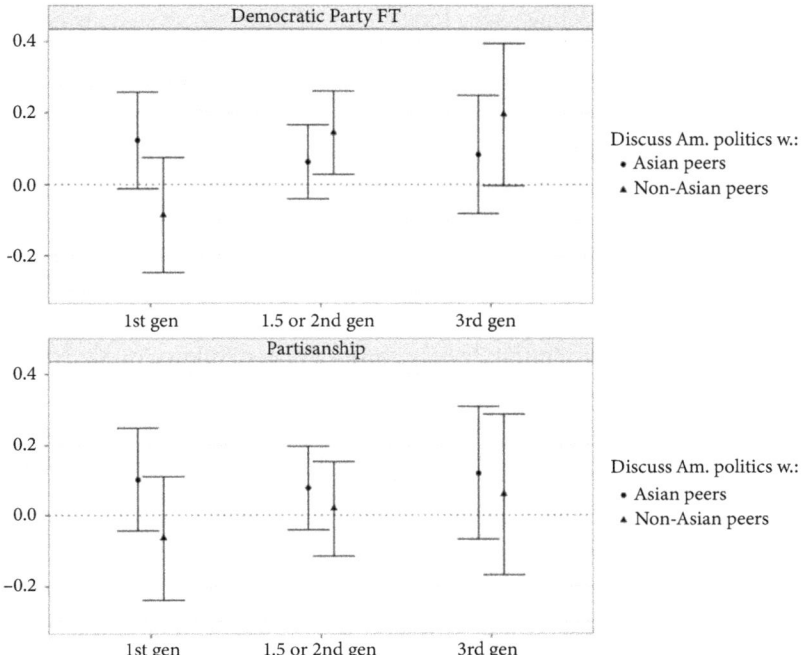

Figure 4.8 Association between political discussion with peers and partisan outcomes by generational status (95% CIs)
Source: The data are drawn from the 2020 Omnibus Asian American Survey (Leung et al. 2020).

consistent with the expectation that racially diverse peer groups play a role in the political socialization of the descendants of Asian American immigrants.

Conclusion

Taken together, the evidence presented in this chapter conveys that the conventional wisdom about political discussion with family during childhood does not fully explain partisan acquisition among Asian Americans. This chapter also offers the first direct evidence of peer influence in the development of Asian American partisan views. In the absence of strong political influence at home, many Asian Americans discuss politics with local peer groups that include close friends, colleagues, neighbors, and varied acquaintances. Beyond these key findings, this chapter has several implications for understanding partisan acquisition among Asian Americans and other immigrant constituencies.

First, this chapter highlights the limited role of the family in shaping partisan views across three generational cohorts and the six largest national origin groups in the Asian American community. It is striking that even third-generation Asian Americans, who are two generations removed from the immigrant experience, report low levels of political discussion with parents and other family members during childhood. Moreover, political discussion with family is not associated with the partisan choices of diverse subgroups of Asian Americans. The fact that these patterns apply across generations conveys that theories of familial political socialization do not apply well to Asian Americans, regardless of their generational status. This suggests that people who grow up with limited political discussion at home during childhood may struggle to develop civic skills and be less likely to discuss politics with their children later in life.

However, this chapter also shows that political learning is a social process for Asian Americans. Asian Americans are open to political influence through social interactions outside the home. In many cases, peers may be more influential than parents in shaping Asian Americans' partisan choices. For example, discussing American politics with peers more frequently than with family members is associated with developing a partisan identity. This suggests that Asian Americans and other immigrants may learn about the political system and develop partisan preferences through conversations with neighbors, friends, colleagues, and even acquaintances in their local environments.

The final sections of the chapter offer evidence that the race of peers who are most politically influential differs across immigrant generations. Asian American immigrants mostly interact with other Asian immigrants and may develop partisan views by discussing American politics with Asian peers. In contrast, those who come of age in the US have more racially diverse peer networks and may develop partisan views through similar discussions with both Asian and non-Asian peers. This finding reflects the different social pathways to partisanship within the Asian American community outlined in Chapter 2.

As the American electorate becomes more racially diverse, standard explanations for partisan acquisition may no longer apply to large swaths of voters. This chapter suggests that peers play a larger role than the nuclear family in shaping Asian Americans' partisan views. One open question includes the nature of the political discussions that immigrants and their children have with peers outside of the home. Do they respond to explicit partisan messages from peer groups, or do they pick up information about the political parties in more subtle ways? In Part II, I focus on a case study of political learning among Asian American youth in college settings to understand the nature of peer influence and the content of political messages. These chapters offer deeper insight into the process of social transmission.

PART II

PEER POLITICAL INFLUENCE ON COLLEGE CAMPUSES

The second part of the book continues to explore the mechanisms of peer influence, turning the lens on political learning and partisan acquisition among Asian American college students. Peer influence is likely to occur on college campuses because they are settings where students live, work, and interact with their peer groups at a critical moment in their personal development (Dey 1996; 1997; Newcomb 1943). Additionally, many Asian Americans who were born or raised in the US attend college at high rates (Digest of Education Statistics 2023). More broadly, Americans' political attitudes are becoming increasingly polarized along lines of college education, suggesting that college settings may play a major role in the political socialization (Grossman and Hopkins 2024).

The chapters in the second part of the book offer a comprehensive investigation of the nature and political consequences of interacting with peer groups in educational settings for the growing population of transitional-, second-, and third-generation Asian Americans who come of age in the United States but experience little in the way of parental political influence. First, what role do social interactions with peers play in the development of political preferences among Asian American college students? Do peer groups have a larger influence on political attitudes among Asian Americans than they do for students from other racial groups? Second, what types of political messages shape partisan attitudes? Does receiving explicitly partisan cues from established peer groups on campus affect Asian Americans' partisan views? Part II explores these questions and others, drawing on innovative evidence from panel surveys and survey experiments.

5
Interactions with College Peers and Political Learning on Campus

This chapter explores whether and how interactions with campus peer groups shape the political perspectives of Asian American youth who attend college in the United States. In a foundational study of political attitude change at Bennington College, then a women's college in Vermont, Theodore Newcomb (1943) found that many students came from conservative households but developed liberal political views through social experiences in a progressive campus environment. Does a similar process occur among Asian American college students on contemporary college campuses, contributing to a trend of Democratic vote choice?

Recall that evidence from interviews presented in Chapter 2 suggests that college peers are an important source of political information for transitional- and second-generation Asian Americans who rarely discussed politics with their parents. For example, several Houston-area Asian Americans reported that they first developed political perspectives through a process akin to osmosis, picking up on the ideas expressed by the people around them during college.

To return to some motivating examples from the Houston case study, a transitional-generation Korean American woman who was in her fifties at the time of the interview recalled that she began to develop liberal political views by picking up on political cues while attending a liberal arts college in the Northeast. Although these experiences occurred several decades before we spoke, she vividly recalled that her parents "never discussed politics" when she was a child and to the extent that American politics came up, "the discussion was just 'don't get involved in politics because it is dirty and corrupt.'" In sharp contrast, her time in college exposed her to a new way of thinking about politics and led her to develop a positive impression of the Democratic Party. As she remembered it, "once I went to [Liberal Arts College], that opened a whole world that I've never been exposed to. I think because I went away from home and I was relatively young, I was like a sponge."

A second-generation Vietnamese American college student who was in his early twenties at the time of the interview also indicated that he learned about American politics through exposure to political discussion on campus. In contrast to the prior respondent, who attended a liberal arts college on the east coast, he was enrolled in a large public university in Texas where he was exposed to a mix of conservative and liberal political attitudes on campus. In describing his experiences ahead of the 2016 presidential election, he said, "I was trying to be in the middle and just observing the people around me, like my classmates and my professors." Although he did not vote, interactions with peers and faculty in his oil engineering program shaped his perspectives on the election outcome. Before Trump unexpectedly won the 2016 presidential election, he recalled that "basically, everyone was saying that if Hillary won, it would be the end of the oil industry." He also recalled that he thought he "should feel happy after the election," to emulate the attitudes of the people around him.

Do the recollections of these two interview respondents reflect a broader process of political learning in campus settings? If so, to what extent do interactions with campus peer groups shape Asian Americans' political views at a time when they are particularly open to peer influence? This chapter systematically investigates whether interacting with college peers influences the political orientations of Asian Americans using a national panel survey of college students. The results offer systematic evidence of peer influence in tightly knit collegiate social environments.

College may be an important setting for political learning for the growing population of Asian American youth who were born or raised in the US. According to the Pew Research Center, there are over 7.9 million second-generation Asian Americans in the US (Chen et al. 2023). Remarkably, nearly two-thirds of this population is under the age of 30 (Chen et al. 2023). This growing cohort of young Asian Americans includes many college graduates. As Figure 5.1 shows, Asian American youth have consistently attended college at much higher rates than their counterparts from other racial groups over the past 30 years. For example, about 80% of Asian American recent high school graduates were enrolled in college in 2022, compared to 64% of whites, 60% of African Americans, and 58% of Latinos (Digest of Education Statistics 2023). These differences in college attendance across racial groups suggest that many Asian American children of immigrants attend college, an important setting for peer group interactions as they come of age.

Coupled with high rates of college attendance, several other factors suggest that Asian Americans may develop lasting political orientations through engagement with campus peer groups. As discussed in earlier chapters, Asian American children of immigrants are unlikely to discuss American politics at home with their parents and arrive on campus open to outside political influence. More generally, colleges are conducive environments for peer influence because

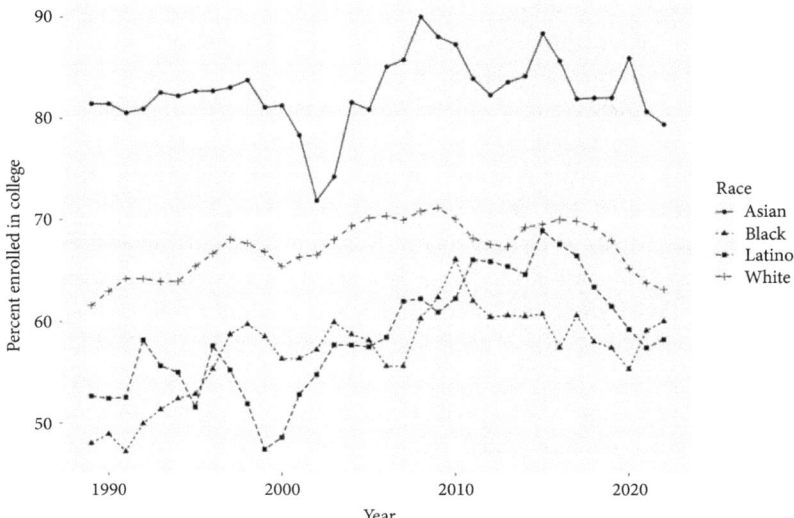

Figure 5.1 Percentage of recent high school graduates enrolled in college (1989–2022, three-year rolling averages)
Source: The data are drawn from National Center for Education Statistics (Digest of Education Statistics 2023).

they are immersive settings where young people spend time together away from home with diverse peer groups. Research on peer influence in college settings supports this point. College peers may shape each other's academic performance, social experiences, and political outlooks through curricular, extracurricular, and social experiences (Carrell et al. 2009; Juvonen et al. 2012; Kremer and Levy 2008; Stinebrickner and Stinebrickner 2006).

Since the social transmission account argues that interactions with peer groups shape political views, this chapter primarily focuses on changes in students' political views from matriculation to graduation. Rather than considering the consequences of college attendance, I explore whether social interactions with campus peer groups are associated with changes in political preferences between freshman and senior year. At the end of the chapter, I briefly consider whether these patterns generalize to a diverse group of young Americans who both attended and did not attend college using a representative national survey.

To test the social transmission explanation, I analyze whether Asian Americans develop political orientations through interactions with college peers using a national panel survey of college students, interviewed twice during their college careers. This longitudinal survey has been conducted by the Cooperative Institutional Research Program (CIRP) since 1966 and is maintained by the Higher

Education Research Institute (HERI) at UCLA. This survey has been used extensively in higher education research and several recent studies of American political behavior, including research on the political orientations of biracial Americans, the policy views of affluent Americans, and civic engagement among low-income college students (Davenport 2018; Mendelberg et al. 2017; Mendelberg et al. 2021). For the purposes of this chapter, the effective CIRP survey sample includes over 250,000 Asian American, African American, Latino, and white college students who attended nearly 600 colleges and universities nationwide between 1987 and 2014. These data allow for comparisons with whites, the majority racial group, African Americans, a predominantly nonimmigrant minority group, and Latinos, a diverse pan-ethnic group that includes many immigrants.

In this chapter, I test several predictions about peer political influence developed from the theory of social transmission. I find that Asian Americans and African Americans enter college with less crystallized political views than their white and Latino peers. The political views of all four racial groups become more coherent and shift in a liberal direction from freshman to senior year, but the largest changes occur among Asian Americans. Turning to peer influence, I find that interacting with peers of a different race drives these changes in political orientations, but only among Asian American and white students. Moreover, these changes are larger for Asian Americans than whites, indicating that peers may play a larger role in political learning among Asian American youth. Finally, campus ideological context influences the direction of political attitude change. In a brief follow-up using the 2016 Collaborative Multi-Racial Post-Election Survey (CMPS), I explore whether college attendance and peer interactions contribute to political socialization for a racially diverse group of young Americans that includes Asian Americans.

Taken together, the evidence presented in this chapter offers several new insights about political socialization among Asian American youth in an era when Democratic preferences solidified within this racial group. First, it shows shifts in the political attitudes of Asian Americans who attend college in the United States that comport with broader partisan trends in the pan-ethnic constituency. The chapter also offers direct evidence that Asian Americans develop political orientations through social interactions with peers. More generally, this chapter shows that exposure to diverse peer groups in college—and potentially in other social environments—has important implications for the development of political views among a wider range of young people from diverse racial groups.

Civic Education, Peer Groups, and Youth Political Engagement

A large body of political science research explores whether civic education initiatives increase political knowledge, civic skills, and political participation among young Americans (Campbell 2006; Holbein and Hillygus 2020; Niemi and Junn 2005; Pasek et al. 2008; Verba et al. 1995). Much of this work focuses on civics curricula in classroom settings. For example, several studies find that taking social science or civics courses—both at the high school and college levels—increases political efficacy and political engagement (Hillygus 2005; Holbein and Hillygus 2020; Pasek et al. 2008). Despite these positive outcomes, research on the political impact of civic education has generally resulted in mixed findings (Willeck and Mendelberg 2022). In fact, several studies find that high school civics curricula do not have large effects on political participation, particularly when it comes to voting (Callahan et al. 2010; Langton and Jennings 1968).

While the political consequences of civic education initiatives are mixed overall, these curricula may play a larger role in shaping participatory norms among young Americans who receive limited political exposure from their parents (Junn 2004). For example, using the Youth Parent Socialization Panel Study, Anja Neundorf, Richard Niemi, and Kaat Smets (2016) show that high school civics courses increased political engagement among children who grew up with little political exposure at home, arguing that "civics classes make up for missing parental socialization" (921). In other work, Rebecca Callahan and Chandra Muller (2013) offer evidence that civic education is associated with increased participation later in life among the children of immigrants but not the children of US-born Americans.

Civic education may also have distinctive political consequences for students from ethno-racial minority groups. For example, standardized civic exams increase political knowledge among children of immigrants attending public schools (Campbell and Niemi 2016, 495). Matthew Nelsen (2021b) finds that civic education content increases political efficacy among whites and political advocacy among African American and Latino youth. In other work, he shows that civic education programs that focus on the experiences of marginalized communities increase political engagement among African American and Latino high school students in Chicago (Nelsen 2021a).

Yet others find that civics programs that encourage peer interactions increase political engagement. For example, "open classroom" settings that facilitate political discussion between peers increase students' interest in politics and desire to vote in future elections (Campbell 2008; Kahne et al. 2013). In *Why We Vote: How Schools and Communities Shape Our Civic Life*, David Campbell (2006) argues that schools and local communities help young Americans develop habits of political participation by exposing them to a culture of civic engagement. Rather than the content of educational curricula, this perspective highlights the role of peer groups and community norms in influencing political attitudes. This echoes conclusions from early work which failed to find strong associations between civic education and political engagement. For example, Kenneth Langton and Kent Jennings (1968) noted that "while the formal curriculum may have little effect, there is still the acquisition of conceptual skills, the social climate of the school, and the presence of peer groups, all of which may play a significant role in the political socialization process" (866).

Taken together, this research conveys that civic education programs do not always lead to political engagement but have the potential to mobilize young voters, especially those from immigrant households and ethno-racial minority groups. However, these programs are particularly likely to increase civic engagement when they facilitate open political discussions. By extension, these initiatives, and the social connections between campus peers that they facilitate, may also shape the development of political ideology, political views, and partisan identities.

Asian American Political Learning in Settings of Higher Education

Research on higher education and political behavior conveys that experiences in college influence the development of political views. While some studies focus on the political effects of academic factors, including test scores and course materials (e.g., Hillygus 2005), others argue that experiences in college shape students' views through cultural norms and social interactions with peers and faculty members (Dey 1996; 1997; Mendelberg et al. 2017; Stevens et al. 2008). For example, Eric Dey (1996; 1997) finds that exposure to the political perspectives of other students and faculty influences students' political views. He concludes that the perspectives of both faculty and peer groups are important and that students' political views "change in the direction of institutional norms" (Dey 1996, 550).

Studies focused on Asian American youth are more limited but indicate that experiences in college provide preliminary exposure to American politics. For example, in a study of students from immigrant families at USC, Janelle Wong and Vivian Tseng (2008) find that political socialization occurs in both directions between immigrant parents and their children (151). While this research does not directly consider peer interactions during college, it conveys that Asian American college students are politically knowledgeable and pass along political information to their parents. In a similar vein, a qualitative study of Asian American youth finds that many learn about politics through experiences with student government in high school (Kiang 2001). Finally, my interviews with Asian Americans in Houston suggest that college is also an important setting for acquiring information about the American political system and mainstream political parties (Raychaudhuri 2018).

In groundbreaking research on the social effects of the college experience, James Sidanius, Shana Levin, Colette Van Laar, and David Sears (2008) explore the impact of experiences with racial diversity on many social and political outcomes. This study surveys UCLA undergraduates six times during college about a range of topics including political ideology, views on racial issues, ethnic identification, and academic achievement (45). Although the sample size is small, it is approximately 35% Asian.[1] This research explores changes in political ideology, among many other outcomes, during college. Relative to white students, Asian Americans enter college with moderate but "less firmly established" political views that become more liberal over time (85, 118). Also, exposure to racial diversity, measured as having a roommate of another race, increases Asian Americans' likelihood of "inter-ethnic friendships and dating" (217).

While this research provides insight into the political views of a racially diverse group of college students at UCLA that includes Asian Americans, it leaves open several questions about campus political socialization. First, it does not identify particular social experiences which lead to political attitude crystallization during college. The authors also do not consider changes in political views beyond perceptions of racial prejudice and views on affirmative action. Second, it is difficult to generalize to Asian American college students nationwide from this study because the sample is small and drawn from a single university during a narrow time frame.

Theory and Hypotheses: Social Transmission of Political Views from Campus Peers

Building on this work, I explore the political consequences of interactions with diverse peer groups during college among Asian Americans and students from other racial groups. The theory of social transmission predicts that Asian Americans develop political orientations through the diffusion of political views from peers in a range of local contexts, including schools, colleges, neighborhoods, workplaces, religious organizations, and other social settings. Of these local

---

[1] About 750 Asian Americans completed the first wave survey and 200 completed the sixth wave survey (Sidanius et al. 2008, 50). The data were collected between 1996 and 2001.

institutions, colleges are particularly conducive environments for peer influence because they are tightly knit settings where students regularly interact with each other in academic, co-curricular, and social contexts. Interactions with campus peer groups may lead to political learning among students from many different racial groups. However, I argue that Asian Americans are particularly open to peer political influence because they are especially likely to enter college without fully formed political perspectives developed by discussing politics with family.

Despite the book's central focus on Asian Americans, exploring the process of peer influence among students from other racial groups provides useful benchmarks for comparison. For example, African American and white students are two predominantly nonimmigrant groups who may enter college with anchored political views developed through political discussion with parents (Jennings and Niemi 1968; Jennings et al. 2009). While whites are the majority racial group, African Americans are a minority group with strong community-based norms of Democratic vote choice, which are linked to feelings of in-group racial solidarity (Dawson 1995; White and Laird 2020). Moreover, Asian Americans are racialized in relation to both African Americans and whites (Kim 2023). Latinos are another diverse pan-ethnic group that includes many immigrants and children of immigrants, which suggests that the social transmission account may also explain how they learn about politics (Zong 2022). However, Latinos attend college at much lower rates than Asian Americans, largely due to financial barriers (Figure 5.1; Zarate and Burciaga 2010). Therefore, peer influence in college settings may play a less central role in the development of the political views among Latino than Asian American youth. I develop hypotheses drawing on these claims which are described below and summarized in Table 5.1.

Focusing first on changes in the consistency of political orientations during college, the *political crystallization hypothesis* predicts that Asian Americans and Latinos enter college with less crystalized (or developed) political views than their African American and white counterparts but experience a larger increase in the coherence of their political attitudes from freshman to senior year. Following James Sidanius and co-authors (2008), I define the crystallization of political views as "the internal consistency of [political] attitudes" (85). In keeping with the partisan preferences expressed on most campuses, the *ideological change* hypothesis predicts that Asian Americans, African Americans, Latinos, and whites become more ideologically liberal during college (Brown et al. 2022). Once again, I expect that Asian Americans and Latinos experience larger changes in political attitudes than members of other racial groups.

What leads to these changes in political attitudes during college? The key mechanism underlying social transmission is interpersonal contact with campus peers. In this chapter, I focus on social interactions with peers from diverse racial groups. Interacting with students of different racial backgrounds is an important part of the college experience that has implications for a range of social and political outcomes, including grades, critical thinking skills, tolerance, cultural awareness, racial policy views, and civic engagement (Brown et al. 2003; Gurin et al. 2009; Johnson and Lollar 2010; Pascarella et al. 2014; Sidanius et al. 2008). Such interactions are particularly formative because college may be the first time that many young people, especially white students, are exposed to peers from different racial backgrounds (Fischer 2011). College may also be the first time

Table 5.1 Summary of Hypotheses

Hypothesis	Description
Changes in political orientations from freshman to senior year	
Political crystallization hypothesis	• Asian Americans and Latinos enter college with less crystallized views than African Americans and whites, but their attitudes become more coherent during college.
Ideological change hypothesis	• The ideological views of all racial groups generally shift in a liberal direction, but these changes are larger for Asian Americans and Latinos than African Americans and whites.
Peer influence on political views	
College peer influence hypothesis	• Interacting with peers of a different race during college shapes the political attitudes of African Americans, Asian Americans, Latinos, and whites.
Direction of effect	• Interacting with peers of a different race is generally associated with a liberal shift in political views.
Moderators of peer influence	
Racial moderator hypothesis	• Interactions with peers of a different race are associated with larger changes in political attitudes among Asian Americans and Latinos than African Americans and whites.
Ideological context hypothesis	• Interactions with peers of a different race are associated with the development of liberal political views among students who enter college with liberal cohorts and conservative views for those who enter college with conservative cohorts.

that Asian Americans are exposed to many other students of color (Fischer 2008; Museus 2008). Through these interactions, college students may transmit the political orientations they arrive with in freshman year to other students. They also may develop new political preferences by experiencing social norms and practices together on campus.

Building on these claims, the *college peer influence hypothesis* predicts that interactions with peers of a different race shape the political orientations of students from multiple racial groups, generally leading to more liberal political views in senior year. Among Asian Americans, interactions with African American, Latino, and white students are influential because non-Asian peers are more likely to arrive on campus with developed political views. A similar process may occur among Latino students, many of whom are the children of immigrants. Among whites, interactions with students of color may affect political views by increasing cultural awareness and positive attitudes toward racial outgroups, even though they enter college with relatively well-formed political predispositions (Fischer 2011). In contrast, interactions with non-Black students may not be as politically formative for African American students who develop political perspectives through in-group social interactions and solidarity building, well before they enter college settings (Dawson 1995; White and Laird 2020).

Finally, I test two hypotheses about factors that may condition how peer interactions affect political orientations: student race and the political norms on campus. The *racial moderator hypothesis* predicts that peer effects are larger for Asian Americans and Latinos than for African Americans and whites because the children of immigrants experience little political exposure in early life (Carlos 2018). A comparison to white Americans offers a difficult test of this hypothesis, since interacting with students of color may be a socially and politically formative experience of intergroup contact (Allport 1954; Fischer 2011; Oliver and Wong 2003; Pettigrew 1997; Pettigrew and Tropp 2006). The second considers the moderating effects of the dominant political ideology on campus. While colleges are often politically liberal environments, this is not always the case. Therefore, the *ideological context hypothesis* predicts that the effects of interactions with peers of a different race are conditioned by the ideological norms in a student's entering freshman cohort.

Drawing Evidence from a Longitudinal National Survey of College Students

I test these hypotheses using CIRP's longitudinal surveys of college students. CIRP's surveys bookend the college experience, interviewing students in the fall of their freshman year, in "The Freshman Survey" (TFS), and the spring of their senior year, in "The College Senior Survey" (CSS) (CIRP Freshman Survey 2023; College Senior Survey 2023). These surveys are housed at the Higher Education Research Institute at UCLA. The multiwave design of these surveys allows for an analysis that explores changes in political attitudes over time.

The full analytical sample includes 263,500 respondents—13,883 Asian Americans, 10,347 African Americans, 10,581 Latinos, and 228,689 whites who attended 571 colleges in 3486 entering first-year cohorts.[2] These respondents entered college between 1987 and 2010 and graduated between 1994 and 2014, a period during which a pattern of consistent Democratic vote choice emerged among Asian Americans (Figure 1.2). The effective sample for the analysis of peer interactions is restricted to a smaller group of nearly 20,000 students who graduated college between 2008 and 2009.[3] These students attended college during Obama's election in 2008, when a racially diverse coalition of young voters supported the Democratic candidate at the highest rates in modern history (Rosentiel 2008). Peer interactions on campus may have been particularly formative during this period and it is possible that the patterns represented are restricted to this distinctive political moment. I address the possibility of such a period effect at the end of the chapter by exploring the possibility of peer political influence with more recent survey data.

To offer a descriptive portrait, the racially diverse group of students who participated in the CIRP survey attended over 500 colleges and universities across the United States. About 88% attended private and 12% attended public institutions, suggesting that the sample tilts heavily toward private universities. However, the colleges that the students attended were geographically diverse. About 41% of respondents were enrolled in schools in Northeastern and Mid-Atlantic states, 19% in the West, 29% in the Midwest, and 11% in the South.

The average entering first-year cohort was about 5% Asian American, 5% African American, 4% Latino, and 81% white. Finally, turning to political norms, the average freshman cohort was ideologically moderate, with 45% of entering students reporting they were "moderate or middle of the road," 28% as "conservative" or "far right," and 27% as "liberal" or "far left" during their freshman year. Although this is not a nationally representative sample of students or colleges, the survey represents the perspectives of a sizable group of young people attending a diverse set of institutions over several decades.

---

[2] Following Tali Mendelberg, Katherine McCabe, and Adam Thal (2017), respondents who did not take both the freshman and senior surveys, spent less than three years in college, or attended two-year colleges were excluded from the sample. I also exclude respondents with missing values on predictors included in the models.

[3] Measures of social contact with peers were only included in these years.

The dependent variables, which measure political attitudes, include political ideology and views on the following policy issues: "abortion should be legal," "the wealthy should pay more in taxes," and "a national healthcare plan is needed to cover everybody's medical costs." To measure ideology, respondents were asked whether they would characterize their political views as far right, conservative, middle of the road, liberal, or far left. The policy attitude questions ask respondents whether they agree or disagree with each statement, measured on a five-point scale. These are continuous measures, rescaled from 0 to 1, with higher values reflecting more liberal attitudes. These questions were asked in both the entering freshman (TFS) and outgoing senior (CSS) surveys. I analyze changes over time in descriptive analyses. In predictive models, I use the senior-year measure as the dependent variable and control for the freshman-year measure. Although the survey does not include questions about partisanship, ideology and the policy questions offer reasonable proxies. Furthermore, the policy questions feature salient social and economic issues.

The primary independent variable is an individual-level measure of social contact with peers of a different race. Interactions with students of a different race is a scaled continuous four-item measure that includes (1) "attending an event sponsored by another racial group, (2) dining with, (3) sharing personal feelings with, and (4) socializing or partying with someone of another race" (alpha = 0.79). These questions, which ask respondents to reflect on their experiences during college, were measured in the senior-year survey.

It is important to note that interactions with peers of a different race is a measure that has different meanings for students from different racial groups. For Asian Americans, the measure represents interactions with non-Asians, who might include African American, Latino, or white peers. For African American students, it represents interactions with non-Black students and among Latinos, it represents interactions with non-Latinos. Among white students, interacting with peers of a different race represents interactions with students of color. Despite this notable difference from the other racial groups in the sample, white students offer a useful point of comparison, since exposure to racial diversity on campus may be socially and politically formative (Fischer 2011).

The Changing Consistency of Political Orientations from Freshman to Senior Year

I begin by exploring the crystallization of political views among students from the four major racial groups represented in the survey. I test the political crystallization hypothesis by analyzing changes in the correlation between the political views respondents expressed in their freshman and senior years. Following Converse (1964) and Sidanius et al. (2008), I use the correlation between political ideology, views on taxing the wealthy, creating a nationalized healthcare plan, and keeping abortion legal to measure the crystallization of political views. Table 5.2 presents the measures of crystallization separately for African Americans, Asian Americans, Latinos, and whites in freshman and senior years.[4]

These results support the political crystallization hypothesis, which predicts that students develop more crystallized political views during college, with larger changes among Asian Americans than other racial groups.[5] Table 5.2 shows that Asian Americans enter college with less crystallized political views than their white and Latino counterparts but more crystallized views than African Americans. The fact that African American students enter and exit college with the least cohesive ideological views is surprising given high rates of political unity within this community (Dawson 1995). However, it may reflect the fact that many African Americans express ideological stances that do not comport with their partisan identification (Jefferson 2024; White and Laird 2020). Turning to a comparison between Asian Americans and whites in freshman year, there is over a 15 percentage-point difference in the correlation between political ideology and policy views ($p < 0.001$). It is also notable that Latinos, another predominantly immigrant group, enter college with political views that are more crystallized than those of Asian Americans.

Table 5.2 Changes in the Crystallization of Political Views During College

Race	Freshman-year value	Senior-year value	Change over time
African American	0.340	0.380	+0.040 (n.s.)
Latino	0.465	0.505	+0.040^
Asian American	0.419	0.478	+0.059**
White	0.574	0.600	+0.026**
Difference: Asian Americans and Whites	−0.155***	−0.122***	−0.033

Note: ***$p < 0.001$; **$p < 0.01$; *$p < 0.05$; ^$p < 0.10$; n.s. = "not significant". P-values extracted from t-tests using cocron package in R.
Source: The data are drawn from the CIRP Freshman Survey and College Senior Survey (CIRP Freshman Survey 2023; College Senior Survey 2023).

---

[4] I make statistical comparisons between correlations using the R package "cocron" (Diedenhofen 2016).
[5] It is possible that these changes are driven by experiences in college or are the consequence of aging, which may lead political views to stabilize (Converse 1969). While I cannot adjudicate between these possibilities using these data, peers may play a role in this process both within and beyond college settings.

Although Asian Americans enter college without fully formed political perspectives, their views became more ideologically coherent during college. Attitude crystallization increases by nearly 6 percentage points among Asian Americans, from 0.419 in freshman year to 0.478 by the end of college ($p < 0.01$). The coherence of the views of African Americans and Latinos also increases from freshman to senior year, but only by about 4 percentage points. Moreover, these differences are not statistically significant at the $p < 0.05$ level. Following a similar pattern, whites' views become more crystallized too. However, the change over time is smaller in magnitude, at just over 2.5 percentage points ($p < 0.01$).

Even though Asian American's political attitudes become more coherent during college, it is important to note that on average, Asian Americans leave college with less crystalized political views than those that their whites peers entered college with. The correlation between political views is 0.478 in senior year among Asian Americans, compared to 0.574 in freshmen year among whites. This difference of nearly 10 percentage points is statistically significant ($p < 0.001$). The senior-year attitudes of Latino students are more crystallized than those of Asian Americans but are also less coherent than those of whites.

These findings support the claim that political socialization may be a prolonged process for immigrants and their immediate descendants (Carlos 2018). Although college is a formative political experience for Asian American and Latino children of immigrants, members of these groups continue to learn about American politics later in life, providing additional opportunities for peer groups to influence ideological positioning.

How Do Political Attitudes Change During College?

Next, I explore the direction and magnitude of changes in political attitudes during college among Asian American, African American, Latino, and white students. It is important to consider the direction that political views change because recent conversations highlight the role of college attendance in shaping vote choice. For example, having a college degree is becoming an increasingly strong predictor of voting for Democratic candidates in elections (Grossman and Hopkins 2024; Zingher 2022). This analysis considers whether college shifts political views in the expected direction across the four major racial groups. According to the ideological change hypothesis, political views become more liberal during college, with larger changes among Asian Americans and Latinos

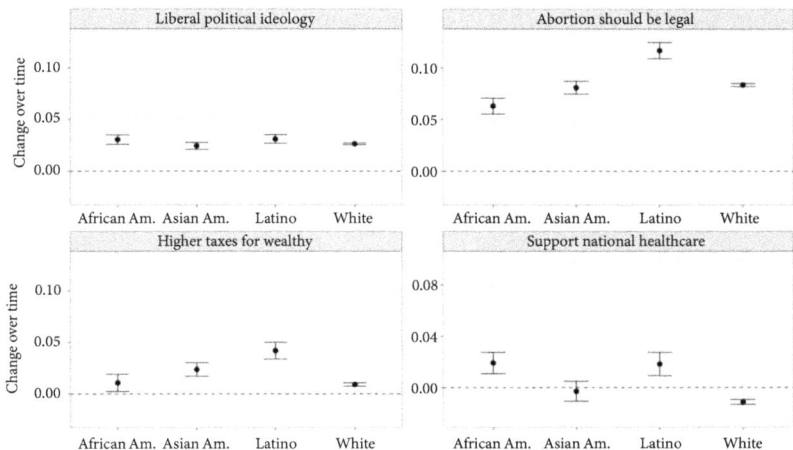

Figure 5.2 Changes in aggregate political views from freshman to senior year
Point estimates of changes over time are plotted with 95% confidence intervals.
Source: The data are drawn from the CIRP Freshman Survey and College Senior Survey (CIRP Freshman Survey 2023; College Senior Survey 2023).

than African Americans and whites. Figure 5.2 presents average changes over time within each racial group.[6]

These aggregate changes in political views support the ideological change hypothesis. The political orientations of African Americans, Asian Americans, Latinos, and whites change significantly overtime, becoming more liberal for nearly all political outcomes. Across these racial groups, students entered college with moderate ideological perspectives and attitudes about abortion, taxing the wealthy, and creating a national healthcare system. With few exceptions, these attitudes shift in a liberal direction and these changes are statistically meaningful at the $p < 0.001$ level (Figure 5.2). These changes are largest for views on keeping abortion legal, which undergo nearly a 12-point shift in a liberal direction among Latinos, an 8-point shift among Asian Americans and whites, and a 6-point shift among African Americans. Political ideology and views on taxing the wealthy shift by 2 or 3 percentage points in a liberal direction.

I also find some support for the prediction that over-time changes in political views are larger among Asian Americans and Latinos than whites and African Americans. Relative to whites, Latinos experienced a larger change in political

---

[6] Appendix Table D.1 presents the mean values in freshman and senior years for each racial group. I identify statistically significant differences using t-tests for differences in means. I used paired tests for analyzing changes within racial groups and unpaired tests for comparing changes over time across racial groups.

ideology (3.1 vs. 2.6 points, $p < 0.05$), perceptions that abortion should be legal (11.7 vs. 8.4 points, $p < 0.001$), perceptions that the wealthy should pay higher taxes (4.2 vs. 1 point, $p < 0.001$), and that a national healthcare system is needed (1.9 points vs. −1.1 points, $p < 0.001$). While Asian Americans experience a larger change in views on taxing the wealthy than whites (2.5 vs. 1.3 points, $p < 0.001$) and that a national healthcare system is needed (about 0 points vs. −1.1 points, $p < 0.05$), there are no other statistically significant differences between the two racial groups.

Taken together, this evidence shows that Asian Americans' political attitudes become more ideologically consistent, and their attitudes shift in a liberal direction during college. While the views of students from other racial groups follow a similar pattern, there is also some evidence that Asian Americans (and Latinos—another predominantly immigrant group) experience larger changes in attitude crystallization and larger shifts in views on economic policies. The next section considers whether experiences interacting with peers from different racial groups during college contribute to these changes in political attitudes.

Do Interactions with Peers of a Different Race Shape Political Views?

Do interactions with peers of a different race during college contribute to these shifts in political attitudes? Do the same patterns of peer influence apply across racial groups? To test the college peer influence hypotheses, I explore the impact of peer interactions on the political views of Asian American, African American, Latino, and white students in senior year. These analyses account for the political views that the same students expressed in the freshman year survey. I consider the relationship between each political outcome and interactions with students of a different race.

This analysis also accounts for a range of individual-, cohort-, and school-level factors that may shape political attitudes (female, Catholic, Protestant, other or no religion, US citizen, English as a first language, and high parental income). I also include controls for the racial and ideological demographics of first-year cohorts, including entering college with a high proportion of Asian American, African American, Latino, white, other race, and ideologically liberal students.[7]

---

[7] Following Mendelberg, McCabe, and Thal (2017), I created binary cohort-level measures using responses from students of all racial backgrounds in the same or the preceding academic cohort as respondents in the analytical sample, drawn from a set of nearly eight million TFS respondents. Freshman-year cohort political ideology is the sole exception to this coding practice because the larger public TFS dataset omits this variable. The models include senior-year fixed effects and random intercepts for freshman cohorts and colleges.

Finally, I include the following school-level controls: public, college, South. See Online Appendix Table 5.1A ⊕ for coding and descriptive information about the control variables.

I use hierarchical regression models, nesting individual students within entering cohorts and colleges. I employ separate models for different racial groups for theoretical and empirical reasons. From a theoretical perspective, interacting with students of a different race has different meanings for African Americans, Asian Americans, Latinos, and whites because of these groups' different positions in the racial hierarchy (Masuoka and Junn 2013; Pérez and Kuo 2021). The results of an empirical test also convey that the relationships are best modeled separately for each racial group.[8,9]

I estimate the effects of interacting with diverse peer groups on senior-year political ideology and views on abortion. The outcomes measuring perceptions that "the wealthy should pay more in taxes" and "a national healthcare plan is needed to cover everybody's medical costs" are omitted from this analysis because there are insufficient cases. Figure 5.3 presents the results visually as the marginal effects of interacting with students of a different race on the two political outcomes for Asian American, African American, Latino and white respondents.[10] The top panel presents peer effects on political ideology and the bottom panel presents peer effects on perceptions that abortion should be legal.

The results support the college peer influence hypothesis among Asian Americans. Recall that this hypothesis predicts that social contact with peers of a different race during college generally leads to liberal political views in senior year. The top panel of Figure 5.3 shows that interacting with non-Asian peers during college increases liberal political ideology by about 12 percentage points for Asian Americans ($p < 0.001$). Among white students, interacting with non-white peers also increased liberal political views in senior year, but by about 8 percentage points ($p < 0.001$). These effects are statistically significant for both Asian Americans and whites, after controlling for freshman-year political ideology and a wide range of characteristics of individuals, their entering freshman cohorts, and their college, such as race, gender, religion, family income, citizenship, and region (Online Appendix Table 5.2A ⊕). In contrast, interacting with

---

[8] The Chow F-test is a statistical technique that compares regression coefficients across subgroups to determine whether the data should be modeled separately or in a single model (Chow 1960). The results convey that the coefficients from regressing the political outcomes onto the peer interactions predictor are significantly different for Asian Americans and the three non-Asian comparison groups. For ideology, $F = 16.65$, $p < 0.001$; for views on abortion, $F = 21.61$, $p < 0.001$.

[9] These model specifications offer several ways to address problems related to selection and endogeneity. First, including freshman-year measures of the dependent variables controls for pre-existing political orientations. Second, individual-level, cohort-level, and school-level predictors control for various alternative explanations and factors associated with college and friend selection. Third, year fixed effects account for changes over time.

[10] The full regression results are included in Online Appendix Table 5.2A.

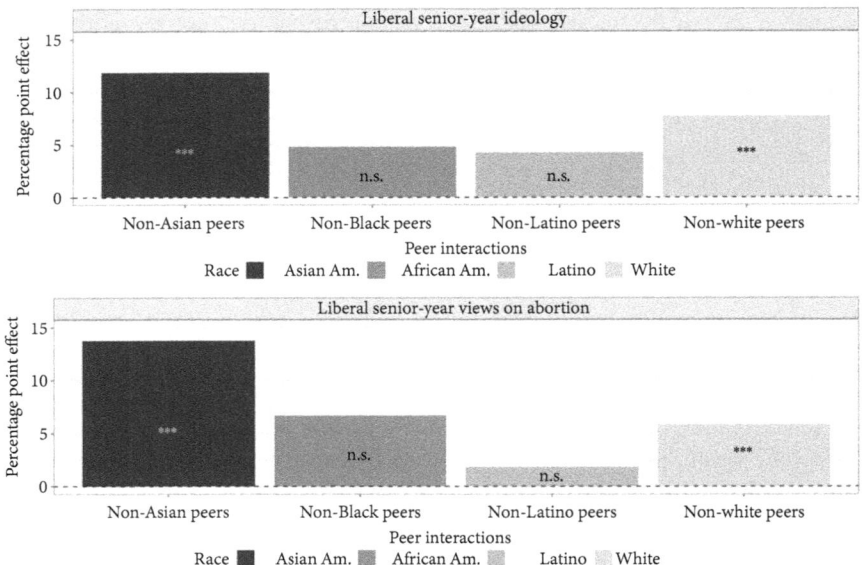

Figure 5.3 Association between interactions with peers of a different race and the political views of students across racial groups

Marginal effects of interacting with peers of a different race extracted from regression models presented in Online Appendix Table 5.2A.
Note: ***p < 0.001; **p < 0.01; *p < 0.05; n.s. = "not significant".
Source: The data are drawn from the CIRP Freshman Survey and College Senior Survey (CIRP Freshman Survey 2023; College Senior Survey 2023).

non-Black or non-Latino peers does not have a meaningful relationship with African American and Latino students' ideological perspectives.

A similar pattern applies for views on whether abortion should be legal. Turning to the bottom panel of Figure 5.3, interacting with non-Asian peers had a large liberalizing effect on Asian American students' attitudes, increasing perceptions that abortion should be legal by about 14 percentage points ($p < 0.001$). Once again, interacting with non-Black or non-Latino peers does not affect African American or Latino students' perceptions that abortion should be legal, despite sizable aggregate shifts in attitudes presented earlier in the chapter. Among white students, interacting with nonwhite peers increased perceptions that abortion should be legal, but the effect is less than half the magnitude of the corresponding effect for Asian Americans, at about 6 percentage points ($p < 0.001$).

Taken together, these results support the peer influence account among Asian American, and to a lesser degree, white college students. Social interactions with peers from a different racial group are associated with the political perspectives of Asian Americans, a predominantly immigrant minority group, and whites, a predominantly nonimmigrant majority group, in senior year. In contrast, interactions with racial outgroup members do not shape the political perspectives of African Americans or Latinos.

The latter finding is unexpected and does not support the college peer influence hypothesis, which predicts that Latinos may learn about American politics through peer groups. While evidence presented earlier in the chapter indicates that the political views of Latinos and African Americans become more coherent and ideologically liberal during college, interacting with non-Black and non-Latino peers does not seem to drive these effects. It is possible that other college experiences, including exposure to new ideas in the classroom or interactions with peers from their own racial group, shape the political perspectives of African Americans and Latinos. Future research should explore these possibilities.

Next, I test the racial moderator hypothesis to explore whether interacting with diverse peer groups has a stronger impact among Asian American than white students.[11] Figure 5.3 shows that interacting with peers of a different race has larger effects (about 4 points larger for ideology and 8 points for abortion) on the political views of Asian American than white youth. To test whether these differences are meaningful, I re-estimate the original regression model on the combined sample of Asian Americans and whites, interacting each respondent's race with the measure of interacting with peers of a different race (Online Appendix Table 5.3A ☛). In both models, the interaction between Asian American racial identification and contact with different-race peers is positive, moderately sized. However, it is important to note that these coefficients are not statistically significant, although they approached the $p < 0.10$ threshold.

The lack of a statistically significant moderating effect of respondent race in the interaction model may be explained by the fact that interacting with students of a different race is politically formative among whites and Asian Americans for different reasons. Among white respondents, interacting with students of color represents exposure to diversity, which may lead to increased tolerance (Brown et al. 2003; Fischer 2011; Johnson and Lollar 2010). In line with other research, the CIRP survey data suggests that social contact with students of color is not very common among white students (Massey et al. 2002; Orfield and Lee 2006). Across survey years, white students' average level of social interaction with African American, Asian American, and Latino students is 0.54, just above the midpoint of the scale.

---

[11] I omit African Americans and Latinos from this analysis since I did not find meaningful peer effects among members of these two racial groups.

In contrast, for Asian Americans, interacting with non-Asian students represents engagement with peers who have strongly anchored political views. This group likely includes many white students given the racial demographics of most college campuses. Furthermore, interacting with non-Asian peers is a daily occurrence for Asian Americans, who make up small percentages of the student body at most colleges and universities. In line with this claim, the average level of social interaction that Asian Americans experience with African American, Latino, and white students is 0.72.[12] Since interacting with students of color is both an unusual and formative experience for whites, it is notable that everyday interactions with non-Asian students have effects of a similar magnitude. This points to the power of non-Asian peer groups in shaping Asian Americans' political views in the absence of strong parental political influence.

Are Peer Effects on Political Views Conditioned by Campus Political Ideology?

Finally, I consider the ideological context hypothesis, which predicts that the effects of peer interactions on political views are contingent on the dominant political ideology in a student's freshman cohort. This analysis takes advantage of variation in the ideological diversity of entering first-year cohorts, re-estimating the models separately for students who entered college in liberal cohorts or in moderate and conservative freshman cohorts. Liberal cohorts are defined as those with more than 66% of the students who identified as liberal or far left. Fewer than 33% of students identify with those ideological labels in moderate or conservative cohorts. Here I focus only on Asian American and white students because meaningful peer effects did not emerge among African American and Latino students earlier in the chapter (Figure 5.3).

Figure 5.4 presents the effects of interacting with peers of a different race on political ideology and abortion for students who entered college in liberal and in moderate or conservative cohorts.[13] The first two panels display peer effects on ideology and views on abortion for Asian Americans who entered college with liberal and conservative cohorts. The third and fourth panels display the corresponding effects for whites.

These results show that peer effects on Asian Americans' political orientations are conditioned by campus ideology. As the first panel of Figure 5.4 shows, interacting with non-Asian students increases liberal political ideology in senior year

---

[12] Although interactions with peers of a different race are not related to political views among African Americans and Latinos, students from these racial groups also report high rates of interaction with non-Black and non-Latino peers, with a mean value of 0.71 among both groups.

[13] The full regression results are included in Tables 5.4A and 5.5A in the Online Appendix ⊕.

by about 14 percentage points among Asian Americans who enter college in liberal cohorts ($p < 0.001$). Among Asian Americans who begin college with moderate or conservative cohorts, the corresponding effect is about 9 points, but it is not statistically distinguishable from 0. The results are similar for views on keeping abortion legal. Contact with non-Asian peers increases perceptions that abortion should be legal by about 16 points ($p < 0.001$) among Asian Americans who entered college with liberal cohorts, but has no statistically significant effect among those who entered college with moderate or conservative cohorts. These results show that the partisan direction of peer influence on Asian Americans' political views is contingent on political norms on campus.

However, this pattern does not hold for white college students. Interacting with students of color leads to more liberal political views in senior year among whites regardless of the political ideology dominant in their first-year cohort. As the third panel of Figure 5.4 shows, interacting with students of color boosts liberal political ideology by about 7 or 8 points for white students who entered college with both liberal and conservative cohorts ($p < 0.001$). The effects for perceptions of abortion are similar in direction but smaller in magnitude. This

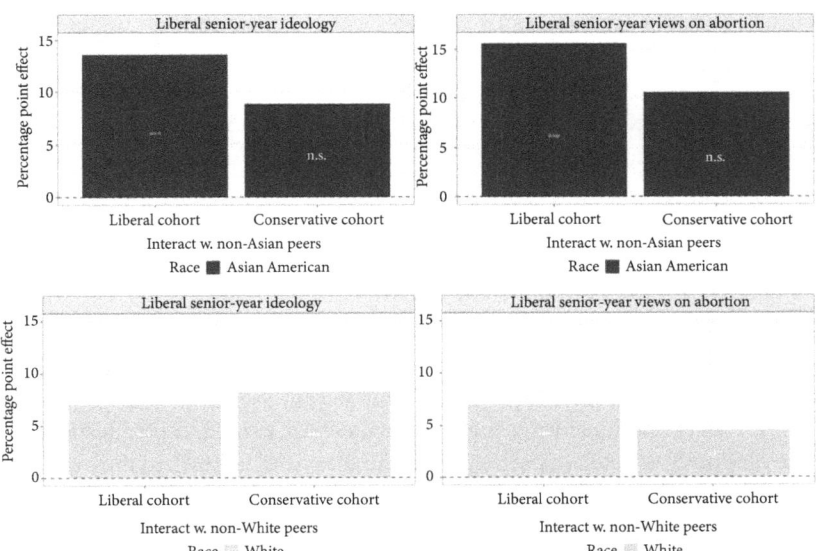

Figure 5.4 Association between interactions with peers of a different race and the political views of Asian American and white students by campus ideology

Marginal effects of interacting with peers of a different race extracted from regression models presented in Online Appendix Tables 5.4A and 5.5A.
Note: ***$p < 0.001$; **$p < 0.01$; *$p < 0.05$; n.s. = "not significant."
Source: The data are drawn from the CIRP Freshman Survey and College Senior Survey (CIRP Freshman Survey 2023; College Senior Survey 2023).

pattern may reflect the fact that interacting with nonwhite peers is a form of exposure to students of color, who may hold more liberal views than their white counterparts regardless of the ideological norms on campus.

These results convey that campus political context shapes peer influence for Asian American students. Interacting with non-Asian students leads Asan Americans to develop more liberal political views, but only on campuses where liberal political norms are commonplace. In contrast, interactions with nonwhite peers consistently move white students' attitudes in a liberal direction, regardless of campus ideological composition.

Peer Influence Beyond College Settings

I end this chapter with a short extension, exploring two open questions that stem from the CIRP college panel survey analysis. First, are over-time changes in college students' views driven by campus social experiences or by the process of coming to political maturity? Second, do peer interactions shape the political attitudes of Asian Americans who do not attend college? To answer these questions, I conduct a brief descriptive analysis focused on Americans under 40 who participated in the 2016 CMPS (Frasure et al. 2016).

The CMPS is a collaborative national political survey fielded in every presidential election year since 2008[14] by researchers at UCLA and other universities. The survey is focused on the political perspectives of an increasingly diverse American public and includes large numbers of minority respondents. This allows for detailed subgroup and cross-group comparisons of their political behavior and attitudes. It also uses a cost-sharing model that involves a large group of collaborators who include questions on the survey.

Respondents to the 2016 survey were randomly selected from lists of voters and nonvoters, using ethnic quotas to ensure sufficient variation in racial demographics. According to the survey documentation, "data for registered voters comes from the national voter registration database email sample. Respondents were randomly selected to participate in the study and confirmed they were registered to vote before starting the survey. For the nonregistered sample, email addresses were randomly selected from various online panel vendors" (Frasure et al. 2016). I restricted the full sample to 5,410 respondents under the age of 40 when the survey was administered. This included 1,722 Asian Americans, 1,569 African Americans, 1,839 Latinos, and 485 white Americans. Among these

---

[14] I use the 2016 survey in this chapter because it is a contemporary survey that included a sizeable sample of Asian Americans and several questions about political exposure from friends and co-workers.

respondents, approximately 205 people identified with more than one racial category.

I begin this analysis by exploring whether young Americans attended college at different rates across racial groups. Although most young CMPS respondents attended college, Asian Americans reported the highest rates of college attendance. Approximately 79.1% of Asian American, 60.0% of African American, 61.1% of Latino, and 65.8% of white respondents under 40 reported that they had at least "some college" education.

Next, I consider whether there are differences in political ideology, partisan identification, support for Obamacare, and perceptions that the wealthy should pay higher taxes by college attendance.[15,16] This analysis offers insight into whether the substantive changes observed in college students' views from freshman to senior year in the CIRP survey are a product of attending college or coming of age. Figure 5.5 presents the average values of these four political attitudes for respondents who attended and did not attend college across racial groups.[17]

Figure 5.5 shows that college educated respondents were somewhat more liberal than those who did not attend college across several measures. Focusing first on all respondents, those who attended college reported significantly higher levels of Democratic partisanship (2.1 points) and support for Obamacare (5.1 points) than those who had not attended college ($p < 0.05$ for both comparisons). Among Asian Americans, those who attended college reported 5.3 points higher levels of Democratic partisanship and 6.6 points of greater support for Obamacare than those who did not ($p < 0.05$ for both comparisons). While there are similar patterns for political ideology, these differences are not statistically meaningful.

Next, I explore the extent to which peers shape the political perspectives of young Americans, regardless of whether they attended college. While colleges and universities are settings where peer influence is likely to occur, peer groups may also exert influence in other social environments, including neighborhoods, workplaces, and religious organizations. This analysis focuses on Asian Americans and Latinos, the two groups for whom social transmission is likely to apply.[18]

---

[15] Policy question wording: (1) "The health care reform law, sometimes called Obamacare, should be amended and improved, not repealed"; (2) "Middle-class families should get a tax cut by having the wealthiest families in America pay a little more in taxes."
[16] Online Appendix Table 5.6A includes detailed descriptive and coded information for the variables included in this analysis.
[17] The measure of college attendance includes respondents who reported the following education levels: (1) "some college, 2-year degree"; (2) "4-year college graduate"; (3) "postgraduate education."
[18] African American and white respondents were not asked these questions.

150 SOCIAL ROOTS OF ASIAN AMERICAN PARTISANSHIP

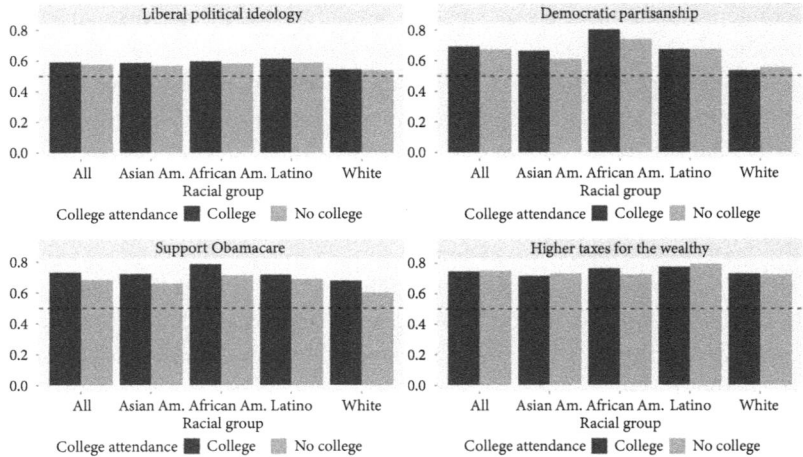

Figure 5.5 Political views by college attendance across racial groups

Source: The data are drawn from the 2016 Collaborative Multiracial Post-election Survey (Frasure et al. 2016).

The 2016 CMPS included a measure of whether friends or co-workers were "important sources of information for learning about U.S. politics." Respondents ranked their importance on a scale from 1 (the least important) to 7 (the most important). I coded the importance of peers in political learning into three categories, each approximately containing one third of the data. Figure 5.6 presents the political views for Asian American and Latino respondents who placed "low," "medium," and "high" levels of importance on peer groups in the process.

The political perspectives of Asian Americans become more ideologically liberal as the importance of peers in their process of learning about US politics increased. In contrast, there is no clear pattern among Latinos. As Figure 5.6 shows, Asian Americans who attributed "high" rather than "low" levels of importance to peers in political learning reported higher levels of liberal political ideology (6.7 points), Democratic partisanship (10.8 points), and support for Obamacare (1.4 points) ($p < 0.05$ for all comparisons). There is a similar pattern of political ideology among Latinos (3.5-point difference, $p < 0.05$). However, surprisingly, the opposite patterns emerge for partisanship. Latinos who relied on peers for political information were 5.3 points less likely to identify as Democrats than those who did not rely on peers ($p < 0.05$). This analysis indicates that young Asian Americans who learned about American politics through peer groups were more politically liberal on average than those who did not rely on peers for political learning. However, this relationship does not extend to

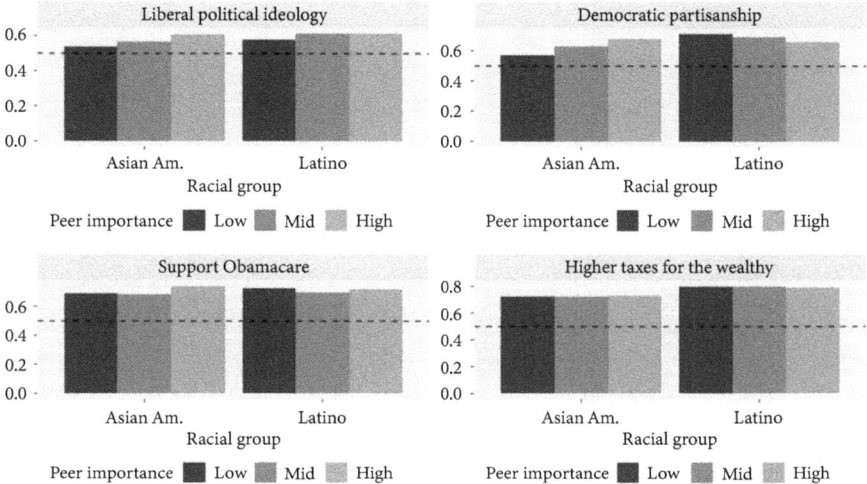

Figure 5.6 Political views by importance of peer groups in political learning for Asian Americans and Latinos

Source: The data are drawn from the 2016 Collaborative Multiracial Post-election Survey (Frasure et al. 2016).

Latinos. It is possible that peers play a less central role in their process of political learning or that their peer groups are more mixed in terms of their partisanship.

Finally, I consider whether the partisan composition of Asian Americans' peer networks conditions the direction of their political perspectives. While evidence presented in prior chapters suggests that many Asian Americans settle in liberal environments and interact with liberal peer groups, the 2016 CMPS included a question about the partisan composition of respondent's social networks.[19] This question was only asked of Asian American respondents. In keeping with prior findings, most Asian Americans had left-leaning social networks. About 14% indicated that their networks tilted toward Republicans, 25% conveyed that their networks were mixed partisan, and 61% stated that their networks tilted toward Democrats.

I find strong evidence that the political perspectives of young Asian Americans vary based on the partisan composition of their social networks. Figure 5.7 presents the political views of young Asian American CMPS respondents who have Republican-, mixed-, and Democratic-leaning social networks. Compared to those who have Republican-leaning networks, Asian Americans with Democratic-leaning networks were more likely to be ideologically liberal (23.7

---

[19] Partisan composition question wording: "Still thinking about your friends and family, how would you generally describe their political affiliation?"

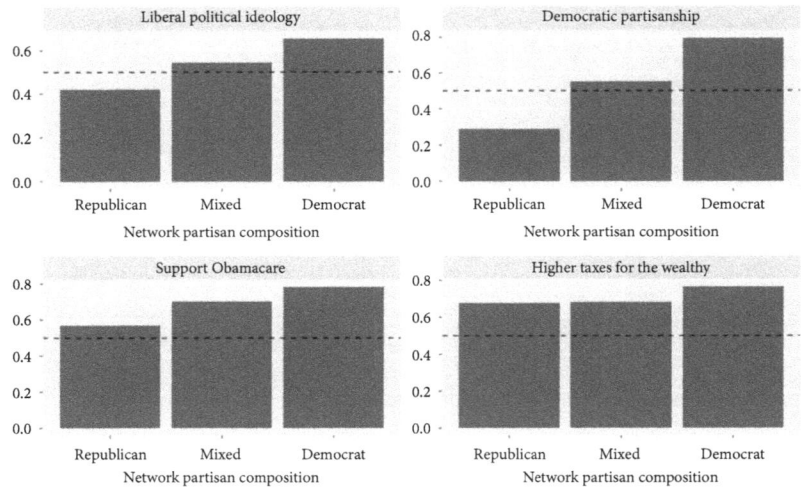

Figure 5.7 Political views by partisan composition of social network for Asian Americans

Source: The data are drawn from the 2016 Collaborative Multiracial Post-election Survey (Frasure et al. 2016).

points), identify as Democrats (50.7 points), support Obamacare (21.2 points), and support higher taxes for the wealthy (8.8 points) ($p < 0.001$ for all comparisons). These stark differences suggest that the direction of peer influence on partisan views, political ideology, and policy attitudes is conditional on the partisan norms reflected within Asian Americans' peer groups. While most Asian Americans are embedded in left-leaning peer groups, those who have more conservative social networks are much more likely to identify as Republicans and be politically conservative.

The patterns that emerge in this descriptive analysis convey that peer interactions are relevant to political attitude formation among Asian American youth beyond college environments. Attributing importance to peer groups in the process of learning about US politics shapes the political perspectives of a wider cohort of young Asian Americans. Moreover, the partisan and ideological direction of their political attitudes is shaped by the partisan composition of peer groups. Finally, those who attended college hold slightly more liberal political views than those who did not. This indicates that campus peer networks largely push Asian American students in a liberal direction, although Republican socialization occurs among young people embedded into conservative social networks.

Conclusion

This chapter offers direct evidence of peer political influence, showing that interactions with peers in college shape Asian Americans' political orientations. As discussed above, college is a useful setting for studying peer influence because it is a social environment away from home that most Asian American children of immigrants enter at an impressionable age. To briefly summarize the findings, Asian Americans develop more liberal political orientations during college and interacting with non-Asian peers contributes to these changes. These peer group effects are strongest when Asian Americans enter college with liberal freshmen cohorts. White students experience similar shifts in political views through interactions with students of color, but they are smaller in magnitude and do not vary based on campus ideological norms. Finally, a similar process of peer influence may shape the partisan perspectives of a diverse young cohort of Asian Americans beyond college settings.

These findings have several implications for understanding how the college experience shapes political learning and how Asian Americans develop political attitudes within tightly knit social environments. First, peer interactions contribute to changes in the political attitudes of the children of Asian American immigrants. In line with the social transmission account, interactions with college peers are associated with changes in political ideology and attitudes about abortion among Asian American students, who enter college without fully formed political orientations. Although this is not direct evidence that peer interactions shape partisan preferences, these findings suggest that peer interactions during college contribute to the development of political ideology among the growing population of Asian Americans who attend college in the United States. Moreover, a follow up analysis focused on young Asian Americans shows that learning about American politics from friends and co-workers increases the likelihood of Democratic partisan identification.

Second, campus ideological context shapes the nature of peer political influence. Since college campuses are typically liberal environments, interacting with non-Asian peers leads to more liberal political views in senior year. However, these interactions have the strongest liberalizing effects on campuses where those views dominate. This comparts with evidence presented in Chapter 3, which shows that political context is important and Asian American political orientations shift in the direction of local partisan norms. Similar patterns emerged in a follow up analysis focused on young Asian Americans who both attended and did not attend college. Those with Democratic-leaning social networks expressed significantly more liberal political views than those with Republican-leaning networks.

Third, comparative analyses convey that the political influence of peers of a different race in college settings applies to white, but not to African American or Latino youth. Interactions with students of color shape the political orientations of whites, a predominantly nonimmigrant constituency that enters college with well-formed political views. This points to the powerful impact that exposure to diversity in college can have on the formation of political views, even among members of the majority racial group. This finding may help to explain the "diploma divide," which points to an increasing gap in vote choice between those with and without a college degree over the past two decades (Grossman and Hopkins 2024; Zingher 2022). According to this account, college graduates are increasingly more likely to vote for Democrats while those without a college degree are more likely to vote for Republicans. While the political views of Latino and African American students also changed over time, interactions with peers from different racial groups did not explain these changes. Future work may explore which aspects of the college experience shape the political perspectives of other students of color.

It is important to note that college represents only one social institution where Asian Americans may learn about American politics and develop political perspectives. While the focus on college as a setting for peer influence is well justified, many Asian Americans, particularly those from working-class backgrounds and immigrants who arrive in the US later in life, do not enroll in American colleges or universities. Even Asian Americans who attend college in the US may not fully develop their partisan perspectives until after college. I expect that a similar process of peer influence occurs in churches, workplaces, neighborhoods, and informal social networks, informing the political views of first-generation immigrants and their children well after they graduate college. While testing these claims is beyond the scope of this chapter, it ends with a brief descriptive analysis which suggests that a similar process may occur beyond college settings. Future research should continue to explore whether peer political influence occurs in other social environments.

Although this chapter offers evidence that interactions with peers during college shape Asian Americans' political views, it has several important limitations. First, even though panel data offer a methodological advantage in studying changes in political attitudes over time, the results are not causally identified. Another limitation is that the political outcomes measured are not explicitly partisan. Although I find direct evidence that experiences in college shape ideological and policy views, I am unable to make claims about how these views translate into vote choice and partisan preferences. Finally, the independent variable, interacting with peers of a different race, does not capture interactions with Asian American peers, which may also be politically formative. Chapter 6 presents the results of two original survey experiments that address many of these limitations. These studies provide a causal test of peer partisan influence on Asian American college students' partisan views by presenting a partisan cue from campus peer groups in a randomized experimental manipulation.

6
Political Endorsements from Peers in Campus Social Networks

In an article published in the *Wall Street Journal* in 2017, Professor George Kuh emphasized the role that students play in each other's college experiences, stating that "peers are the single most important influential group on campus, in terms of how students spend their time, what classes they take, how much they study, and what habits they pick up" (Belkin 2017). Campus peers live, work, and interact with each other in a tightly knit environment, shaping each other's social and academic outcomes. A similar logic may also apply to the political realm. If campus peers have the power to influence students' academic and social realities, can they also shape each other's political perspectives? This chapter investigates this possibility, focusing specifically on the partisan influence of campus peer groups for Asian American students.

Do Asian American college students learn about American politics through partisan cues from their peers? A growing number of Asian American children of immigrants who come of age in the United States and experience limited partisan socialization through the family may be open to political information expressed by peers in educational settings. The evidence presented earlier in the book indicates that Asian Americans discuss American politics more frequently with peers during adulthood than with family members during childhood, which in turn shapes the development of partisan orientations. What role do interactions with campus peer groups play in this process? To what extent do Asian American college students observe the people around them and soak up the political perspectives expressed on campus, as several of the Houston interview participants indicated?

The previous chapter builds on these qualitative insights and explores the process of political socialization among Asian Americans who attend colleges and universities nationwide. Evidence from a national panel survey of college students indicates that interacting with diverse peer groups during college leads to changes in ideological and policy views. Despite the broad scope and longitudinal nature of the survey, the prior analysis left open several questions that are addressed in the current chapter. First, it is unclear whether changes in ideology and policy preferences extend to partisan preferences. Second, Chapter 5 offers several examples in which left-leaning campus peer groups push Asian

The Social Roots of Asian American Partisanship. Tanika Raychaudhuri, Oxford University Press.
© Oxford University Press (2025). DOI: 10.1093/9780197826560.003.0006

Americans in a liberal direction, but limited evidence of socialization in a conservative direction, a potential outcome when Asian Americans are exposed to pro-Republican cues from peers. Finally, while panel surveys offer several advantages over cross-sectional surveys, they do not definitively address the possibility of self-selection.

This chapter extends these observational tests and explores whether endorsements of policy initiatives proposed by the Democratic or Republican Party from college peer networks change Asian Americans' partisan attitudes. Drawing on the theory of social transmission, I predict that learning that an established campus peer network supports a policy proposal attributed to a particular political party will lead Asian Americans to express greater support for the policy and party in question. I test this hypothesis and several additional expectations in two pre-registered survey experiments. Both experiments exposed college students to an infographic about a higher education policy proposal purportedly circulating on social media websites. In each study, I randomly varied the partisan direction of the infographic (e.g., whether the policy was attributed to Democrats or Republicans) and whether members of the respondents' undergraduate peer network on campus support the policy.

The studies were conducted with complementary student populations. The first focused on over 400 Asian Americans and non-Asian students at the University of Houston, a large and diverse public university in the city. The second study was conducted on a national sample of nearly 800 Asian American and non-Asian college students, recruited from several hundred public and private universities by the survey firm College Pulse. African Americans, Latinos, and whites were also included as comparison groups in both studies, to test whether peer endorsements have a stronger impact among Asian Americans or whether peer influence reflects a more general process of youth socialization in campus environments.

The experiments offer direct causal evidence that partisan cues from peer groups shape Asian Americans' partisan preferences, even when the party in question is unpopular on campus. First, peer endorsements of both Democratic and Republican proposals affect policy views and willingness to sign a petition endorsing the policy across studies. However, only the Republican treatment infographic significantly altered partisan preferences. Across both studies, the Republican treatment with an endorsement from campus peer groups increased Asian Americans' ratings of the Republican Party, relative to an identical version of the infographic that described the policy but omitted the social endorsement.

These findings highlight the power of social cues in shaping Asian Americans' partisan preferences. An unusual positive message for peers about Republicans increased positive evaluations of the party. In contrast, a similar positive cue from peers about Democrats, which respondents are more likely to be exposed to on a regular basis on most college campuses, had no influence. This is direct evidence that partisan messages from peer groups can influence Asian Americans' partisan leanings at the individual level.

Testing the Theory of Social Transmission Experimentally

Social identity accounts of partisanship suggest that attachments to political parties are social, emotional, and expressive and are often driven by affective considerations rather than ideological or policy views (Achen and Bartels 2016; Green et al. 2004; Greene 2004). Taken together with research on the social flow of political information, this work finds that partisan attachments are often laden with emotion and developed through social interactions (Anspach 2017; Berelson et al. 1954; Huckfelt and Sprague 1995; Mutz 2002; Mutz and Mondak 2006). The theory of social transmission draws on these social accounts of partisanship and predicts that people develop favorable attitudes about a political party through the influence of peers in local contexts. Individuals may develop a preference for a given party because their friends support that party and endorse it in daily social interactions. Put differently, people develop partisan attitudes and identities through the social transmission of partisan cues from friends and acquaintances within established peer networks.

I argue that this explanation applies more readily to Asian Americans than many non-Asian groups. This is because most Asian American adults are immigrants or the children of immigrants, who are unlikely to develop partisan attitudes through the family, as described in detail in previous chapters. Without strong familial partisan anchoring, Asian Americans may be more open to political beliefs expressed by friends and acquaintances than similarly positioned whites, African Americans, and even Latinos.[1]

Although social transmission from peers could generate partisan views across the political spectrum, the theory predicts most Asian Americans will develop Democratic rather than Republican preferences because many settle in liberal metropolitan areas where they are more likely to interact with Democratic peers (Gebeloff et al. 2021; Logan and Zhang 2013). Although Republican socialization is less common, it is likely to occur when Asian Americans settle in conservative areas or interact with Republican-leaning peer groups (Leonhardt 2023).

---

[1] I do not have strong theoretical expectations about whether the social transmission account applies to Latinos. It is possible that peers play an important role in their political learning but Chapter 5 offers mixed evidence of this claim. Future work should test this claim in studies focused on Latino immigrants and children of immigrants.

This chapter offers an important innovation over observational tests of social transmission presented in earlier chapters that cannot fully account for the possibility that people choose their peer groups based on partisan considerations. That is, rather than developing partisan attitudes through social interactions, perhaps Asian Americans select into social networks based on existing political leanings. The survey experiments presented in this chapter help adjudicate between these different explanations for the association between local partisan norms and partisan preferences observed in early chapters by randomizing exposure to partisan cues from peers. By randomly varying the partisan direction of these cues, the studies also provide a test of peer socialization in a Republican direction, which is less common in real-world settings.

The experiments test several hypotheses developed from the broader theoretical account. Most centrally, these studies investigate the core expectation that Asian Americans develop partisan views through peer influence. To that end, I experimentally manipulated a visual infographic presenting information about a policy intended to make higher education more affordable. I randomly manipulated two aspects of the infographic: (1) whether the policy was proposed by the Democratic or Republican Party, and (2) whether the infographic contained an endorsement from peers on campus. Table 6.1 summarizes the four

Table 6.1 Overview of Experimental Conditions

	Endorsement: None	Endorsement: Campus peer network
Party that proposed policy: Democratic	Control 1 (C1): Democratic proposal with no endorsement Title: "Democrats promote strategy to increase access to higher education"	Treatment 1 (T1): Democratic proposal with peer endorsement Title: "Democrats' strategy to increase access to higher education finds strong support in the UH [Study 1]/your campus community" [Study 2]
Party that proposed policy: Republican	Control 2 (C2): Republican proposal with no endorsement Title: "Republicans promote strategy to increase access to higher education"	Treatment 2 (T2): Republican proposal with peer endorsement Title: "Republicans' strategy to increase access to higher education finds strong support in the UH [Study 1]/your campus community" [Study 2]

experimental conditions. I describe the research design in more detail in the next section.

Presented in the context of the experimental design, the *peer endorsement hypothesis* predicts that viewing either partisan treatment version of the infographic with the peer endorsement increases support for the policy in question and the party proposing it, relative to the identical control version with no social endorsement. This expectation applies to both the Democratic and Republican versions of the treatments, which are each compared to the control versions for the same party. The control versions of the infographics are identical to the treatment versions but they do not contain a social endorsement. For policy outcomes, I also compare the effects of the combined partisan treatments against both partisan controls because the peer endorsement should increase support for the policy in question regardless of which party proposed it.

I also predict that peer partisan endorsements have stronger effects among Asian Americans than students from other racial groups, who are more likely to enter college with strongly anchored political views. This expectation draws on the theoretical underpinnings of the social transmission account and the findings presented in the prior chapter, which indicate that peer group interactions are particularly formative for Asian American college students when compared to their African American, white, and Latino peers. Therefore, I consider whether the peer endorsement treatment effects differ by respondent race. The *respondent race hypothesis* predicts that peer endorsements have stronger political effects among Asian American than non-Asian respondents.

Finally, I test additional hypotheses about the moderating effects of factors that may shape whether students are open to partisan endorsements from peers.[2] These include reported levels of political discussion and feeling a sense of belonging on campus. First, the *family political discussion hypothesis* predicts that peer endorsements have stronger political effects among students who report limited (vs. frequent) discussion of American politics with family during childhood. In contrast, the *peer political discussion hypothesis* predicts that peer endorsements have stronger political effects among students who report frequent (vs. limited) discussion of American politics with other students on campus. Finally, the *campus belonging hypothesis* predicts that peer endorsements carry more social meaning and have stronger political effects among students who report a high (vs. low) sense of belonging with other students on campus.

---

[2] These moderator hypotheses were pre-registered for both studies, but the first study was insufficiently powered to effectively test them.

Experimental Design: Social Media Infographics With and Without Peer Endorsements

The purpose of the experiments was to test whether Asian American college students are pushed in the expected partisan direction after being informed that many of their campus peers support a partisan policy proposal. College students are a useful population for this study for theoretical and practical reasons. First, students' partisan attitudes may be malleable because they enter college while their political views are still developing (e.g., Dey 1996; Dey 1997; Mendelberg et al. 2017). Second, Asian American students are overrepresented on many college campuses, which helps to mitigate the challenges associated with sampling this "hard to reach" minority group that comprises less than 6% of the national population (Jaschik 2017).

The experimental manipulations were visual infographics describing a policy to make higher education more affordable. The infographics were modeled off actual graphics shared by political nonprofits and other organizations on social media to promote policy initiatives. The language used in the infographics draws on statements about higher education from both political parties (e.g., "Democratic Party on Education" and "Republican Party on Education" 2021). As described above, I randomly varied the partisan direction of the policy and whether it was endorsed by other undergraduate students on campus, an established peer group. All other dimensions of the infographics, including the substantive information describing the policy, were identical. This design choice makes for a difficult test of the social transmission account because both treated and control respondents read the same substantive information about the policy.

Both studies used a between-subjects design with four experimental conditions (Table 6.1). Each respondent was randomly assigned to view just one of the four versions of the infographic and answered questions about some of the political outcomes before and after viewing the experimental manipulation. Both the Democratic and Republican partisan conditions included the same policy idea. In the treatment versions, the policy proposal was supplemented with additional text and an image indicating that indicating that 70% of undergraduate students on campus support the policy.

The experimental design was largely identical across the two studies except for the specific policy featured in the infographics. In the first study, the infographics featured a debt-forgiveness initiative targeting students from middle-class families. The second study featured a policy to expand access to federal grants for college tuition, like Pell Grants. I changed the featured policy due to changes in the political climate in late 2022, when college debt forgiveness became strongly associated with the Biden administration's policy agenda (US Department of Education 2022). The full text of the experimental manipulations and infographic images from both studies are included in the Online Appendix (Online Appendix Figures 6.1A–6.8A ⊕).

The infographics focus on higher education because this topic is highly salient to college students, which may increase their attentiveness to the information presented in it. Additionally, social endorsements from other students may act as a heuristic, informing respondents of whether they should support the policy (e.g., Berelson et al. 1954 on opinion leaders and Mondak 1993 on endorsements). Political cues from college peers may be particularly meaningful because campuses are tightly knit communities where students live and work together.

The policies could also plausibly be attributed to either party because reducing the costs of higher education is less polarizing than many other political issues. Although Democrats are currently stronger proponents of policies to make higher education more affordable, several high-profile Republicans have supported initiatives to offer debt forgiveness to military veterans and qualified students from low-income families (Morris 2021; NASFAA 2019). Moreover, Republican Members of Congress recently proposed a bill expanding access to Pell Grants (Baime and Gimbroys 2022; Carrasco 2022). Finally, ordinary Americans are not highly polarized about higher education. For example, a recent poll found that 78% of Democrats and 58% of Republicans support some form of widespread student loan forgiveness (Winter 2020). According to another national survey, 82% of all voters, including 91% of Democrats and 77% of Republicans, support expanding access to Pell Grants (National Association of Independent Colleges and Universities 2021).

Both survey experiments began with questions about demographics, levels of political discussion with campus peers and family members, sense of belonging on campus, and pre-treatment questions about select political outcomes. Next, respondents were randomly assigned to view one of the four experimental conditions. Afterward, they answered several manipulation checks and questions about the political outcomes of interest. Respondents were informed that the infographic was fictional and debriefed about the purpose of the study at the end of the survey. Both studies were approved by the Institutional Review Board at the researcher's university prior to data collection.

Although both studies utilize a between-subjects design, several political outcome questions were also asked pre-treatment to analyze within-subject changes in policy views and partisan preferences. Prior research finds that this design choice helps to overcome challenges associated with identifying substantively meaningful and statistically significant treatment effects with small samples (Clifford et al. 2021).

Study 1: Peer Endorsements of Tuition Debt Forgiveness at a Diverse Public University

The first study was conducted with 456 undergraduate students at the University of Houston, a large and diverse public university in the city. The University of Houston is recognized as both an Asian American and Native American Pacific Island-Serving as well as a Hispanic-Serving institution by the US Department of Education. The analytical sample included 138 Asian American and 318 non-Asian respondents.[3] The Asian American sample was diverse and reflected the ethnic composition of Houston, which is home to large South and Southeast Asian populations (Appendix Table A.2). About 10.9% of Asian American respondents identified as East Asian, 44.9% as South Asian, and 40.5% as Southeast Asian. About 3.6% of respondents indicated they were from some other region of Asia.[4] The non-Asian comparison group was also very diverse, reflecting the racial demographics of the university. About 22.3% of students identified as African American, 44.0% as Latino, 7.9% as Middle Eastern or North African, and 23.9% as white, and 1.9% identified with another racial category.

Data collection occurred in March and April of 2022. The study was preregistered through the Open Science Framework[5] (OSF) prior to the start of data collection. These data offer an initial assessment of peer influence at a minority-serving university. Respondents were recruited from several sections of two large introductory political science courses, which all undergraduate students at the university are required to take prior to graduating. Over 5,000 students enroll in these courses each year. Therefore, eligible participants represent a diverse cross-section of the undergraduate population. Survey respondents were invited to take the survey on Qualtrics through email solicitations from course instructors. The survey took between 7 and 10 minutes to complete. Respondents who completed the survey received extra credit in their political science course.

---

[3] Due to issues with subject recruitment, this study reached about a quarter of the target sample size. Power analyses using the R package "pwr" indicate that study 1 is sufficiently powered to estimate post-treatment effects of approximately 0.12 (e.g., 12 points on a scale from 0 to 100) and pre-post treatment effects of 0.09. These calculations assume a standard deviation of 0.18, a power level of 0.80, and an alpha of 0.05.

[4] While the Asian American sample is diverse in terms of region of origin, the sample is too small for further subgroup differentiation in either study.

[5] See https://osf.io/cn584.

Study 2: Peer Endorsements of Tuition Grants Among a National College Student Sample

The second study was conducted with 688 full-time undergraduate students enrolled in four-year colleges and universities across the country. This experiment extends the first study and tests whether the findings generalize to a larger representative sample of college students beyond a single campus with a sizable Asian American population. Respondents were recruited from a verified and racially diverse panel of college students managed by the research firm, College Pulse. Of the 688 respondents who participated in the study, 392 identified as Asian American and 296 identified with other racial groups.[6]

The Asian American respondents represent a diverse range of regional subgroups and approximate the demographics of Asian Americans nationwide (Figure 1.1). About 41.1% identified as East Asian, 26.5% as South Asian, 30.6% as Southeast Asian, and 1.8% indicated they were from some other region of Asia. Of the non-Asian respondents, approximately 11.5% identified as African American, 12.2% as Latino, 62.2% as white, and 14.2% with some other group. The racial composition of the national sample offers a point of contrast from the single campus sample, where white students did not account for most non-Asians on campus.

The survey[7] was hosted online on the College Pulse platform and took between 5 and 7 minutes to complete. Respondents who completed the survey received compensation in the form of points that could be redeemed for gift cards. The data were collected between December 2022 and January 2023. The study was pre-registered through OSF prior to the start of data collection.[8]

The sample represents a diverse cross-section of undergraduates attending four-year colleges and universities nationwide. The participants attended 205 distinct schools including large public institutions (e.g., Florida State University, Ohio State University, University of California Los Angeles, University of Connecticut, University of Maryland College Park, and University of Oregon), elite private universities (e.g., George Washington University, New York University, Syracuse University, and Vanderbilt University), liberal arts colleges (e.g., Ithaca College, Oberlin College, Smith College, Williams College), and Ivy League universities (e.g., Brown University, Cornell University, Dartmouth University, and Princeton University). Approximately 11.2% of students in the sample attended

---

[6] The minimum target sample size was 250 students from each racial group. Power analyses using the R package "pwr" indicate that study 2 is sufficiently powered to estimate post-treatment effects of approximately 0.08 (e.g., 8 points on a scale from 0 to 100) and pre-post treatment effects of 0.055. These calculations assume a standard deviation of 0.18, a power level of 0.80, and an alpha of 0.05.

[7] The survey is also known as the University of Houston/College Pulse Study.

[8] See https://osf.io/exp7g.

schools in the Northeast, 21.7% in the Mid-Atlantic, 29.1% in the Midwest, 20.1% in the South, and 18.0% in the West. About 69.8% of students attended public institutions while 30.2% attended private institutions. The diversity of colleges represented in the sample indicates that the results are not driven by institutional or regional norms.

Turning to individual characteristics, about 61.9% of respondents identified as female and 20.7% as first-generation immigrants. The average respondent was 21 years old. The sample skewed toward those from middle- and higher-class backgrounds. About 28.8% identified as upper or upper-middle class, 42.0% as middle class, and 29.2% as working or lower class. In terms of majors, 12.3% studied business, 23.7% engineering, 9.5% humanities, 32.3% math and natural sciences, 14.2% social sciences, and 8% studied some other discipline. About 15.9% of respondents participated in Greek life. The sample included students from all college years but skewed toward juniors and seniors. While only 4.2% were freshmen, 23.0% were sophomores, 33.3% were juniors, and 39.5% were seniors.

Variables and Measures Included in the Survey Experiments

The following demographic variables were measured in both studies, before respondents were exposed to the experimental manipulation: race, age, gender, socioeconomic status,[9] generational status, division of study, and college year. Self-identified Asian American respondents were also asked about their region of origin. The second study included several additional demographic questions, such as whether respondents were registered to vote, participated in Greek life, received financial aid, and their perceptions that the cost of education is the most important issue. Finally, since the second study was conducted at multiple institutions, it included the following school-level variables: whether the institution is public or private and the institution's geographic region (Northeast, Mid-Atlantic, Midwest, South, West).

I also included measures of factors that might condition the peer endorsement treatment effects, including the frequency of discussing American politics with parents and family members during childhood and with other students on campus; both continuous measures, coded from 0 ("Never") to 1 ("Frequently"). Finally, I included a measure of sense of belonging on campus, a continuous variable scaled from 0 ("Strongly disagree") to 1 ("Strongly agree"). These questions were asked before respondents viewed the experimental manipulations.

[9] Measured as family income in the first study and class background in the second study.

Next, each respondent was randomly assigned to view one of the four experimental conditions. Randomization was conducted separately for Asian American and non-Asian students to ensure that a roughly equal number of students from each racial group was assigned to each experimental condition. After viewing the experimental infographics, respondents answered manipulation checks to ensure that they interpreted the information presented in the infographic. These questions ask respondents to recall which political party proposed the policy and what percentage of undergraduates on campus support the policy if they viewed a treatment infographic with the peer endorsement. To heighten uptake of the treatment, responses to these questions were followed by automated statements of the correct answers. The question wording and coding details of the manipulation checks are included in Table 6.1A in the Online Appendix ⊕.

The first set of post-treatment outcomes measure support for the policy described in the infographic. Respondents were asked to indicate their level of support for the higher education policy (debt forgiveness in Study 1, expanding access to Pell Grants in Study 2). Responses were coded on a five-point scale and rescaled from 0 ("Strongly oppose") to 1 ("Strongly support"). Next, respondents were asked if they would be willing to sign a petition supporting the policy, a three-point measure: 0 ("No"), 0.5 ("Not sure,") and 1 ("Yes").

The second set of outcomes measure partisan preferences. The primary partisan outcomes are 10-point feeling thermometer ratings of the Democratic and Republican Parties, rescaled from 0 ("Least favorable") to 1 ("Most favorable"), five-point measures of viewing each party in a positive light, rescaled from 0 ("Strongly disagree") to 1 ("strongly agree"), and partisanship on the standard seven-point scale, rescaled from 0 ("Strong Republican") to 1 ("Strong Democrat"). Four-point measures of perceptions that each major party represents the interests of people like the respondent, coded from 0 ("Not very likely") to 1, ("Very likely") were included as additional partisan outcomes in both studies.[10]

Several political outcomes were measured before and after the experimental manipulation in both studies. When analyzing these outcomes, the dependent variable was modeled as within-subject change over time. In Study 1, pre-treatment measures were included for policy support, feeling thermometer ratings of the political parties, and whether the respondent views each party in a positive light. In Study 2, pre-treatment measures were included for policy support, feeling thermometer ratings of the parties, and partisan identification.[11] The pre- and post-treatment measures used identical question wording and response options.

---

[10] The first study also included open-ended statements of likes and dislikes of each party. These questions were drawn from the American National Election Study.

[11] College Pulse respondents reported their partisan identification when they first joined the panel.

Evidence of Peer Partisan Influence Across Two Survey Experiments

In line with narratives about the growing diploma divide, most participants expressed more favorable attitudes about Democrats than Republicans, regardless of whether they viewed the treatment or control versions of the infographics (Grossman and Hopkins 2024). Online Appendix Table 6.2A ⊕ describes the data, displaying the mean values of political outcomes across experimental conditions. In general, respondents expressed more positive evaluations of the Democratic than Republican Party. Most participants also expressed fairly high levels of support for the policies described in the experimental infographics, which are intended to make higher education more affordable, across the four experimental conditions.[12]

Did Respondents Understand the Information Presented in the Infographics?

Next, I evaluate whether respondents understood the information presented in the experimental conditions. I compare the proportion of respondents who answered the manipulation checks correctly across conditions (Appendix E Tables E.3 and E.4). Across both studies, over 65% of respondents correctly identified the party that proposed the policy across experimental conditions. Although there are no differences in recall rates between treatment and control conditions when holding party constant, respondents were generally better able to recall the party that proposed the policy in the Democratic than the Republican versions of the infographic. This may be because Democratic politicians have been more likely to propose such policies. Turning to the peer endorsement manipulation, most respondents in the treatment conditions correctly identified the percentage of undergraduates on campus who supported the policy across racial groups, with lower levels of correct responses among Asian American respondents in the Republican treatment condition in the second study (Appendix Table E.4).

Taken together, this evidence shows that most respondents understood both the partisan signals and peer endorsements presented in the experimental infographics. However, the policies to make higher education more affordable were more strongly linked to the Democratic Party in the minds of many respondents, especially among Asian Americans in the second study.

---

[12] Both samples were also balanced on several observable pre-treatment covariates (Appendix Table E.2).

Peer Endorsement Treatment Effects on Policy Support and Partisan Preferences

Next, I consider the peer endorsement hypothesis, which predicts that respondents who viewed the treatment infographics with endorsements from campus peer groups will express more support for the policy and the party proposing it than those who viewed the control versions without a peer endorsement. To test this hypothesis, I regress each political outcome onto the treatment indicator(s) using OLS models. For outcomes that were measured before and after the experimental manipulation, the dependent variable is modeled as a change over time.

I present the peer endorsement treatment effects for the partisan and policy outcomes in Figures 6.1 through 6.4.[13] These figures visually display the effect of each social endorsement treatment infographic relative to the control version of the infographic for the following outcomes: support for the higher education policy and a willingness to a sign a petition supporting the policy (Figure 6.1), ratings of the Democratic and Republican parties (Figure 6.2), partisanship (Figure 6.3), and perceptions of the Democratic and Republican parties (Figure 6.4). In each figure, the effects are presented separately for the Democratic treatment infographic relative to the Democratic control as well as for the Republican treatment infographic relative to the Republican control. Since Figure 6.1 focuses on nonpartisan outcomes, it also presents the pooled treatment effects of both the Democratic and Republican treatments relative to the combined controls.

Focusing first on policy outcomes, peer endorsements increase support for the higher education policy and a willingness to support it publicly among Asian Americans regardless of whether it was proposed by Democrats or Republicans (Figure 6.1). In the first study, the pooled treatments (e.g., combined Democratic and Republican) with social endorsements from peers increased support for debt forgiveness by 4.9 percentage points among Asian Americans, compared to the combined controls (Figure 6.1, panel 1). It is important to note that this effect is only marginally significant at the $p < 0.10$ level. In the second study, the Democratic treatment with the social endorsement increased willingness to sign the petition among Asian Americans by over 11 points, relative to the Democratic control (Figure 6.1, panel 4, $p < 0.10$). These results offer suggestive evidence that peer endorsements of both the Democratic and Republican

---

[13] Treatment effects are plotted separately for Asian American and non-Asian participants of each study with 95% confidence intervals These values are extracted from regression models presented in Appendix E (Appendix Tables E.5–E.23). In each model, the treatment(s) are represented with binary indicators and the associated control(s) serve as the omitted baseline. Regression models are estimated separately for Asian Americans and non-Asians.

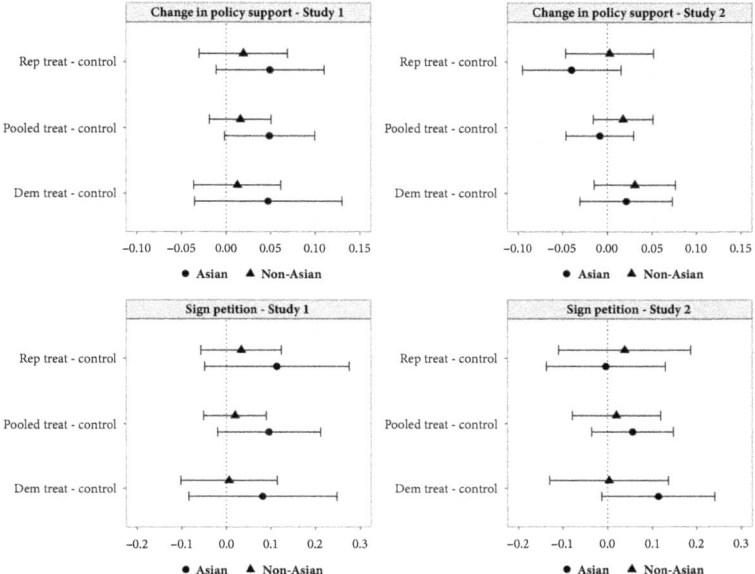

Figure 6.1 Peer social endorsement treatment effects on policy outcomes (95% CIs)

parties shape Asian Americans' policy views and willingness to express them publicly.

Turning to partisan outcomes, the social endorsement treatment effects on ratings of the political parties offer the strongest evidence that peer endorsements change Asian Americans' partisan preferences, increasing positive evaluations of the Republican Party. First, as the peer endorsement hypothesis predicts, the Republican treatment leads to net positive changes in thermometer ratings of the Republican Party of nearly 8 percentage points among Asian American students in the first study, relative to the control without a peer endorsement (Figure 6.2, Panel 1, $p < 0.05$). There is a similar effect among Asian American college students nationwide. In the second study, the Republican treatment increases net positive changes in ratings of the Republican Party by about 5 percentage points among Asian Americans (Figure 6.2, Panel 2, $p < 0.05$). I also find evidence that this positive message about Republicans from peer groups reduces ratings of Democrats among Asian Americans. The Republican treatment also leads to net negative changes in thermometer ratings of the Democratic Party by 3.6 percentage points among Asian Americans in the second study (Figure 6.2, Panel 4, $p < 0.05$).

The social endorsement treatment effects on changes in partisan feeling thermometer ratings offer evidence that a single partisan message from an

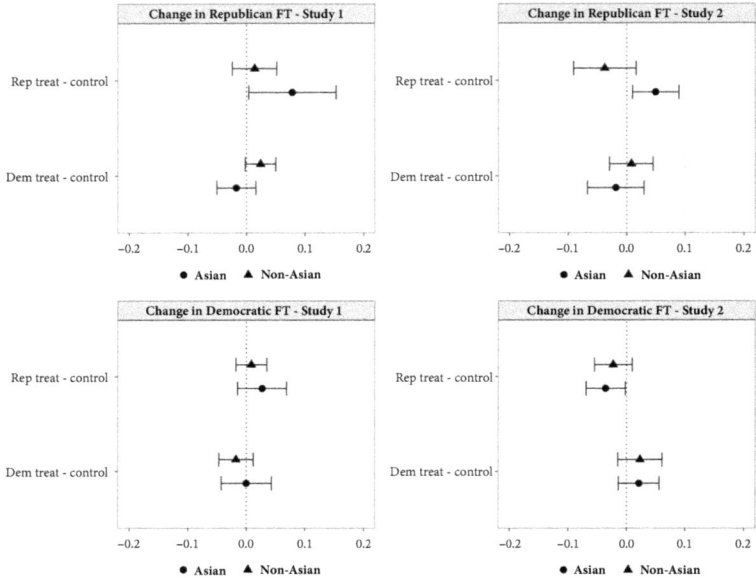

Figure 6.2 Peer social endorsement treatment effects on changes in party ratings (95% CIs)

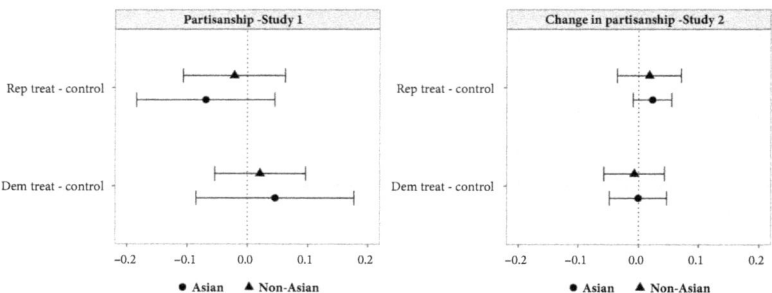

Figure 6.3 Peer social endorsement treatment effects on partisanship (95% CIs)

established peer group can alter Asian American college students' evaluations of both political parties. This represents a difficult test of the hypothesis since the treatment and control versions of the infographics include identical information except for the social endorsement from campus peer groups. It is also important to note that these effects are driven by versions of the infographic that attribute this popular policy to the Republican Party. There are no corresponding effects of the Democratic versions of the infographic or among non-Asians.

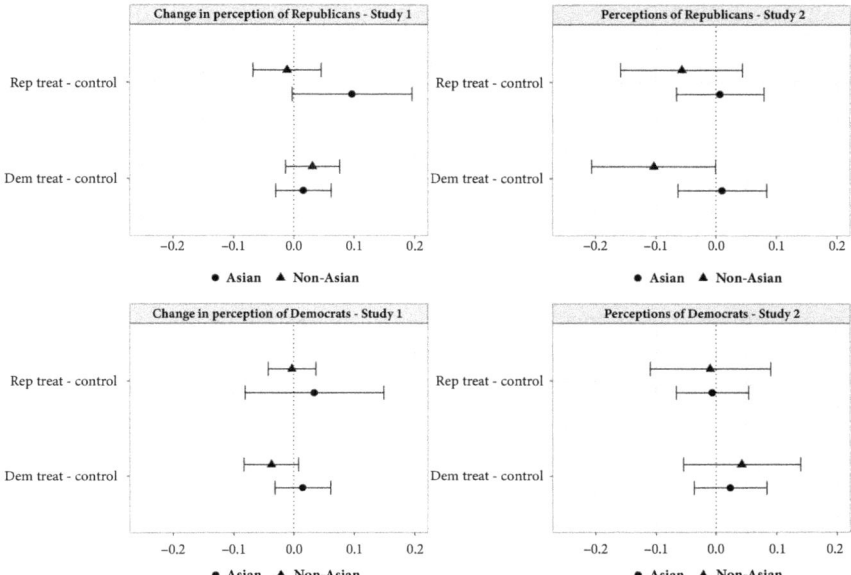

Figure 6.4 Peer social endorsement treatment effects on perceptions of the parties (95% CIs)

Next, there are no statistically significant treatment effects of either the Democratic or Republican infographics with peer endorsements on partisanship (Figure 6.3). However, viewing the Republican treatment with a social endorsement from peers increased Republican identification by nearly 7 points among Asian Americans, relative to the Republican control without a social endorsement in the first study (Figure 6.3, panel 1, $p = 0.25$). While this effect falls short of the standard threshold for statistical significance, it is notable because partisanship is a stable and deeply held attachment that rarely changes over the course of individuals' lives (Campbell et al. 1960; Hopkins et al. 2023).

There are some suggestive treatment effects on viewing the parties in a positive light. In particular, the Republican treatment leads to positive changes in perceptions of the Republican Party by almost 10 percentage points over time among Asian Americans, relative to the Republican control without the peer endorsement in the first study (Figure 6.4, panel 1, $p < 0.10$). In the second study, the Democratic treatment leads to about a 10 point decrease in positive perceptions of the Republican Party over time among non-Asians (Figure 6.4, panel 2, $p < 0.10$). Finally, neither treatment affects perceptions that each party represents the interests of people like the respondent (Appendix Tables E.12–E.14; E.22–E.23).

These results indicate that peer endorsements have the power to shape the policy views and partisan preferences of college students. However, the effects are asymmetric across political parties and racial groups. Peer endorsements of both the Democratic and Republican versions of the infographic affect policy outcomes among Asian Americans. However, these endorsements only affect Asian Americans' ratings of the political parties when the policy is attributed to Republicans. The Republican treatment may be particularly influential because many Asian American college students already have positive views of the Democratic Party (Online Appendix Table 6.2A ⊕). While there is room for Republicans to improve their image, it may be difficult to increase support for Democrats among young people who already support the party at high rates.

Among non-Asian respondents, the Democratic version of the treatment affected just one partisan outcome at the margins. This suggests that partisan cues from peers have the power to shape the political perspectives of college students across racial groups. However, peer groups may be particularly politically influential for Asian American students, who enter college with less political exposure through the family.

Do Race, Political Discussion, and Sense of Belonging on Campus Condition Peer Effects?

While the previous analysis identifies several meaningful treatment effects on partisan outcomes among Asian Americans, it does not definitively indicate whether the treatments have a stronger impact on Asian Americans than non-Asians. To test the respondent race hypothesis, I re-estimate the main models, interacting Asian American racial identification with each treatment indicator.[14]

As the respondent race hypothesis predicts, the treatment effects for party feeling thermometer ratings are stronger for Asian Americans than non-Asians. The Republican infographic increases ratings of the Republican Party among Asian Americans but not among members of other racial groups in both studies. As the interaction models presented in Table 6.2 show, these peer endorsement treatment effects are conditioned by respondent race.

In the interactive models, the Republican treatment does not have a direct effect on ratings of the Republican Party but significantly increases this outcome among Asian Americans in the first study at the $p < 0.10$ level (Table 6.2, Column 2). In the second study, this interaction term is larger and statistically

---

[14] The full regression results are included in the Online Appendix (Tables 6.3A—6.10A ⊕). I omit perceptions that the parties represent the interests of people like the respondent from this analysis because it is a secondary outcome without statistically significant main treatment effects.

Table 6.2 Moderating Effects of Race on Change in Republican Party Ratings

	Dependent variable: Change in Republican Party feeling thermometer ratings			
	Study 1		Study 2	
	(1)	(2)	(3)	(4)
Dem Treatment	0.024^	—	0.008	—
	(0.013)	—	(0.024)	—
Rep Treatment	—	0.014	—	−0.037
	—	(0.021)	—	(0.025)
Asian	0.017	−0.017	0.011	−0.062**
	(0.017)	(0.027)	(0.022)	(0.022)
Treatment x Asian	−0.041^	0.064^	−0.027	0.087**
	(0.023)	(0.039)	(0.033)	(0.033)
Constant	−0.010	0.048**	−0.009	0.063***
	(0.009)	(0.015)	(0.017)	(0.017)
Observations	225	225	396	329
Adjusted R²	0.007	0.017	−0.006	0.020

Note: ***p < 0.001 **p < 0.01; *p < 0.05; ^p < 0.10. Treatments compared to associated control conditions.

significant at the $p < 0.05$ level (Table 6.2, Column 4). This suggests that the Republican treatment with a social endorsement from other undergraduates on campus has a larger impact on ratings of the Republican Party among Asian Americans than students from other racial groups.

Next, I consider the possibility that the results are conditioned by levels of political discussion with family during childhood. As expected, Asian Americans reported lower levels of political discussion with parents during childhood than their non-Asian counterparts. There is an 8 percentage point difference in reported levels of political discussion with parents during childhood between Asian Americans and non-Asians in Study 1 and a 14 point difference in Study 2. These differences are both statistically significant at the $p < 0.01$ level. To test whether these differences have implications for how persuasive social endorsements from peer groups are, I re-estimate the main models for the full sample and Asian American respondents to the second study, including an interaction between the political discussion measures and each treatment indicator (Online Appendix, Tables 6.11A–6.17A ⊚).

Although few moderating effects emerge, there are several instances in which the peer endorsement treatments have stronger effects among those who reported frequent political discussion with parents during childhood (Online

Appendix Tables 6.11A; 6.12A; 6.14A ⊛). This pattern does not support the family political discussion hypothesis and instead suggests that Asian Americans who discussed politics at home are also more likely to be persuaded by partisan messages from their peer groups. This unexpected finding suggests that Asian Americans who discussed politics with family during childhood may be more open to political cues from peer groups than their counterparts who rarely discussed politics at home.

Turning to the moderating role of political discussion with peers, I test whether the treatment effects are stronger among Asian Americans who report frequent discussion of American politics with peers on campus. There are no major differences in levels of political discussion with campus peers between Asian Americans and respondents from other racial groups. In addition, levels of political discussion with peers do not consistently moderate the treatment effects (Online Appendix, Tables 6.18A–6.24A ⊛). Finally, feeling a sense of belonging on campus does not moderate the treatment effects (Online Appendix Tables 6.25A–6.31A ⊛). Taken with the inconclusive results for political discussion with peers, these findings indicate that levels of social integration on campus may not condition the impact of endorsements from campus peer groups.

Conclusion

The survey experiments presented in this chapter offer direct causal evidence that partisan cues from peer groups shape Asian Americans' partisan attitudes. These studies build on observational tests presented in earlier chapters and offer an important methodological advantage, using randomization to rule out peer-network selection effects. Even in a stylized environment, learning that many of their undergraduate peers support a policy promoted by the Republican Party affects evaluations of the policy and party among Asian American college students. This finding holds at different points in time among students enrolled in a diverse public institution and other universities across the country.

This finding is notable against a backdrop of weak support for Republicans among students in both samples. Although most Asian American respondents did not report objectively positive evaluations of the Republican Party, exposure to a peer endorsement of a popular higher education policy endorsed by Republicans improved their perceptions of the party. It is important to note that this change in political attitudes is driven by the peer endorsement rather than the policy cue itself, which was identical in the treatment and control versions of the infographic.

At first glance, it is surprising that the Democratic version of the treatment infographic with the peer endorsement did not affect Asian Americans' political views. Given trends of strong support for Democrats within this community, shouldn't peer endorsements of the Democratic Party increase Asian Americans' support for Democrats? It is important to note that the Asian American students who participated in the experiments already held positive views about the Democratic Party. Moreover, many Asian American college students likely receive positive messages about the Democratic Party from their peers in daily life. Therefore, a single stylized peer endorsement of the Democratic Party may not be enough to fundamentally alter their partisan views, especially on liberal campuses.

This points to a limitation of one-shot surveys for testing social transmission, a contextual theory about political socialization, which is a long-term social process that unfolds over years. In the real world, the effects of these messages do not manifest immediately but accrue overtime. Even though exposure to a single partisan message is unlikely to fundamentally alter partisan views and identities, these survey experiments provide insight into the process of peer partisan influence, suggesting that even a single positive cue from peer groups about Republicans alters Asian Americans' partisan preferences at the margins.

Nevertheless, these experiments have implications for both political parties' ability to appeal to Asian American voters. The lack of peer endorsement treatment effects when the policy is attributed to Democrats indicates there may be a ceiling on Democrats' ability to improve Asian Americans' perceptions of their party by highlighting policy initiatives in messages from peer groups. Most Asian Americans who participated in these studies already had a favorable image of Democrats and already associated policies to make higher education more affordable with the Democratic Party. However, peer endorsements may be an effective way of engaging with and mobilizing Asian Americans, particularly ahead of elections. On the other hand, Republicans may be able to leverage peer endorsements of their policy agenda to increase their favorability among Asian Americans. Although immigrants and racial minorities have not traditionally been the focus of contemporary Republican mobilization initiatives, they may be quite effective at garnering Asian American support through targeted policy initiatives.

Turning to non-Asian groups, I find little evidence that similar partisan messages from campus peer groups affect the partisan preferences or policy views of African American, Latino, and white students. It is notable that peer effects do not emerge because some of these non-Asian respondents may also be immigrants or the children of immigrants. This offers suggestive evidence that the theory of social transmission may be better suited to explain the process of political learning among Asian Americans than members of other immigrant constituencies. However, further research is needed to explore this possibility.

More broadly, this chapter contributes to understanding the mechanisms of partisan acquisition among Asian Americans. Although this chapter focuses on campus environments, a similar process may occur in other social settings. Immigrants and their children make up over 25% of the American population and a growing percentage of the electorate (Radford and Budiman 2018). At the same time, the political parties have become increasingly polarized on issues related to race and immigration. Although many assume that the Democratic Party is the obvious choice for immigrant constituencies, neither party directly appeals to immigrant voters (Hajnal and Lee 2011; Wong 2006). These results show that direct partisan appeals from both sides of the aisle may be effective at garnering Asian American support if they are endorsed by a respondent's proximate social network. Such endorsements of Republicans, even if they are few and far between, may explain movement toward the Republican Party within the Asian American and Latino communities in recent years (Leonhardt 2023; Sesin 2022).

7
Conclusion and Implications for Asian American Political Incorporation

Returning to the book's motivating example, the 2020 senate run-off elections in Georgia represented one of the first election cycles in which candidates took notice of the pivotal role that Asian American voters could play in electoral outcomes and tailored their campaign strategies to appeal to this diverse pan-ethnic community. Several Asian American political organizers and leaders stressed the importance of engaging the AAPI community in mobilization initiatives during that race. As Margaret Fung of AALDEF put it, "Asian American voters must no longer be ignored in the political process" (Asian American Legal Defense and Education Fund 2021).

Since that election cycle, political candidates and campaigns are turning their focus to Asian Americans as the voting-eligible population rapidly grows. For example, during the 2022 congressional midterm races, candidates attempted to mobilize Asian American voters across the country, including in Orange County, California; Las Vegas, Nevada; and Sugar Land, Texas (Goldenstein 2022; Lai 2022b; Qin 2022). In the 2024 presidential election cycle, the Kamala Harris campaign focused get out the vote messaging on Asian American voters, especially in Georgia, where they were part of Joe Biden's 2020 winning coalition (Zeleny 2024). On the Republican side, a pro-Trump PAC called Asians Making America Great Again also courted Asian American voters, publishing a multilingual voter guide (Samson 2024).

While candidates from both parties attempted to draw members of the community into their coalitions, most Asian Americans voted for Democrats nationwide in 2024. However, the margin of support for Democratic candidates is eroding. Growing numbers of Asian Americans have voted for Republicans in every election since 2012, when three-quarters of Asian American voters supported Barack Obama. English-language exit polls estimate that approximately 63% of Asian Americans voted for Biden in 2020, 65% voted for Democratic congressional candidates in the 2022 midterms, and about 55% voted for Harris in 2024, the first Asian American presidential candidate running in a general election (Lichtenstein 2022; Yam 2024). The theory and evidence presented in this book can help explain these partisan trends and offers insights about the political behavior of Asian Americans in the contemporary period.

In this final chapter, I consider the broader implications of this book for understanding political learning within and beyond Asian American communities. While Asian American political learning and partisan acquisition is a complex process, the arguments and evidence presented in the book lend themselves to several general conclusions. I also consider the extent to which social transmission offers a compelling explanation for political learning among other social groups beyond Asian Americans. Throughout these sections, I discuss avenues for future research based on the new questions this book raises.

At the end of the chapter, I turn to the practical implications of this research for campaigns and civic organizations seeking to mobilize Asian Americans. The political parties and civic campaigns have historically paid limited attention to Asian Americans. Emergent efforts to mobilize Asian American voters must be informed by the perspectives and interests of community members. I conclude by discussing the implications of this book for Asian American political incorporation and the future of American politics as the electorate diversifies.

Political Learning Within the Asian American Community

The evidence presented in this book leads to several important conclusions about political learning and partisan acquisition among Asian Americans. First, Asian Americans are a Democratic-leaning constituency in the current political moment, although there has been meaningful movement toward the Republican Party over the past decade. The evidence from national surveys presented in the first part of the book indicates that Asian Americans consistently vote for Democrats and rate the party favorably. In the second part of the book, evidence from a multidecade panel survey of college students shows that Asian Americans develop more liberal ideological preferences and policy views during college. These descriptive findings align with the results of exit polls, which reflect similar partisan trends in Asian American vote choice but are often conducted only in English and may be inaccurate for geographically concentrated minority groups (Barreto et al. 2006; Ramakrishnan 2020).

Despite this long-standing trend of Democratic voting among Asian Americans, there has been a noticeable uptick in support for Republican candidates in recent years. Support for Democratic presidential candidates peaked at nearly 75% when President Obama was re-elected in 2012 ("How Groups Voted" 2025). Since then, polls indicate that support for Democratic candidates decreased by about 10 percentage points across the next few presidential and midterm election cycles.[1] Democratic vote choice was even more anemic among Asian Americans, much like the electorate at large, during the 2024 election cycle.

Recent news stories indicate that Asian Americans may be shifting even further to the right in ways that could exacerbate the decline in Democratic voting (Edsall 2022; Leonhardt 2023). Although this trend may be overstated in media accounts and by English-language exit polls (see Bacon Jr. 2023 and Ramakrishnan 2020), it is nonetheless surprising given a spate of hate crimes and violence against Asian Americans during the COVID-19 pandemic, which theories of social exclusion argue should push Asian American voters toward the Democratic Party (Chan et al. 2022).

The arguments presented in this book may help to explain these partisan dynamics as they unfold. In contrast to other theoretical accounts which primarily explain partisan acquisition in a Democratic direction, in the social transmission account, the direction of partisan socialization differs based on the dynamics of local peer groups. While most Asian Americans settle in liberal metropolitan areas where they are more likely to interact with peer groups that hold Democratic views, increasing numbers of Asian Americans are settling in suburban areas where some members of their peer groups may be politically conservative (Lai 2011; Lung-Amam 2017). Moreover, as the political mood shifts within local environments, the political messages Asian Americans are exposed to from peer groups may change over time. For example, voter sentiment has been shifting in a conservative direction within traditional urban liberal strongholds like New York City, which have large Asian American populations (Rubinstein and Chen 2024). Asian Americans may be responding to these shifting allegiances as they develop partisan perspectives.

The evidence presented in Chapter 3 conveys that Asian Americans who settle in politically conservative areas are more likely to support Republican candidates than those who settle in liberal areas. Furthermore, the survey experiments in Chapter 6 demonstrate that even Asian American college students on liberal campuses are receptive to pro-Republican messages from peer groups. Future research should explore emerging settlement patterns among Asian Americans and consider whether local partisan dynamics map onto changes in partisan views.

The social transmission account offers a fresh perspective on changing partisan dynamics in the Asian American community. The theory suggests that Asian American settlement patterns happened to benefit the Democratic Party over

---

[1] Although English-language national exit polls suggest a shift toward Republicans at the margins, targeted multilingual polls estimate that 70%–80% of Asian Americans supported Democratic candidates in recent elections (Asian American Legal Defense and Education Fund 2017; 2020).

the past few decades even though the party has done little to actively recruit members of this constituency. The evidence presented in this book indicates that the Democratic trend in Asian American vote choice can largely be attributed to settlement patterns and osmosis effects rather than meaningful mobilization and alignment on policy goals. Most Asian Americans live in liberal metropolitan areas where they develop positive evaluations of the Democratic Party through interactions with the people around them rather than by direct communication from the parties. However, their political attitudes may change if the political dynamics of their social networks and local environments shift in a conservative direction. This suggests that Democrats may not be able to maintain high levels of support among Asian Americans without investing further in recruiting and engaging members of these communities. Recent declines in Democratic vote choice within Asian American communities reflect this possibility.

Another major implication of this book is that peer groups outside of the home are important sources of political information for Asian Americans as they navigate the American political system and develop partisan preferences. This departs from standard accounts of political learning in the American context that center the nuclear family and political discussion at home during childhood (Beck and Jennings 1991; Jennings and Niemi 1968; Jennings et al. 2009). It is also distinctive from explanations that focus on the role of political parties in the mobilization of immigrants at the local level (Allswang [1977] 2019; Andersen 1979; Cornwell 1960; Dahl 1961; Wong et al. 2011).

The empirical chapters offer several pieces of evidence supporting this conclusion. First, qualitative illustrations from in-depth interviews with Asian Americans in Houston indicate that both Asian American immigrants and children of immigrants rarely discuss American politics at home with their parents during childhood. Chapter 4 offers the strongest evidence for this claim, demonstrating that Asian Americans discuss American politics more frequently with peers than family, which in turn is associated with the development of partisan views. These results are notable because they hold for first-generation immigrants, the transitional- and second-generation children of immigrants, and the third-generation grandchildren of immigrants. Although the third generation currently accounts for a small fraction of the Asian American adult population, familial models of political socialization may remain a poor fit for Asian Americans as the US-born population grows. This comports with recent work finding that most Americans do not accurately perceive their parents' partisan attachments, questioning the applicability of theories of intergenerational partisan transmission more broadly (Ojeda and Hatemi 2015).

The second part of the book shows how interactions within peer networks during college shape the political views of Asian Americans who come of age in the US. In Chapter 5, I find that interactions with peers of a different race are associated with changes in political views among a diverse cohort of Asian Americans attending colleges and universities across the country. Finally, Chapter 6 offers direct causal evidence of peer partisan influence. Across two survey experiments, Asian American college students' perceptions of the Republican Party become more favorable when exposed to an endorsement of a policy proposed by the party from other undergraduates on their campus, relative to similar information without a social endorsement. Moreover, there is no corresponding effect among members of other racial groups, indicating that social transmission from peers shapes partisan views more strongly for Asian Americans, who experience limited political discussion at home. The experiments directly address concerns about self-selection through randomization and offer evidence that social transmission can occur in a Republican direction.

Although colleges and universities are useful settings for testing the social transmission account, one open question for future research is whether social transmission from peers shapes the political views of Asian Americans in other social environments. Evidence offered in the second part of the book does not directly apply to Asian Americans who did not attend college in the US, but I expect that peers are an important source of partisan information beyond campus environments. Chapter 5 concludes with an analysis of peer networks among young Asian Americans that supports this claim.

To better understand partisan acquisition among all Asian Americans, future work should directly explore the role of peer groups in providing political information among diverse subgroups. Analyses of peer partisan influence among first-generation Asian Americans may focus on social interactions with other Asian American immigrants through cultural organizations and friendship groups, leveraging social network data and analysis techniques (Carlson et al. 2020). Disaggregating the Asian American community to identify that differences in political socialization across national origin groups will be particularly important in such studies.

Implications for Political Socialization in Other Immigrant and Nonimmigrant Groups

Exploring the political dynamics of a minority group like Asian Americans also offers insights about political socialization for other social groups within the American electorate. Perhaps most centrally, this book conveys that the process of political socialization is substantively different in immigrant and nonimmigrant communities. While existing literature on immigrant political behavior makes a similar point, the comparison is often between US-born and foreign-born Americans (e.g., Fernandez and Dempsey 2017; Hajnal and Lee 2011; Phan and Garcia 2009).

Instead, this research suggests that differences in political socialization occur between immigrant and nonimmigrant families. Taken together, the evidence presented in this book shows that the poor fit of familial theories of partisan socialization extends from first-generation immigrants to their children's generation, and in some cases, even their grandchildren's generation. While Asian Americans represent just one immigrant constituency in the United States, this finding has important implications for understanding political socialization for immigrants and their children, a growing segment of the American population (Radford and Budiman 2018).

However, peer groups may also contribute to political socialization in predominantly nonimmigrant communities. The comparative analyses presented throughout the book offer evidence that social transmission from peers, at least in part, explains partisan preferences among various non-Asian groups. For example, Chapter 5 demonstrates that interacting with students from a different racial group is associated with changes in the political views of both Asian American and white students. Finally, Chapter 6 offers evidence that exposure to peer endorsements of the Democratic Party increases positive perceptions of Democrats among African American, Latino, and white college students. Taken together, these findings show that peer groups contribute to political socialization among young people from various racial groups who may also be exposed to discussion of American politics through the family. Moreover, they offer a point of contrast to previous findings of weak peer effects on the political views of (primarily white) American adolescents (Campbell 1980; Tedin 1980).

In light of these findings, it is important to reevaluate the relative impact of peer groups and the family on the development of political views among young people during a moment of increasing partisan polarization. Most of the evidence supporting theories of family socialization is drawn from surveys conducted several decades ago (e.g., Beck and Jennings 1991; Jennings and Niemi 1968) and their applicability in the contemporary period is an open question. On the one hand, family members hold more similar political views in the current era than they did several decades ago, suggesting a potential strengthening of the familial transmission model as the public becomes more polarized (Iyengar et al. 2018; Tyler and Iyengar 2023). If this is the case, then peer networks may act as echo chambers, reinforcing the partisan messages that nonimmigrants receive at home.

On the other hand, it is possible that polarization weakens the familial transmission model. For example, the children of strong partisans are more likely to stray from their parents' views later in life because they have the information and skills to develop their own political perspectives (Dinas 2014). In this case, peer groups may offer new political ideas and challenge political perspectives passed along through the family. Future research should explore these possibilities among an increasingly diverse American population.

The Scope Conditions of the Social Transmission Account

Although this book focuses on political learning and partisan acquisition among Asian Americans, social transmission is a general explanation that could apply to any group that experiences limited political socialization through the family. Therefore, social transmission from peers in local contexts may contribute to the partisan socialization of immigrants from Latin America, Africa, the Caribbean, Europe, and the Middle East.

Since many immigrants in the US are Latino or Hispanic, future research may consider whether social transmission explains political learning and partisan acquisition in this similarly diverse pan-ethnic community. Research on the political behavior of Latinos in the United States suggests that they are also unlikely to develop political views through the family in a traditional top-down approach (Carlos 2018; Hajnal and Lee 2011). In fact, Fernandez and Dempsey (2017) show that external factors like local partisan context influence Latino partisan attachments. However, it is possible that Latino immigrant families discuss politics more frequently than their Asian American counterparts. If this is the case, familial political socialization may play a more important role in the political socialization of Latinos than Asian Americans.

While this book does not focus on Latinos, evidence presented in Chapter 5 shows that the political attitudes of Latino college students shift during college. However, interactions with non-Latino peer groups do not seem to drive these effects. Yet this is not definitive evidence that Latinos do not learn about American politics from peer groups. Rather, it suggests that different types of peer groups may be politically formative for Asian Americans and Latinos. Future research should explore the role of peer groups in political learning for Latinos with a focus on the diversity of social experiences and networks within this pan-ethnic community.

While social transmission is not distinctive to Asian Americans, this account applies most readily to groups that include large numbers of immigrants and children of immigrants. Theories of family political socialization can accommodate alternative mechanisms as they relate to immigrant families (e.g., Wong and Tseng 2008), but immigrant families may also be less strongly partisan than nonimmigrant families. Moreover, immigrant families have a shorter history in the United States, so partisan preferences rest on weaker foundations than those passed down in nonimmigrant families. Therefore, the social transmission perspective is most relevant to the partisan socialization of contemporary immigrant constituencies.

Nevertheless, to a lesser extent, social transmission from peers may also contribute to partisan socialization among members of predominantly nonimmigrant groups. Social input from peers may reinforce the partisan views that Americans inherit from their parents (Tedin 1980). Alternatively, peer influence may fill a void in partisan socialization for Americans who break from the partisan preferences of their family members for various reasons. For example, although many LGBT individuals grow up in liberal homes (e.g., Egan 2012), social input from peers may shape the partisan views of LGBT youth. A similar argument might also apply to others who move far away from home at a young age or whose parents were not at all interested in American politics.

It is important to note that social transmission does not unilaterally predict Democratic partisan preferences across social groups. To the contrary, social transmission predicts Democratic preferences among most Asian Americans because they settle in left-leaning partisan environments. However, recent shifts to the right within this group suggest that these dynamics are continually evolving. Other social groups may not follow this geographical distribution and could interact more frequently (relative to Asian Americans) with peers who have Republican partisan preferences. For example, a growing number of Latino immigrants have settled in rural farming communities over the past 20 years (Kandel and Cromartie 2004; Lichter and Johnson 2021). Future work may explore whether new patterns of settlement and local partisan norms are contributing to recent increases in support for Republican candidates among Latino voters (Fraga et al. 2024; Martinez 2023).

Implications for the Political Mobilization of Asian Americans

Moving beyond these scholarly contributions, this book also has practical implications for political mobilization efforts targeting Asian Americans and members of other immigrant communities. First, political campaigns, parties, interest groups, and community organizations may consider relaying political messages to these communities through established peer networks. For example, political organizations could engage Asian Americans who are politically active as community liaisons and ask them to share tailored messages with other Asian

Americans in their social networks on an ad hoc basis. Since Asian Americans are a diverse pan-ethnic group, it is important that these materials are offered in a variety of Asian languages and in culturally sensitive formats ("Language Access" 2023). Likewise, political events targeting immigrant groups should involve trusted community members who can offer endorsements of these messages. Employing specialized campaign staff from these communities will make this possible.

In this context, it is noteworthy that the composition of established peer networks varies substantially across generations and ethnic groups within the Asian American community. Candidates and political organizers should be aware of these differences and include an array of community members in the outreach process. For example, Asian American immigrants are most likely to respond to political messages and appeals from members of their own national origin group. As such, politically engaged Asian American immigrants who have lived in the United States for long periods but still maintain strong connections within their national origin communities might be helpful liaisons. In contrast, younger Asian Americans may be open to messages from Asian Americans and non-Asian peers in educational settings. Therefore, college campuses may be a useful environment to focus outreach efforts targeting Asian American children of immigrants.

Campaigns and political organizations might also consider engaging the adult children of Asian American immigrants to mobilize their parents. Theories of reverse intergenerational transmission predict that the children of immigrants develop political views outside of the home and may inform their parents' political views (Wong and Tseng 2008). Although many Asian American children of immigrants did not discuss American politics with their parents during childhood, excerpts from qualitative interviews presented in Chapter 2 indicate that occasional discussions occur between parents and children later in life. As such, reaching out to immigrants through their children could be a useful way to engage first-generation Asian Americans who have limited socioeconomic resources, English proficiency, or interest in American politics. Such initiatives would also have to be targeted and use campaign messages and materials that are relevant to immigrant communities.

Turning to the domain of partisan politics, this book confirms findings from previous research indicating that although Asian Americans are currently a Democratic-leaning constituency, their long-term partisan attachments are still emerging (Hajnal and Lee 2011). For example, Chapter 3 shows that Asian Americans vote for Democratic candidates at higher rates than they identify as Democratic partisans. Furthermore, the fact that Asian American college students responded favorably to positive messages about the Republican Party across two survey experiments presented in Chapter 6 conveys that many members of this racial group are not wedded to either political party. This suggests that careful mobilization initiatives from across the political spectrum that target the interests and needs of the group may be effective.

To that end, political initiatives that are nonpartisan and focused on civic engagement may be most successful at engaging Asian American immigrants. As Janelle Wong finds in *Democracy's Promise* (2006), the political parties have not made major efforts to engage Asian Americans and other contemporary immigrant groups in the political process. Therefore, community organizations, including groups that do not have an explicit political purpose, play a major role in exposing Asian Americans to the political system. As the number of nonpartisan civic engagement initiatives that aim to increase the political participation of various minority groups increases, such organizations should consider targeting their messages to Asian Americans using some of the strategies described above. These efforts may be particularly effective if they are focused on providing information about how the political system works. Organizations focused on civic engagement may fill an important gap by providing basic information about American politics and how to get involved in the political system.

Similar strategies may also be effective for engaging members of other immigrant communities. However, further research is needed to confirm whether peer groups play a major role in political socialization outside of the Asian American community. Most generally, it is important that political organizations and campaigns understand these communities and use tailored approaches and appeals to engage with members of these groups. This requires that political organizations and candidates recognize the demographic profiles of the constituencies they serve and respond to the needs of growing immigrant subgroups.

Conclusion: Implications for the Future of (Asian) American Politics

Most broadly, this research has important implications for understanding American politics as the electorate rapidly diversifies. According to the National Populations Project, Asian Americans are one of the fastest growing racial groups in the United States, largely due to "high net international migration" (Vespa et al. 2018, 3). In fact, the population of people who identify as Asian alone is projected to grow from about 21 million in 2022 to over 34 million by 2060 ("2023 National Population Projections Tables" 2023). Population projections in a scenario with high immigration indicate that the Asian American population may nearly double in size over the next 35 years ("2023 National Population Projections Tables"

2023). Despite the rapid growth of the Asian American population and the central role they play in the demographic transformation of the electorate, relatively little is known about the dynamics of their partisan socialization. This research contributes toward filling this gap by advancing a social explanation for partisan socialization focused on political learning.

Perhaps the most important conclusion that can be drawn from this book is that the Asian American population will emerge as an influential political constituency in communities across the United States, regardless of the direction of their partisan socialization. In the domain of electoral politics, Asian American voters could contribute to close victories for Democratic candidates if they continue to vote for Democrats at high rates. It is also possible they will contribute to Republican electoral victories if partisan views shift meaningfully in a conservative direction. These dynamics will likely vary across local contexts.

I end the book by considering how this process plays out on both the local and national levels. An implication of the social transmission account is that the role Asian American voters play in elections varies across localities. While Asian Americans may vote consistently for members of one party in solidly Democratic or Republican contexts, their partisan views may be more varied in mixed partisan environments. To offer two localized examples that highlight the potential complexity of these partisan dynamics, I consider the role of Asian American voters in a mixed-partisan congressional district in Southern California and largely Asian American neighborhoods in New York City during recent election cycles.

First, voters in California's 45th congressional district, which includes parts of Orange and Los Angeles Counties, decided between two Asian American candidates during the 2022 midterms: Michelle Steel, a Korean American Republican incumbent, and Jay Chen, a Taiwanese American Democratic challenger. Although Representative Steel won the election with 52.4% of the final vote, most voters in this district supported Biden in the 2020 presidential election ("California 45th Congressional District Election Results" 2022). Asian Americans, who make up about 25% of eligible voters in this district, were a focus of both campaigns and many crossed party lines to vote for Steel, the Korean American Republican candidate (Lai 2022b). Steel's electoral success in 2022 may be partly due to the history of right-leaning politics in this district, which may have pushed Asian American voters' preferences in a Republican direction.

However, these dynamics shifted in 2024, when Steel faced a tough challenge from Democrat Derek Tran, a Vietnamese American. In this cycle, Steel came up short in a very tight race, losing the election to the Democratic challenger by less than 700 votes (Mason 2024). Her loss was notable in an election year in which Democrats performed poorly nationwide. Tran's candidacy resonated with many Vietnamese Americans, who make up a large proportion of voters in the district (Mason 2024). This reflects the strength of shared national origin between Asian American candidates and voters (Sadhwani 2022). Tran is a Democrat and Vietnamese Americans are a right-leaning constituency, although younger generations are shifting toward the left (Le and Su 2017). Tran's victory also reflects the increasingly competitive nature of elections in this mixed-partisan district that used to be a Republican stronghold.

In contrast, voting patterns in Asian American neighborhoods of New York City reflect the slow erosion of solid Democratic support in a diverse and liberal city (Kao 2023). Governor Kathy Hochul, the Democratic incumbent, won most of the votes in predominantly Asian American neighborhoods in the 2022 gubernatorial election. However, these constituencies "shifted to the right by 23 percentage points, compared with 2018, after more than a decade of reliably backing Democrats" (Kao 2023). Notably, there were sharper shifts toward Republicans in Asian American neighborhoods in Brooklyn and Queens than Manhattan, where the Chinese American community has deeper roots and may have established stronger partisan loyalties to the Democrats.

In an article covering this surprising change in voting patterns, Jason Kao (2023) argues that Republicans have cultivated more support in these communities through increased outreach efforts and their stances on crime and education. Although only about "22% of eligible Asian voters in the city live in these areas," these patterns indicate that Asian Americans' allegiances may change with the partisan dynamics of their local environments or direct contact from political candidates (Kao 2023). These trends extended to the 2024 presidential election, when Harris's margin of victory in East and South Asian neighborhoods in Brooklyn and Queens eroded relative to Biden's in 2020 (Rubinstein and Chen 2024).

Turning to the national political scene, the increasing presence of Asian American candidates and the continued barriers they face offer mixed signals about the political incorporation of Asian Americans in the future. On the one hand, a growing number of Asian American candidates from both parties are running for and securing political office ("AA & NH/PI Candidate Pipeline" 2024). However, many of these candidates fail to receive strong support from Asian American voters or the broader electorate (Ulloa 2023). In fact, Asian Americans remain one of the most under-represented racial groups at all levels of political office (Reflective Democracy Campaign 2021; Kistner and Raychaudhuri 2025).

Perhaps no example better encapsulates these complexities than Vice President Kamala Harris's unsuccessful bid as the Democratic presidential nominee in the 2024 election cycle. Harris's ascension to the top of the ticket was a historic moment from the perspective of race and gender, as she was the first woman of color, African American woman, and Asian American candidate in a general presidential election. In the week after President Biden suddenly ended his campaign, Democratic Party elites quickly consolidated support for Vice President Harris. In turn, Asian American voters reacted with excitement for her candidacy. For example, a survey conducted by AAPI Data in September 2024 indicated that 66% of Asian Americans planned to vote for Harris while only 28% planned to vote for Trump ("Sep 2024 AAPI Voter Survey" 2024). These numbers reflected an increase in Asian American support for the Democratic candidate of nearly 20 percentage points compared to when Biden was in the race earlier that year.

Although Democratic Party elites offered Asian Americans a central position in the 2024 political coalition, Asian American voters may have ultimately supported Harris at lower rates than this survey predicted. As mentioned earlier in the chapter, NBC exit polls estimate that 54% of Asian Americans voted for Harris and 39% for Trump (Yam 2024). The decline in Asian American support for the Democratic candidate between 2020, when 63% of Asian Americans voted for Biden, and 2024 is particularly notable because Harris was the first Asian American presidential candidate in a general election.

This example highlights the complexities of Asian American vote choice. It suggests that Asian Americans may not be poised to become a core constituency of the Democratic Party as they become more politically incorporated, even though many reside in left-leaning political contexts and have voted for Democrats over the past 20 years. Instead, Asian Americans may evolve into a competitive political constituency whose support could be marshaled by candidates from both major parties in different ways at the local, state, and national levels.

Analyzing how political parties, candidates, the family, and peer groups shape political learning will help to clarify the role that Asian Americans will play in future elections. Insights about the process of political learning within and across local political contexts will become increasingly important as diverse Asian American populations become politically incorporated and their influence grows in communities across the United States.

APPENDIX A

Interview Methodology and Houston Case Study Information (Chapter 2)

Table A.1 Metropolitan Statistical Areas with Largest Asian American Populations

	Metropolitan Statistical Area	Total population estimate	Asian American population estimate	Percentage of population that is Asian American
1	New York–Newark–Jersey City, NY–NJ–PA Metro Area	20,011,812	2,548,735	12.74%
2	Los Angeles–Long Beach–Anaheim, CA Metro Area	13,202,558	2,442,392	18.50%
3	San Francisco–Oakland–Berkeley, CA Metro Area	4,725,584	1,454,616	30.78%
4	San Jose–Sunnyvale–Santa Clara, CA Metro Area	1,995,351	803,811	40.28%
5	Washington–Arlington–Alexandria, DC–VA–MD–WV Metro Area	6,332,069	784,055	12.38%
6	Chicago–Naperville–Elgin, IL–IN–WI Metro Area	9,607,711	764,681	7.96%
7	Seattle–Tacoma–Bellevue, WA Metro Area	3,971,125	716,293	18.04%
8	Dallas–Fort Worth–Arlington, TX Metro Area	7,543,340	630,636	8.36%
9	Houston–The Woodlands–Sugar Land, TX Metro Area	7,048,954	628,796	8.92%
10	Urban Honolulu, HI Metro Area	1,015,167	617,202	60.80%
11	San Diego–Chula Vista–Carlsbad, CA Metro Area	3,296,317	495,882	15.04%
12	Boston–Cambridge–Newton, MA–NH Metro Area	4,912,030	470,059	9.57%
13	Philadelphia–Camden–Wilmington, PA–NJ–DE–MD Metro Area	6,215,222	444,552	7.15%
14	Atlanta–Sandy Springs–Alpharetta, GA Metro Area	6,026,734	430,323	7.14%
15	Sacramento–Roseville–Folsom, CA Metro Area	2,379,368	412,851	17.35%

Source: The data are drawn from five-year American Community Survey estimates (2017–2021) using "Census Data API" for Metropolitan Statistical Areas (US Census Bureau 2024b).

Interview Methodology

Interview subjects were recruited through solicitation emails sent to community organizations, student organizations at the University of Houston, solicitations by academics and community leaders, and snowball sampling. Before beginning fieldwork, I identified local Asian American serving community organizations and student organizations at the University of Houston (UH) through internet research. I obtained contact information for 19 local Asian American and seven UH student organizations and reached out to describe the study and my intention to recruit local Asian American residents to participate in interviews. I received responses from six community organizations and two student organizations, who shared information about the study with their members.

In the first round of interviews, I spoke with members of these organizations who volunteered to participate in the study. Next, I reached out to additional participants through connections with Asian American community leaders and contacts identified by prior interview respondents through snowball sampling.

Interviews were scheduled in advance and were conducted in person or over video conferencing software in July and August of 2017. Prior to each interview, respondents completed an informed consent form and a short demographic questionnaire. Interviews followed a semistructured protocol, which included questions about their family's immigration history, places they had lived and life in Houston, professional experiences, social experiences, educational experiences, and political perspectives. In some cases, interviews deviated from these questions if interviewees brought up different topics. Such cases were clearly marked.

Interviews were conducted in English and lasted between 35 and 90 minutes. The average duration was 60 minutes. All interviews were audio-recorded, after receiving the subject's permission. The interviews were manually transcribed from audio files and then coded into qualitative categories based on the major topics and themes.

Demographic Characteristics of Interview Respondents

Table A.2 Demographic Profile of Houston-Area Asian American Interview Respondents

Source	Age	Household Income	Gender	National Origin	Generation	US Citizen
Houston-area Interview Respondents	Min: 21 Max: 65 Median: 39	Less than $20,000: 4.5% $20,000–59,999: 13.6% $60,000–79,999: 14% $80,000–99,999: 13.6% $100,000–119,999: 13.6% $120,000–219,999: 13.6% $220,000–499,999: 18% $500,000–$1,000,000: 4.5% No response: 4.6%	Female: 55% Male: 45%	Chinese: 23% Filipino: 9% Indian: 18% Japanese: 4.5% Korean: 4.5% Pakistani: 14% Singaporean: 4.5% Taiwanese: 4.5% Vietnamese: 18%	Foreign-born: 64% US-born: 36%	Citizen: 86% Noncitizen: 14%
ACS 5-year estimates (2017–2021)	Median age (Asian Alone): 37.6	Median household income (in 2021 inflation adjusted dollars Asian Alone): $96,947	Female: 51.5% Male: 48.5%	Chinese: 16.8% Filipino: 9.7% Indian: 26.3% Japanese: 1.2% Korean: 3.3% Pakistani: 7.8% Singaporean: No estimate Taiwanese: 1.3% Vietnamese: 25.1%	Foreign-born: 67.8% US-born: 32.2%	Citizen: 73.6% Noncitizen: 26.4%

Source: ACS five-year estimates (years: 2017–2021) procured using Census Data API for Houston–The Woodlands–Sugar Land, TX Metro Area (US Census Bureau 2024b). National origin values drawn from ACS five-year estimates (years 2017–2021) for residents of the Houston–The Woodlands–Sugar Land, TX Metro Area who selected one Asian national origin category using Social Explorer (US Census Bureau 2021).

APPENDIX B

NAAS Cross-Tabulations and Additional Survey Results (Chapter 3)

Table B.1 Asian American Vote Choice by Local Partisan Context

	All Asian Americans		Chinese Americans		Indian Americans		Filipino Americans	
	Majority Republican county	Majority Democratic county	Majority Republican county	Majority Democratic county	Majority Republican county	Majority Democratic county	Majority Republican county	Majority Democratic county
Republican vote choice	47.5%	34.1%	39.4%	25.5%	33.3%	15.5%	50.0%	50.7%
Democratic vote choice	52.5%	65.9%	60.6%	74.5%	66.7%	84.5%	50.0%	49.3%
Total	100%	100%	100%	100%	100%	100%	100%	100%

	All Asian Americans		Korean Americans		Japanese Americans		Vietnamese Americans	
	Majority Republican county	Majority Democratic county	Majority Republican county	Majority Democratic county	Majority Republican county	Majority Democratic county	Majority Republican county	Majority Democratic county
Republican vote choice	47.5%	34.1%	53.6%	34.7%	41.7%	20.9%	77.5%	73.9%
Democratic vote choice	52.5%	65.9%	46.4%	65.3%	58.3%	79.1%	22.5%	26.1%
Total	100%	100%	100%	100%	100%	100%	100%	100%

Source: The data are drawn from the 2008 National Asian American Survey (Ramakrishnan et al. 2008).

Table B.2 Asian American Vote Choice by Local Asian American Context

	All Asian Americans		Chinese Americans		Indian Americans		Filipino Americans	
	Low Asian county	High Asian county	Low Asian county	High Asian county	Low Asian county	High Asian county	Low Asian county	High Asian county
Republican vote choice	38.1%	36.1%	26.4%	26.9%	19.9%	14.6%	62.6%	45.7%
Democratic vote choice	61.9%	63.9%	73.6%	73.1%	80.1%	85.4%	37.4%	54.3%
Total	100%	100%	100%	100%	100%	100%	100%	100%

	All Asian Americans		Vietnamese Americans		Korean Americans		Japanese Americans	
	Low Asian county	High Asian county	Low Asian county	High Asian county	Low Asian county	High Asian county	Low Asian county	High Asian county
Republican vote choice	38.1%	36.1%	75.1%	74.2%	37.9%	40.4%	25.0%	21.8%
Democratic vote choice	61.9%	63.9%	24.9%	25.8%	62.1%	59.6%	75.0%	78.2%
Total	100%	100%	100%	100%	100%	100%	100%	100%

Note: Low Asian county = Fewer than 14% of county residents are Asian; High Asian county = More than 14% of county residents are Asian.
Source: The data are drawn from the 2008 National Asian American Survey (Ramakrishnan et al. 2008).

Table B.3 Association Between County Partisan Context and Vote Choice

Subset:	Dependent variable: Intention to vote for Democratic candidate							
	All Asians	Chinese	Indian	Filipino	Vietnamese	Korean	Japanese
County partisan context: Majority Democratic county	0.161**	0.190*	0.129*	−0.106	0.018	0.173^	0.164
	(0.035)	(0.085)	(0.061)	(0.129)	(0.057)	(0.100)	(0.127)
Length of residence: 1–4 years	−0.186**	−0.126	0.002	−0.514*	−0.154	−0.095	−0.245
	(0.065)	(0.158)	(0.099)	(0.201)	(0.203)	(0.155)	(0.149)
Length of residence: 5 or more years	−0.211**	−0.157	−0.025	−0.520**	−0.166	−0.174	−0.226^
	(0.061)	(0.147)	(0.093)	(0.189)	(0.197)	(0.142)	(0.131)
Percentage Asian American in county	0.198	−0.110	0.325	0.900*	−0.054	0.254	0.272
	(0.123)	(0.25)	(0.232)	(0.373)	(0.258)	(0.492)	(0.261)
Constant	0.653**	0.740**	0.680**	0.937**	0.399^	0.581**	0.778**
	(0.068)	(0.165)	(0.106)	(0.220)	(0.207)	(0.168)	(0.181)
Observations	1,669	337	381	195	308	192	197
Adjusted R^2	0.021	0.007	0.012	0.048	−0.010	0.010	0.015

Note: *** $p < 0.001$; ** $p < 0.01$; * $p < 0.05$; ^ $p < 0.10$.
Omitted county partisan context category: Majority Republican county. Omitted length of residence category: less than 1 year
Source: The data are drawn from the 2008 National Asian American Survey (Ramakrishnan et al. 2008).

APPENDIX C

OAAS Cross-Tabulations and Additional Survey Results (Chapter 4)

Table C.1 Democratic Party Ratings Across Levels of Political Discussion

Group	Level of political discussion with family			Level of political discussion with peers		
	Low (0–24)	Medium (25–49)	High (50–100)	Low (0–25)	Medium (26–49)	High (50–100)
All Asian Americans	55.2	58.7	60.5	54.9	57.4	63.1
Chinese Americans	55.7	55.6	54.1	52.5	53.5	58.7
Indian Americans	58.0	67.3	70.1	60.0	67.0	71.1
Filipino Americans	47.2	55.9	58.3	49.1	57.6	60.7
Vietnamese Americans	58.2	60.2	54.8	57.0	51.1	61.1
Korean Americans	57.0	55.6	58.3	53.7	60.4	58.4
Japanese Americans	54.0	55.5	61.9	55.1	55.5	62.3

Source: The data are drawn from the 2020 Omnibus Asian American Survey (Leung et al. 2020).

Table C.2 Democratic Partisans and Leaners Across Levels of Political Discussion

Group	Level of political discussion with family			Level of political discussion with peers		
	Low (0–24)	Medium (25–49)	High (50–100)	Low (0–25)	Medium (26–49)	High (50–100)
All Asian Americans	54.0%	55.3%	55.1%	49.0%	54.5%	60.6%
Chinese Americans	57.9%	51.0%	48.3%	47.8%	52.0%	55.7%
Indian Americans	48.6%	61.7%	57.4%	45.3%	50.9%	65.9%
Filipino Americans	41.7%	46.7%	48.3%	32.5%	51.1%	58.7%
Vietnamese Americans	56.0%	55.1%	45.6%	47.8%	50.0%	55.9%
Korean Americans	52.6%	60.7%	60.3%	56.8%	64.7%	56.4%
Japanese Americans	54.9%	56.5%	68.8%	57.9%	58.6%	65.6%

Source: The data are drawn from the 2020 Omnibus Asian American Survey (Leung et al. 2020).

Table C.3 Cross-Tabulation of Political Discussion with Peers and Any Partisan Identification

Any Party Identification	Level of political discussion with peers		
	Low (0–25)	Medium (26–49)	High (50–100)
No	27.2%	18.6%	15.5%
Yes	72.8%	81.4%	84.5%
Total	100.0 %	100.0%	100.0%

Source: The data are drawn from the 2020 Omnibus Asian American Survey (Leung et al. 2020).

Table C.4 Cross-Tabulation of Political Discussion with Family and Any Partisan Identification

Any Party Identification	Level of political discussion with family		
	Low (0–24)	Medium (25–49)	High (50–100)
No	19.6%	22.0%	20.0%
Yes	80.4%	78.0%	80.0%
Total	100.0%	100.0%	100.0%

Source: The data are drawn from the 2020 Omnibus Asian American Survey (Leung et al. 2020).

Table C.5 Association Between Discussing American Politics with Family or Peers and Partisan Outcomes

Outcome:	Democratic Party feeling thermometer rating		Partisan identification	
	OLS	Weighted model	OLS	Weighted model
Political discussion with peers during adulthood	0.181*** (0.036)	0.185*** (0.040)	0.108** (0.041)	0.118** (0.044)
Political discussion with family during childhood	0.008 (0.032)	0.020 (0.037)	−0.056 (0.037)	−0.065 (0.040)
Female	0.018 (0.015)	0.015 (0.015)	0.021 (0.017)	0.023 (0.018)
Age	−0.001 (0.001)	−0.001 (0.001)	−0.001* (0.001)	−0.001* (0.001)

Outcome:	Democratic Party feeling thermometer rating		Partisan identification	
	OLS	Weighted model	OLS	Weighted model
Education	−0.015	−0.018	0.009	0.001
	(0.037)	(0.037)	(0.042)	(0.046)
Income	−0.037	−0.036	0.008	0.022
	(0.026)	(0.027)	(0.030)	(0.032)
Homeowner	−0.015	−0.003	−0.022	−0.011
	(0.017)	(0.016)	(0.019)	(0.020)
Married	−0.031	−0.030	−0.071***	−0.084***
	(0.016)	(0.017)	(0.018)	(0.020)
Foreign-born	−0.019	−0.022	−0.048**	−0.040*
	(0.015)	(0.016)	(0.017)	(0.019)
Constant	0.612***	0.607***	0.694***	0.697***
	(0.035)	(0.037)	(0.040)	(0.043)
Observations	1,535	1,535	1,535	1,535
Adjusted R^2	0.035	—	0.032	—

Note: ***$p < 0.001$; **$p < 0.01$; *$p < 0.05$.
Source: The data are drawn from the 2020 Omnibus Asian American Survey (Leung et al. 2020).

Table C.6 Association Between Discussing American Politics with Asian or Non-Asian Peers and Partisan Outcomes Across Generational Subsets

Outcome:	Democratic Party feeling thermometer rating			Partisan identification		
Subset:	1st gen	Transitional or 2nd gen	3rd gen	1st gen	Transitional or 2nd gen	3rd gen
Political discussion with Asian peers during adulthood	0.123^ (0.069)	0.063 (0.053)	0.084 (0.084)	0.102 (0.075)	0.078 (0.061)	0.121 (0.096)
Political discussion with non-Asian peers during adulthood	−0.086 (0.082)	0.144* (0.059)	0.196^ (0.102)	−0.064 (0.089)	0.020 (0.069)	0.061 (0.116)
Political discussion with family during childhood	0.014 (0.064)	0.023 (0.044)	−0.022 (0.071)	−0.081 (0.069)	−0.042 (0.051)	−0.031 (0.082)
Female	−0.020 (0.031)	0.003 (0.020)	0.087** (0.032)	−0.010 (0.034)	0.018 (0.023)	0.078* (0.036)
Age	−0.002* (0.001)	−0.0004 (0.001)	−0.0001 (0.001)	−0.002 (0.001)	−0.001 (0.001)	0.00004 (0.001)
Education	−0.005 (0.075)	−0.030 (0.050)	−0.034 (0.085)	0.005 (0.082)	0.002 (0.057)	0.036 (0.097)
Income	−0.017 (0.054)	−0.041 (0.035)	−0.041 (0.059)	0.084 (0.058)	0.006 (0.041)	−0.085 (0.067)
Homeowner	−0.050 (0.034)	0.010 (0.023)	−0.002 (0.039)	−0.074* (0.037)	0.009 (0.027)	−0.036 (0.044)
Married	−0.034 (0.036)	−0.059* (0.023)	−0.011 (0.034)	−0.046 (0.039)	−0.113*** (0.026)	−0.017 (0.039)
Constant	0.731*** (0.097)	0.592*** (0.045)	0.519*** (0.080)	0.674*** (0.105)	0.674*** (0.052)	0.589*** (0.091)
Observations	434	747	354	434	747	354
Adjusted R^2	0.017	0.041	0.049	0.011	0.029	0.017

Note: ***$p<0.001$; **$p<0.01$; *$p<0.05$; ^$p<0.10$.
Source: The data are drawn from the 2020 Omnibus Asian American Survey (Leung et al. 2020).

APPENDIX D
Additional CIRP Survey Results (Chapter 5)

Table D.1 Changes in Aggregate Political Views from Freshman to Senior Year

Political view	Student race	Mean values			
		Freshman year	Senior year	Change over time	Difference (vs. white)
Liberal political ideology	African American	0.570	0.601	0.031***	0.005 (n.s.)
	Latino	0.544	0.575	0.031***	0.005*
	Asian American	0.540	0.564	0.024***	−0.002 (n.s.)
	White	0.490	0.516	0.026***	—
Abortion should be legal	African American	0.559	0.622	0.063***	−0.021***
	Latino	0.465	0.582	0.117***	0.033***
	Asian American	0.557	0.638	0.081***	−0.003 (n.s.)
	White	0.474	0.558	0.084***	—
The wealthy should pay higher taxes	African American	0.654	0.665	0.011*	0.001 (n.s.)
	Latino	0.590	0.632	0.042***	0.032***
	Asian American	0.585	0.608	0.023***	0.013***
	White	0.544	0.554	0.010***	—
Need for a national healthcare plan	African American	0.773	0.793	0.020***	0.031***
	Latino	0.702	0.721	0.019***	0.030***
	Asian American	0.691	0.689	−0.002 (n.s.)	0.009*
	White	0.604	0.593	−0.011***	—

Note: ***p < 0.001; **p < 0.01; *p < 0.05; ^ p < 0.10. P-values derived from t-tests for difference in means.
Source: The data are drawn from the CIRP Freshman Survey and College Senior Survey (CIRP Freshman Survey 2023; College Senior Survey 2023).

APPENDIX E
Additional Experimental Results (Chapter 6)

Descriptive and Variable Coding Information

Table E.1 Sample Size Across Experimental Conditions

	Dem Control	Dem Treatment	Rep Control	Rep Treatment
Study 1 (UH Student sample)				
Full sample	111	117	114	114
Asian American	31	37	34	36
Non-Asian	80	80	80	78
Study 2 (National student sample)				
Full sample	197	162	186	143
Asian American	112	89	110	81
Non-Asian	85	73	76	62

Table E.2 Balance Across Experimental Conditions

Covariate	Dem Control	Dem Treatment	Rep Control	Rep Treatment	F-statistic and p-value (One-way ANOVA)
Study 1 (UH student sample)					
Race (Asian)	0.28	0.32	0.30	0.32	$F = 0.17, p = 0.91$
Age	20.1	20.5	20.7	20.4	$F = 0.30, p = 0.82$
Gender (Female)	0.55	0.57	0.58	0.61	$F = 0.24, p = 0.87$
Family income	0.47	0.53	0.50	0.49	$F = 0.70, p = 0.55$
Grad year (Senior)	0.20	0.15	0.17	0.28	$F = 2.21, p = 0.08$
Generation (First generation)	0.20	0.15	0.17	0.28	$F = 2.21, p = 0.08$
Division (Social science)	0.27	0.22	0.26	0.22	$F = 0.43, p = 0.73$

Covariate	Dem Control	Dem Treatment	Rep Control	Rep Treatment	F-statistic and p-value (One-way ANOVA)
Study 2 (National student sample)					
Race (Asian)	0.57	0.55	0.59	0.57	F = 0.21, p = 0.88
Age	20.9	21.6	20.6	21.1	F = 2.11, p = 0.10
Gender (Female)	0.63	0.69	0.60	0.54	F = 2.25, p = 0.08
Class status	0.49	0.51	0.48	0.47	F = 2.25, p = 0.08
Grad year (Senior)	0.41	0.44	0.38	0.34	F = 1.09, p = 0.35
Generation (First generation)	0.21	0.15	0.23	0.24	F = 1.60, p = 0.18
Division (Social science)	0.13	0.21	0.13	0.10	F = 2.14, p = 0.09
College region (Northeast)	0.09	0.12	0.10	0.14	F = 0.75, p = 0.52
Public institution	0.70	0.66	0.70	0.73	F = 0.55, p = 0.65

Table E.3 Manipulation Check Results (Study 1)

Group	Dem Control	Dem Treatment	Rep Control	Rep Treatment
Manipulation check: Identified correct party				
Full sample	0.95	0.97	0.86	0.87
T-test	No sig. difference (p = 0.47)		No sig. difference (p = 0.85)	
Asian Am	0.94	1	0.85	0.94
T-test	No sig. difference (p = 0.12)		No sig. difference (p = 0.21)	
Non-Asian	0.95	0.95	0.86	0.83
T-test	No sig. difference (p = 1.00)		No sig. difference (p = 0.61)	
Manipulation check: Identified correct endorsement				
Full sample	NA	0.92	NA	0.94
T-test	No sig. difference (p = 0.49)			
Asian Am	NA	0.89	NA	0.92
T-test	No sig. difference (p = 0.73)			
Non-Asian	NA	0.93	NA	0.95
T-test	No sig. difference (p = 0.54)			

Table E.4 Manipulation Check Results (Study 2)

Group	Dem Control	Dem Treatment	Rep Control	Rep Treatment
Manipulation check: Identified correct party				
Full sample	0.93	0.94	0.75	0.76
T-test	No sig. difference (p = 0.59)		No sig. difference (p = 0.84)	
Asian Am	0.93	0.93	0.66	0.68
T-test	No sig. difference (p = 0.91)		No sig. difference (p = 0.82)	
Non-Asian	0.92	0.95	0.88	0.87
T-test	No sig. difference (p = 0.50)		No sig. difference (p = 0.85)	
Manipulation check: Identified correct endorsement				
Full sample	NA	0.89	NA	0.78
T-test	Sig. difference (p = 0.007)			
Asian Am	NA	0.91	NA	0.69
T-test	Sig. difference (p = 0.00026)			
Non-Asian	NA	0.86	NA	0.89
T-test	No sig. difference (p = 0.68)			

Study 1: Average Treatment Effects

Table E.5 Treatment Effects on Change in Support for Debt Forgiveness Policy (Study 1)

	Dependent variable: Change in support for debt forgiveness policy								
	Full sample			Asian			Non-Asian		
Subset:	(1)	(2)	(3)	(4)	(5)	(6)	(7)	(8)	(9)
Dem Treatment	0.023	—	—	0.047	—	—	0.013	—	—
	(0.021)			(0.042)			(0.025)		
Rep Treatment	—	0.029	—	—	0.049	—	—	0.019	—
		(0.020)			(0.031)			(0.025)	
Pooled Treatment	—	—	0.026^	—	—	0.049^	—	—	0.016
			(0.015)			(0.026)			(0.018)
Constant	0.009	−0.002	0.003	−0.000	−0.015	−0.008	0.012	0.003	0.008
	(0.015)	(0.014)	(0.010)	(0.031)	(0.022)	(0.019)	(0.018)	(0.018)	(0.013)
Observations	228	228	456	68	70	138	160	158	318
Adjusted R2	0.001	0.005	0.005	0.004	0.022	0.018	−0.005	−0.003	−0.001

Note: *** p < 0.001; ** p < 0.01; * p < 0.05; ^ p < 0.10. Treatments compared to associated control conditions.

Table E.6 Treatment Effects on Willingness to Sign Petition (Study 1)

	Dependent variable:								
	Willingness to sign petition supporting debt forgiveness policy								
Subset:	Full sample			Asian			Non-Asian		
	(1)	(2)	(3)	(4)	(5)	(6)	(7)	(8)	(9)
Dem Treatment	0.026	—	—	0.082	—	—	0.006	—	—
	(0.046)			(0.085)			(0.055)		
Rep Treatment	—	0.057	—	—	0.114	—	—	0.033	—
		(0.041)			(0.083)			(0.046)	
Pooled Treatment	—	—	0.041	—	—	0.096	—	—	0.020
			(0.031)			(0.059)			(0.036)
Constant	0.748***	0.772***	0.760***	0.661***	0.706***	0.685***	0.781***	0.800***	0.791***
	(0.033)	(0.029)	(0.022)	(0.063)	(0.059)	(0.043)	(0.039)	(0.032)	(0.025)
Observations	228	228	456	68	70	138	160	158	318
Adjusted R^2	−0.003	0.004	0.002	−0.001	0.013	0.012	−0.006	−0.003	−0.002

Note: *** $p < 0.001$; ** $p < 0.01$; * $p < 0.05$; ^ $p < 0.10$. Treatments compared to associated control conditions.

Table E.7 Treatment Effects on Change in Republican Party Feeling Thermometer Ratings (Study 1)

	Dependent variable:					
	Change in Republican Party feeling thermometer ratings					
Subset:	Full sample		Asian		Non-Asian	
	(1)	(2)	(3)	(4)	(5)	(6)
Dem Treatment	0.012	—	−0.017	—	0.024^	—
	(0.011)	—	(0.017)	—	(0.013)	—
Rep Treatment	—	0.033^	—	0.079*	—	0.014
	—	(0.018)	—	(0.038)	—	(0.019)
Constant	−0.006	0.042***	0.007	0.030	−0.010	0.048***
	(0.008)	(0.013)	(0.013)	(0.027)	(0.010)	(0.014)
Observations	225	225	67	67	158	158
Adjusted R^2	0.001	0.011	0.001	0.047	0.014	−0.003

Note: *** $p < 0.001$; ** $p < 0.01$; * $p < 0.05$; ^ $p < 0.10$. Treatments compared to associated control conditions.

Table E.8 Treatment Effects on Change in Democratic Party Feeling Thermometer Ratings (Study 1)

	Dependent variable:					
	Change in Democratic Party feeling thermometer ratings					
Subset:	Full sample		Asian		Non-Asian	
	(1)	(2)	(3)	(4)	(5)	(6)
Dem Treatment	−0.012	—	−0.0003	—	−0.018	—
	(0.012)	—	(0.022)	—	(0.015)	—
Rep Treatment	—	0.014	—	0.027	—	0.009
	—	(0.011)	—	(0.021)	—	(0.013)
Constant	0.020*	−0.014^	0.030^	−0.015	0.016	−0.014
	(0.009)	(0.008)	(0.016)	(0.015)	(0.011)	(0.009)
Observations	226	224	67	67	159	157
Adjusted R^2	−0.001	0.003	−0.015	0.009	0.002	−0.004

Note: *** $p < 0.001$; ** $p < 0.01$; * $p < 0.05$; ^ $p < 0.10$. Treatments compared to associated control conditions.

Table E.9 Treatment Effects on Partisan Identification (Study 1)

	\multicolumn{6}{c}{*Dependent variable:*}
Subset:	\multicolumn{6}{c}{*Partisan identification (Higher values = Democratic)*}
	Full sample		Asian		Non-Asian	
	(1)	(2)	(3)	(4)	(5)	(6)
Dem Treatment	0.027	—	0.046	—	0.021	—
	(0.033)	—	(0.067)	—	(0.039)	—
Rep Treatment	—	−0.037	—	−0.069	—	−0.022
	—	(0.035)	—	(0.059)	—	(−0.043)
Constant	0.664***	0.649***	0.634***	0.667***	0.675***	0.642***
	(0.024)	(0.025)	(0.049)	(0.042)	(0.027)	(0.030)
Observations	228	228	68	70	160	158
Adjusted R^2	−0.001	0.0005	−0.008	0.006	−0.004	−0.005

Note: *** $p < 0.001$; ** $p < 0.01$; * $p < 0.05$; $p < 0.10$. Treatments compared to associated control conditions.

Table E.10 Treatment Effects on Change in Viewing Republican Party in a Positive Light (Study 1)

	\multicolumn{6}{c}{*Dependent variable:*}
Subset:	\multicolumn{6}{c}{*Change in viewing Republican Party in a positive light*}
	Full sample		Asian		Non-Asian	
	(1)	(2)	(3)	(4)	(5)	(6)
Dem Treatment	0.027	—	0.016	—	0.031	—
	(0.018)	—	(0.024)	—	(0.023)	—
Rep Treatment	—	0.022	—	0.096^	—	−0.011
	—	(0.025)	—	(0.051)	—	(0.029)
Constant	−0.020	0.050**	−0.016	0.015	−0.022	0.066**
	(0.013)	(0.018)	(0.017)	(0.036)	(0.016)	(0.020)
Observations	228	228	68	70	160	158
Adjusted R^2	0.006	−0.001	−0.008	0.037	0.005	−0.005

Note: *** $p < 0.001$; ** $p < 0.01$; * $p < 0.05$; ^ $p < 0.10$. Treatments compared to associated control conditions.

Table E.11 Treatment Effects on Change in Viewing the Democratic Party in a Positive Light (Study 1)

	Dependent variable:					
	Change in viewing Democratic Party in a positive light					
Subset:	Full sample		Asian		Non-Asian	
	(1)	(2)	(3)	(4)	(5)	(6)
Dem Treatment	−0.022	—	0.015	—	−0.037	—
	(0.018)	—	(0.024)	—	(0.023)	—
Rep Treatment	—	0.009	—	0.034	—	−0.003
	—	(0.023)	—	(0.059)	—	(0.020)
Constant	0.020	0.004	−0.008	0.015	0.031^	0.000
	(0.013)	(0.016)	(0.017)	(0.042)	(0.016)	(0.014)
Observations	228	228	68	70	160	158
Adjusted R^2	0.003	−0.004	−0.009	−0.010	0.010	−0.006

Note: *** $p < 0.001$; ** $p < 0.01$; * $p < 0.05$; ^ $p < 0.10$. Treatments compared to associated control conditions.

Table E.12 Treatment Effects on Democrats Represent People "Like Me" (Study 1)

	Dependent variable:					
	Democrats represent people like me					
Subset:	Full sample		Asian		Non-Asian	
	(1)	(2)	(3)	(4)	(5)	(6)
Dem Treatment	0.005	—	0.033	—	−0.004	—
	(0.039)	—	(0.072)	—	(0.047)	—
Rep Treatment	—	0.012	—	0.103	—	−0.028
	—	(0.037)	—	(0.064)	—	(0.046)
Constant	0.562***	0.541***	0.516***	0.471***	0.579***	0.571***
	(0.028)	(0.026)	(0.053)	(0.046)	(0.033)	(0.032)
Observations	228	228	68	70	160	158
Adjusted R^2	−0.004	−0.004	−0.012	0.023	−0.006	−0.004

Note: *** $p < 0.001$; ** $p < 0.01$; * $p < 0.05$; ^ $p < 0.10$. Treatments compared to associated control conditions.

Table E.13 Treatment Effects on Republicans Represent People "Like Me" (Study 1)

	\multicolumn{6}{c}{Dependent variable:}					
	\multicolumn{6}{c}{Republicans represent people like me}					
Subset:	Full sample		Asian		Non-Asian	
	(1)	(2)	(3)	(4)	(5)	(6)
Dem Treatment	−0.016	—	−0.045	—	−0.004	—
	(0.039)	—	(0.071)	—	(0.047)	—
Rep Treatment	—	−0.003	—	0.078	—	−0.038
	—	(0.039)	—	(0.065)	—	(0.048)
Constant	0.252***	0.316***	0.280***	0.265***	0.242***	0.337***
	(0.028)	(0.027)	(0.052)	(0.046)	(0.033)	(0.034)
Observations	228	228	68	70	160	158
Adjusted R^2	−0.004	−0.004	−0.009	0.007	−0.006	−0.002

Note: *** $p < 0.001$; ** $p < 0.01$; * $p < 0.05$; ^ $p < 0.10$. Treatments compared to associated control conditions.

Table E.14 Treatment Effects on Parties Represent People "Like Me" (Combined Measure) (Study 1)

	\multicolumn{6}{c}{Dependent variable:}					
	\multicolumn{6}{c}{Parties represent people like me (combined measure–Pro-Democrat)}					
Subset:	Full sample		Asian		Non-Asian	
	(1)	(2)	(3)	(4)	(5)	(6)
Dem Treatment	0.011	—	0.039	—	0.000	—
	(0.032)	—	(0.061)	—	(0.038)	—
Rep Treatment	—	0.007	—	0.013	—	0.005
	—	(0.030)	—	(0.051)	—	(0.037)
Constant	0.655***	0.613***	0.618***	0.603***	0.669***	0.617***
	(0.023)	(0.021)	(0.045)	(0.037)	(0.027)	(0.026)
Observations	228	228	68	70	160	158
Adjusted R^2	−0.004	−0.004	−0.009	−0.014	−0.006	−0.006

Note: *** $p < 0.001$; ** $p < 0.01$; * $p < 0.05$; ^ $p < 0.10$. Treatments compared to associated control conditions.

Study 2: Average Treatment Effects

Table E.15 Treatment Effects on Change in Support for Pell Grant Policy (Study 2)

	\multicolumn{9}{c}{Dependent variable:}
	\multicolumn{9}{c}{Change in support for Pell Grant policy}
Subset:	Full sample			Asian			Non-Asian		
	(1)	(2)	(3)	(4)	(5)	(6)	(7)	(8)	(9)
Dem Treatment	0.025 (0.018)	—	—	0.021 (0.026)	—	—	0.031 (0.023)	—	—
Rep Treatment	—	−0.022 (0.019)	—	—	−0.040 (0.028)	—	—	0.003 (0.025)	—
Pooled Treatment	—	—	0.003 (0.013)	—	—	−0.008 (0.019)	—	—	0.018 (0.017)
Constant	−0.018 (0.012)	0.003 (0.013)	−0.008 (0.009)	−0.016 (0.018)	0.009 (0.018)	−0.003 (0.013)	−0.021 (0.016)	−0.007 (0.017)	−0.014 (0.012)
Observations	359	329	688	201	191	392	158	138	296
Adjusted R^2	0.003	0.001	−0.001	−0.002	0.005	−0.002	0.005	−0.007	0.0003

Note: *** $p < 0.001$; ** $p < 0.01$; * $p < 0.05$; ^ $p < 0.10$. Treatments compared to associated control conditions.

Table E.16 Treatment Effects on Willingness to Sign Petition (Study 2)

	Dependent variable: Willingness to sign petition supporting Pell Grant policy								
Subset:	Full sample			Asian			Non-Asian		
	(1)	(2)	(3)	(4)	(5)	(6)	(7)	(8)	(9)
Dem Treatment	0.067 (0.047)	—	—	0.114^ (0.065)	—	—	0.004 (0.068)	—	—
Rep Treatment	—	0.016 (0.050)	—	—	−0.004 (0.068)	—	—	0.039 (0.076)	—
Pooled Treatment	—	—	0.042 (0.034)	—	—	0.056 (0.047)	—	—	0.020 (0.050)
Constant	0.609*** (0.032)	0.645*** (0.033)	0.627*** (0.023)	0.549*** (0.043)	0.627*** (0.044)	0.588*** (0.031)	0.688*** (0.046)	0.671*** (0.051)	0.680*** (0.034)
Observations	359	329	688	201	191	392	158	138	296
Adjusted R^2	0.003	−0.003	0.001	0.010	−0.005	0.001	−0.006	−0.005	−0.003

Note: *** $p < 0.001$; ** $p < 0.01$; * $p < 0.05$; ^ $p < 0.10$. Treatments compared to associated control conditions.

Table E.17 Treatment Effects on Change in Republican Party Feeling Thermometer Ratings (Study 2)

Subset:	\multicolumn{6}{c}{*Dependent variable:*}					
	\multicolumn{6}{c}{Change in Republican Party feeling thermometer ratings}					
	Full sample		Asian		Non-Asian	
	(1)	(2)	(3)	(4)	(5)	(6)
Dem Treatment	−0.007	—	−0.019	—	0.008	—
	(0.016)	—	(0.025)	—	(0.019)	—
Rep Treatment	—	0.014	—	0.050*	—	−0.037
	—	(0.017)	—	(0.020)	—	(0.027)
Constant	−0.003	0.026*	0.002	0.001	−0.009	0.063***
	(0.011)	(0.011)	(0.017)	(0.013)	(0.013)	(0.018)
Observations	359	329	201	191	158	138
Adjusted R^2	−0.002	−0.001	−0.002	0.026	−0.005	0.006

Note: *** $p < 0.001$; ** $p < 0.01$; * $p < 0.05$; ^ $p < 0.10$. Treatments compared to associated control conditions.

Table E.18 Treatment Effects on Change in Democratic Party Feeling Thermometer Ratings (Study 2)

Subset:	\multicolumn{6}{c}{*Dependent variable:*}					
	\multicolumn{6}{c}{Change in Democratic Party feeling thermometer ratings}					
	Full sample		Asian		Non-Asian	
	(1)	(2)	(3)	(4)	(5)	(6)
Dem Treatment	0.022^	—	0.021	—	0.023	—
	(0.013)	—	(0.018)	—	(0.019)	—
Rep Treatment	—	−0.030*	—	−0.036*	—	−0.023
	—	(0.012)	—	(0.017)	—	(0.017)
Constant	−0.006	0.003	−0.010	0.000	−0.001	0.007
	(0.009)	(0.008)	(0.012)	(0.011)	(0.013)	(0.011)
Observations	359	329	201	191	158	138
Adjusted R^2	0.005	0.015	0.002	0.017	0.003	0.006

Note: *** $p < 0.001$; ** $p < 0.01$; * $p < 0.05$; ^ $p < 0.10$. Treatments compared to associated control conditions.

Table E.19 Treatment Effects on Change in Partisanship (Study 2)

Subset:	Dependent variable:					
	Change in partisan identification (Higher values = Democratic)					
	Full sample		Asian		Non-Asian	
	(1)	(2)	(3)	(4)	(5)	(6)
Dem Treatment	−0.002	—	−0.001	—	−0.007	—
	(0.018)	—	(0.024)	—	(0.026)	—
Rep Treatment	—	0.021	—	0.023	—	0.018
	—	(0.015)	—	(0.016)	—	(0.027)
Constant	−0.000	−0.021*	−0.014	−0.019^	0.020	−0.024
	(0.012)	(0.010)	(0.016)	(0.011)	(0.018)	(0.018)
Observations	323	300	182	172	141	128
Adjusted R^2	−0.003	0.003	−0.006	0.006	−0.007	−0.004

Note: *** $p < 0.001$; ** $p < 0.01$; * $p < 0.05$; ^ $p < 0.10$. Treatments compared to associated control conditions.

Table E.20 Treatment Effects on Viewing the Republican Party in a Positive Light (Study 2)

Subset:	Dependent variable:					
	Viewing Republican Party in a positive light					
	Full sample		Asian		Non-Asian	
	(1)	(2)	(3)	(4)	(5)	(6)
Dem Treatment	−0.040	—	0.010	—	−0.103^	—
	(0.031)	—	(0.038)	—	(0.052)	—
Rep Treatment	—	−0.021	—	0.007	—	−0.057
	—	(0.031)	—	(0.037)	—	(0.052)
Constant	0.343***	0.306***	0.321***	0.311***	0.371***	0.299***
	(0.021)	(0.020)	(0.025)	(0.024)	(0.036)	(0.035)
Observations	359	329	201	191	158	138
Adjusted R^2	0.002	−0.002	−0.005	−0.005	0.018	0.002

Note: *** $p < 0.001$; ** $p < 0.01$; * $p < 0.05$; ^ $p < 0.10$. Treatments compared to associated control conditions.

Table E.21 Treatment Effects on Viewing the Democratic Party in a Positive Light (Study 2)

	Dependent variable:					
	Viewing Democratic Party in a positive light					
Subset:	Full sample		Asian		Non-Asian	
	(1)	(2)	(3)	(4)	(5)	(6)
Dem Treatment	0.030	—	0.023	—	0.043	—
	(0.028)	—	(0.031)	—	(0.050)	—
Rep Treatment	—	−0.010	—	−0.006	—	−0.010
	—	(0.028)	—	(0.031)	—	(0.051)
Constant	0.595***	0.625***	0.645***	0.655***	0.529***	0.582***
	(0.019)	(0.019)	(0.021)	(0.020)	(0.034)	(0.034)
Observations	359	329	201	191	158	138
Adjusted R^2	0.0003	−0.003	−0.002	−0.005	−0.002	−0.007

Note: *** $p < 0.001$; ** $p < 0.01$; * $p < 0.05$; ^ $p < 0.10$. Treatments compared to associated control conditions.

Table E.22 Treatment Effects on "Republicans Represent People Like Me" (Study 2)

	Dependent variable:					
	Republicans represent people like me					
Subset:	Full sample		Asian		Non-Asian	
	(1)	(2)	(3)	(4)	(5)	(6)
Dem Treatment	−0.018	—	−0.020	—	−0.018	—
	(0.031)	—	(0.038)	—	(0.051)	—
Rep Treatment	—	−0.013	—	0.018	—	−0.053
	—	(0.032)	—	(0.041)	—	(0.052)
Constant	0.269***	0.260***	0.241***	0.258***	0.306***	0.263***
	(0.021)	(0.021)	(0.025)	(0.027)	(0.035)	(0.035)
Observations	359	329	201	191	158	138
Adjusted R^2	−0.002	−0.003	−0.004	−0.004	−0.006	0.0003

Note: *** $p < 0.001$; ** $p < 0.01$; * $p < 0.05$; ^ $p < 0.10$. Treatments compared to associated control conditions.

Table E.23 Treatment Effects on "Democrats Represent People Like Me" (Study 2)

Subset:	*Dependent variable:*					
	Democrats represent people like me					
	Full sample		Asian		Non-Asian	
	(1)	(2)	(3)	(4)	(5)	(6)
Dem Treatment	0.047	—	0.040	—	0.058	—
	(0.030)	—	(0.036)	—	(0.051)	—
Rep Treatment	—	−0.005	—	0.019	—	−0.032
	—	(0.033)	—	(0.042)	—	(0.051)
Constant	0.558***	0.566***	0.589***	0.594***	0.518***	0.526***
	(0.020)	(0.022)	(0.024)	(0.028)	(0.035)	(0.034)
Observations	359	329	201	191	158	138
Adjusted R^2	0.004	−0.003	0.001	−0.004	0.002	−0.004

Note: *** $p < 0.001$; ** $p < 0.01$; * $p < 0.05$; ^ $p < 0.10$. Treatments compared to associated control conditions.

References

"1988 Democratic Party Platform." 2023. The American Presidency Project. https://www.presidency.ucsb.edu/documents/1988-democratic-party-platform.

AAPI Data. 2020. "2020 Asian American Voter Survey (National)." AAPI Data. https://aapidata.com/wp-content/uploads/2024/02/aavs2020_crosstab_national.pdf.

AAPI Data. 2022. "Houston-The Woodlands-Sugar Land, TX Metro Area." AAPI Data. https://censusmaps.aapidata.com/pages/houston.

"AA & NH/PI Candidate Pipeline." 2024. Asian Pacific American Institute for Congressional Studies. https://www.apaics.org/aapi-candidate-pipeline.

Abdelkader, Rima, and Shako Liu. 2020. "'Binded by Blood,' Split over Election: Asian American Family Embodies Generational Shift in Politics." *NBC News*. https://www.nbcnews.com/news/asian-america/binded-blood-split-over-election-asian-american-family-embodies-generational-n1244077.

Abrajano, Marisa, and R. Michael Alvarez. 2010. *New Faces, New Voices: The Hispanic Electorate in America*. Princeton University Press.

Abramowitz, Alan. 2018. *The Great Alignment: Race, Party Transformation, and the Rise of Donald Trump*. Yale University Press.

Achen, Christopher H., and Larry M. Bartels. 2016. *Democracy for Realists: Why Elections Do Not Produce Responsive Government*. Princeton University Press.

Alba, Richard, and Victor Nee. 2003. *Remaking the American Mainstream: Assimilation and Contemporary Immigration*. Harvard University Press.

Aleksynska, Mariya. 2011. "Civic Participation of Immigrants in Europe: Assimilation, Origin, and Destination Country Effects." *European Journal of Political Economy* 27(3): 566–85.

Allport, Gordon W. 1954. *The Nature of Prejudice*. Addison-Wesley.

Allswang, John M. [1977] 2019. *Bosses, Machines, and Urban Voters*. Johns Hopkins University Press.

Alvarez, R. Michael, and Lisa García Bedolla. 2003. "The Foundations of Latino Voter Partisanship: Evidence from the 2000 Election." *Journal of Politics* 65(1): 31–49.

Amlani, Sharif, and Carlos Algara. 2021. "Partisanship & Nationalization in American Elections: Evidence from Presidential, Senatorial, & Gubernatorial Elections in the U.S. Counties, 1872–2020." *Electoral Studies* 73: 1-13. https://doi.org/10.1016/j.electstud.2021.102387.

Andersen, Kristi. 1979. *The Creation of a Democratic Majority, 1928–1936*. University of Chicago Press.

Anoll, Allison P. 2022. *The Obligation Mosaic: Race and Social Norms in US Political Participation*. University of Chicago Press.

Anoll, Allison P., Lauren D. Davenport, and Rachel Lienesch. 2024. "Racial Context(s) in American Political Behavior." *American Political Science Review*: 1–17. doi:10.1017/S0003055424000832.

Ansolabehere, Stephen, and Brian F. Schaffner. 2017. "CCES Common Content, 2016." https://dataverse.harvard.edu/dataset.xhtml?persistentId=doi%3A10.7910/DVN/GDF6Z0.

Anspach, Nicolas M. 2017. "The New Personal Influence: How Our Facebook Friends Influence the News We Read." *Political Communication* 34(4): 590–606.

Aoki, Andrew L., and Don T. Nakanishi. 2001. "Asian Pacific Americans and the New Minority Politics." *PS: Political Science and Politics* 34(3): 605–10.

Archdeacon, Thomas J. 1983. *Becoming American: An Ethnic History*. Free Press.

Asian Americans Advancing Justice-Atlanta and Asian American Advocacy Fund. 2022. *The Future of Voting: A Profile of Asian American and Pacific Islander Voters in Georgia*. https://www.advancingjustice-atlanta.org/aapi-data-2022.

Asian American Legal Defense and Education Fund. 2017. *New AALDEF Report: The Asian American Vote in 2016*. AALDEF. https://www.aaldef.org/press-release/new-aaldef-report-the-asian-american-vote-in-2016/.

Asian American Legal Defense and Education Fund. 2020. "AALDEF Exit Poll: Asian Americans Favor Biden Over Trump 68% to 29%; Played Role in Close Races in Georgia and Other Battleground States." AALDEF. https://www.aaldef.org/press-release/aaldef-exit-poll-asian-americans-favor-biden-over-trump-68-to-29-played-role-in-close-races-in-georgia-and-other-battleground-states/.

Asian American Legal Defense and Education Fund. 2021. "AALDEF Exit Poll: 2/3 of Asian American Voters Favored Senators-Elect Raphael Warnock and Jon Ossoff in 2021 Georgia Runoff Elections." AALDEF. https://www.aaldef.org/press-release/aaldef-exit-poll-2-3-of-asian-american-voters-favored-senators-elect-raphael-warnock-and-jon-ossoff-in-2021-georgia-runoff-elections/.

Astin, Alexander W. 1977. *Four Critical Years. Effects of College on Beliefs, Attitudes, and Knowledge*. Jossey-Bass.

Bacon Jr., Perry. 2023. "The GOP Gains Among 'Voters of Color' Are Overhyped." *Washington Post*. https://www.washingtonpost.com/opinions/2023/03/21/black-asian-latino-voters-shift/.

Baime, David, and Katherine Gimbroys. 2022. "Washington Watch: House GOP Plan for Short-Term Pell, Loan Policies." *Community College Daily*. https://www.ccdaily.com/2022/08/washington-watch-house-gop-plan-for-short-term-pell-loan-policies/.

Bakker, Bert N., Yphtach Lelkes, and Ariel Malka. 2020. "Understanding Partisan Cue Receptivity: Tests of Predictions from the Bounded Rationality and Expressive Utility Perspectives." *Journal of Politics* 82(3): 1061–77.

Bakshy, Eytan, Solomon Messing, and Lada A. Adamic. 2015. "Exposure to Ideologically Diverse News and Opinion on Facebook." *Science* 348(6239): 1130–32.

Bankert, Alexa, Ryan Powers, and Geoffrey Sheagley. 2023. "Trade Politics at the Checkout Lane: Ethnocentrism and Consumer Preferences." *Political Science Research and Methods* 11(3): 605–12.

Barberá, Pablo, John T. Jost, Jonathan Nagler, Joshua A. Tucker, and Richard Bonneau. 2015. "Tweeting From Left to Right: Is Online Political Communication More Than an Echo Chamber?" *Psychological Science* 26(10): 1531–42.

Barker, David C., Adam B. Lawrence, and Margit Tavits. 2006. "Partisanship and the Dynamics of 'Candidate Centered Politics' in American Presidential Nominations." *Electoral Studies* 25(3): 599–610.

Barreto, Matt A. 2007. "¡Sí Se Puede! Latino Candidates and the Mobilization of Latino Voters." *American Political Science Review* 101(3): 425–41.

Barreto, Matt A., Fernando Guerra, Mara Marks, Stephen A. Nuño, and Nathan D. Woods. 2006. "Controversies in Exit Polling: Implementing a Racially Stratified Homogenous Precinct Approach." *PS: Political Science and Politics* 39(3): 477–83.

Barreto, Matt A., and José A. Muñoz. 2003. "Reexamining the 'Politics of In-between': Political Participation among Mexican Immigrants in the United States." *Hispanic Journal of Behavioral Sciences* 25(4): 427–47.

Barrón-López, Laura. 2020. "Democratic Organizers Set Their Sights on Asian American Voters to Win Control of the Senate." *Politico*. https://www.politico.com/news/2020/12/18/georgia-senate-runoffs-asian-american-voters-448287.

Bartel, Ann P. 1989. "Where Do the New U.S. Immigrants Live?" *Journal of Labor Economics* 7(4): 371–91.
Bartel, Ann P., and Marriane J. Koch. 1991. "Internal Migration of U.S. Immigrants." In *Immigration, Trade, and the Labor Market*, ed. John M. Abowd and Richard B. Freeman. University of Chicago Press, 121–34.
Bartels, Larry M. 2008. *Unequal Democracy: The Political Economy of the New Gilded Age*. Princeton University Press.
Bauman, Anna. 2021. "Asian Americans Are the Fastest Growing Demographic in Houston's Suburbs. Here's Why." *Houston Chronicle*. https://www.houstonchronicle.com/news/houston-texas/houston/article/Asian-Americans-fastest-growing-Fort-Bend-Houston-16486256.php.
Beck, Paul Allen, and M. Kent Jennings. 1991. "Family Traditions, Political Periods, and the Development of Partisan Orientations." *Journal of Politics* 53(3): 742–63.
Belkin, Douglas. 2017. "Where College Students Are Most Inspired by Their Peers." *Wall Street Journal*. https://www.wsj.com/articles/where-college-students-are-most-inspired-by-their-peers-1506467221.
Berelson, Bernard R., Paul S. Lazarsfeld, and William N. McPhee. 1954. *Voting: A Study of Opinion Formation in a Presidential Campaign*. University of Chicago Press.
Bloch, Matthew, Keith Collins, Robert Gebeloff, Marco Hernandez, Malika Khurana, and Zach Levitt. 2024. "Election Results Show a Red Shift Across the U.S. in 2024." *New York Times*. https://www.nytimes.com/interactive/2024/11/06/us/politics/presidential-election-2024-red-shift.html.
Bloemraad, Irene. 2006. "Citizenship Lessons from the Past: The Contours of Immigrant Naturalization in the Early 20th Century." *Social Science Quarterly* 87(5): 927–53.
Bosch, Mary. 2024. "Bipartisan Organization Works to Increase Asian American Voter Participation, Target Hmong in Wisconsin." *The Daily Cardinal*. https://www.dailycardinal.com/article/2024/07/bipartisan-organization-works-to-increase-asian-american-voter-participation-target-hmong-in-wisconsin.
Bowler, Shaun, Stephen P. Nicholson, and Gary M. Segura. 2006. "Earthquakes and Aftershocks: Race, Direct Democracy, and Partisan Change." *American Journal of Political Science* 50(1): 146–59.
Bowman, Nicholas A., and Julie J. Park. 2014. "Interracial Contact on College Campuses: Comparing and Contrasting Predictors of Cross-Racial Interaction and Interracial Friendship." *Journal of Higher Education* 85(5): 660–90.
Brown, Heath. 2016. *Immigrants and Electoral Politics: Nonprofit Organizing in a Time of Demographic Change*. Cornell University Press.
Brown, Kendrick T. Tony N. Brown, James. S Jackson, Robert M. Sellers, and Warde J. Manuel. 2003. "Teammates On and Off the Field? Contact With Black Teammates and the Racial Attitudes of White Student Athletes." *Journal of Applied Social Psychology* 33(7): 1379–403.
Brown, Sarah, Carolyn Kuimelis, and Grace Mayer. 2022. "College Is a Dividing Line in Politics. Here's What You Need to Know." *The Chronicle of Higher Education*. https://www.chronicle.com/article/college-is-a-dividing-line-in-politics-heres-what-you-need-to-know.
Brust, Amelia. 2017. "MAP: See How Houston Area's Demographics Have Changed Since 1980." *Community Impact*. https://communityimpact.com/data-reference/2017/06/09/latest-kinder-survey-shows-demographics-attitudes-changing-in-houston/.
Budiman, Abby. 2020. "Asian Americans Are the Fastest-Growing Racial or Ethnic Group in the U.S. Electorate." Pew Research Center. https://www.pewresearch.org/fact-tank/2020/05/07/asian-americans-are-the-fastest-growing-racial-or-ethnic-group-in-the-u-s-electorate/.
Budiman, Abby, Luis Noe-Bustamante, and Mark Hugo Lopez. 2020. "Naturalized Citizens Make Up Record One-in-Ten U.S. Eligible Voters in 2020." Pew Research

Center's Hispanic Trends Project. https://www.pewresearch.org/hispanic/2020/02/26/naturalized-citizens-make-up-record-one-in-ten-u-s-eligible-voters-in-2020/.

Budiman, Abby, and Neil G. Ruiz. 2021a. "Asian Americans Are the Fastest-Growing Racial or Ethnic Group in the U.S." Pew Research Center. https://www.pewresearch.org/fact-tank/2021/04/09/asian-americans-are-the-fastest-growing-racial-or-ethnic-group-in-the-u-s/.

Budiman, Abby, and Neil G. Ruiz. 2021b. "Key Facts about Asian Americans, a Diverse and Growing Population." Pew Research Center. https://www.pewresearch.org/fact-tank/2021/04/29/key-facts-about-asian-americans/.

Budiman, Abby, and Neil G. Ruiz. 2021c. "Key Facts about Asian Origin Groups in the U.S." Pew Research Center. https://www.pewresearch.org/short-reads/2021/04/29/key-facts-about-asian-origin-groups-in-the-u-s/.

Bueker, Catherine Simpson. 2005. "Political Incorporation Among Immigrants from Ten Areas of Origin: The Persistence of Source Country Effects." *International Migration Review* 39(1): 103–40.

Cain, Bruce E., D. Roderick Kiewiet, and Carole J. Uhlaner. 1991. "The Acquisition of Partisanship by Latinos and Asian Americans." *American Journal of Political Science* 35(2): 390–422.

Calavita, Kitty. 1989. "The Contradictions of Immigration Lawmaking: The Immigration Reform and Control Act of 1986." *Law & Policy* 11(1): 17–47.

"California 45th Congressional District Election Results." 2022. *The New York Times*. https://www.nytimes.com/interactive/2022/11/08/us/elections/results-california-us-house-district-45.html.

Callahan, Rebecca M., and Chandra Muller. 2013. *Coming of Political Age: American Schools and the Civic Development of Immigrant Youth*. Russell Sage Foundation.

Callahan, Rebecca M., Chandra Muller, and Kathryn S. Schiller. 2010. "Preparing the Next Generation for Electoral Engagement: Social Studies and the School Context." *American Journal of Education* 116(4): 525–56.

Campbell, Angus, Philip E. Converse, Warren E. Miller, and Donald E Stokes. 1960. *The American Voter*. University of Chicago Press.

Campbell, Bruce A. 1980. "A Theoretical Approach to Peer Influence in Adolescent Socialization." *American Journal of Political Science* 24(2): 324–44.

Campbell, David. 2006. *Why We Vote: How Schools and Communities Shape Our Civic Life*. Princeton University Press.

Campbell, David E. 2008. "Voice in the Classroom: How an Open Classroom Climate Fosters Political Engagement Among Adolescents." *Political Behavior* 30(4): 437–54.

Campbell, David E. 2019. "What Social Scientists Have Learned About Civic Education: A Review of the Literature." *Peabody Journal of Education* 94(1): 32–47.

Campbell, David E., and Richard G. Niemi. 2016. "Testing Civics: State-Level Civic Education Requirements and Political Knowledge." *American Political Science Review* 110(3): 495–511.

Carlos, Roberto F. 2018. "Late to the Party: On the Prolonged Partisan Socialization Process of Second-Generation Americans." *Journal of Race, Ethnicity and Politics* 3(2): 381–408.

Carlos, Roberto F. 2021. "The Politics of the Mundane." *American Political Science Review* 115(3): 775–89.

Carlson, Taylor N., Marisa Abrajano, and Lisa García Bedolla. 2020. *Talking Politics: Political Discussion Networks and the New American Electorate*. Oxford University Press.

Carmines, Edward G., and James A. Stimson. 1989. *Issue Evolution: Race and the Transformation of American Politics*. Princeton University Press.

Carrasco, Maria. 2022. "House Republicans Propose Student Loan Reforms, Pell Grants for Short-Term Programs, and Limits on ED Authority." NASFAA. https://

www.nasfaa.org/news-item/27724/House_Republicans_Propose_Student_Loan_Reforms_Pell_Grants_for_Short-Term_Programs_and_Limits_on_ED_Authority.

Carrell, Scott E., Richard L. Fullerton, and James E. West. 2009. "Does Your Cohort Matter? Measuring Peer Effects in College Achievement." *Journal of Labor Economics* 27(3): 439–64.

Casellas, Jason P. 2010. *Latino Representation in State Houses and Congress*. Cambridge University Press.

Chan, Nathan K. 2021. "Political Inequality in the Digital World: The Puzzle of Asian American Political Participation Online." *Political Research Quarterly* 74(4): 882–98.

Chan, Nathan K., and Benjamin Hoyt. 2021. "The Changing Landscape: The Role of Civic Education on Political Efficacy Among Latina/Os and Asian Americans." *Journal of Political Science Education*: 983–1000.

Chan, Nathan Kar Ming, Jae Yeon Kim, and Vivien Leung. 2022. "COVID-19 and Asian Americans: How Elite Messaging and Social Exclusion Shape Partisan Attitudes." *Perspectives on Politics* 20(2): 618–34.

Chan, Nathan, Joyce H. Nguy, and Natalie Masuoka. 2024. "The Asian American Vote in 2020: Indicators of Turnout and Vote Choice." *Political Behavior* 46(1): 631–55.

Chang, Michael. 2004. *Racial Politics in an Era of Transnational Citizenship: The 1996 "Asian Donorgate" Controversy in Perspective*. Lexington Books.

Charmaz, Kathy, and Linda Liska Belgrave. 2012. "Qualitative Interviewing and Grounded Theory Analysis." In *The SAGE Handbook of Interview Research: The Complexity of the Craft*, ed. Jaber F. Gubrium. SAGE, 347–66.

Chaudhary, Ali R. 2017. "Voting Here and There: Political Integration and Transnational Political Engagement among Immigrants in Europe." *Global Networks* 18(3): 437–60.

Chen, Juan, Gilbert C. Gee, Michael S. Spencer, Sheldon H. Danziger, David T. Takeuchi. 2009. "Perceived Social Standing among Asian Immigrants in the US: Do Reasons for Immigration Matter?" *Social Science Research* 38(4): 858–69.

Chen, Rachel, Sono Shah, and Neil G. Ruiz. 2023. "Among Asian Americans, U.S.-Born Children of Immigrants Are Most Likely to Have Hidden Part of Their Heritage." *Pew Research Center*. https://www.pewresearch.org/short-reads/2023/09/11/among-asian-americans-us-born-children-of-immigrants-are-most-likely-to-have-hidden-part-of-their-heritage/.

Chiswick, Barry R., and Paul W. Miller. 2004. "Where Immigrants Settle in the United States." *Journal of Comparative Policy Analysis: Research and Practice* 6(2): 185–97.

Cho, Wendy K. Tam. 1999. "Naturalization, Socialization, Participation: Immigrants and (Non-)Voting." *Journal of Politics* 61(4): 1140–55.

Cho, Wendy K. Tam, and Bruce E. Cain. 2001. "Asian Americans as the Median Voters: An Exploration of Attitudes and Voting Patterns on Ballot Initiatives." In *Asian Americans and Politics: Perspectives, Experiences, and Prospects*, ed. Gordon H. Chang. Stanford University Press, 133–52.

Cho, Wendy K. Tam, James G. Gimpel, and Joshua J. Dyck. 2006. "Residential Concentration, Political Socialization, and Voter Turnout." *Journal of Politics* 68(1): 156–67.

Chow, Gregory C. 1960. "Tests of Equality Between Sets of Coefficients in Two Linear Regressions." *Econometrica* 28(3): 591–605.

"CIRP Freshman Survey." 2023. Higher Education Research Institute. https://heri.ucla.edu/cirp-freshman-survey/.

Clifford, Scott, Geoffrey Sheagley, and Spencer Piston. 2021. "Increasing Precision without Altering Treatment Effects: Repeated Measures Designs in Survey Experiments." *American Political Science Review* 115(3): 1048–65.

Cohn, Nate. 2021. "How Educational Differences Are Widening America's Political Rift." *New York Times*. https://www.nytimes.com/2021/09/08/us/politics/how-college-graduates-vote.html.

"College Senior Survey." 2023. *Higher Education Research Institute*. https://heri.ucla.edu/college-senior-survey/.
Collet, Christian, and Pei-te Lien. 2009. *The Transnational Politics of Asian Americans*. Temple University Press
Converse, Philip E. 1964. "The Nature of Belief Systems in Mass Publics." In *Ideology and Discontent*, ed. David Apter. Free Press, 206–61.
Converse, Philip E. 1969. "Of Time and Partisan Stability." *Comparative Political Studies* 2(2): 139–71.
Cornwell, Elmer E. 1960. "Party Absorption of Ethnic Groups: The Case of Providence, Rhode Island." *Social Forces* 38(3): 205–10.
Cramer, Katherine. 2004. *Talking about Politics: Informal Groups and Social Identity in American Life*. University of Chicago Press.
Dahl, Robert A. 1961. *Who Governs?* Yale University Press.
Davenport, Lauren D. 2018. *Politics beyond Black and White: Biracial Identity and Attitudes in America*. Cambridge University Press.
Davies, James C. 1965. "The Family's Role in Political Socialization." *The Annals of the American Academy of Political and Social Science* 361(1): 10–19.
Dawson, Michael C. 1995. *Behind the Mule: Race and Class in African-American Politics*. Princeton University Press.
Debenedetti, Gabriel. 2017. "Obama's Party-Building Legacy Splits Democrats." *Politico*. https://www.politico.com/story/2017/02/obama-democrats-party-building-234820.
De Benedictis-Kessner, Justin, Matthew A. Baum, Adam J. Berinsky, and Teppei Yamamoto. 2019. "Persuading the Enemy: Estimating the Persuasive Effects of Partisan Media with the Preference-Incorporating Choice and Assignment Design." *American Political Science Review* 113(4): 902–16.
"Democratic Party on Education." 2021. *On the Issues*. https://www.ontheissues.org/celeb/democratic_party_education.htm.
Desai, Saahil. 2018. "The Untapped Potential of the Asian Voter." *Washington Monthly* April/May/June 2018. https://washingtonmonthly.com/magazine/april-may-june-2018/the-untapped-potential-of-the-asian-voter/.
Desilver, Drew. 2014. "Chart of the Week: The Most Liberal and Conservative Big Cities." Pew Research Center. https://www.pewresearch.org/short-reads/2014/08/08/chart-of-the-week-the-most-liberal-and-conservative-big-cities/.
DeSipio, Louis. 1996. *Counting on the Latino Vote: Latinos as New Electorate*. University of Virginia Press.
de Graauw, Els. 2016. *Making Immigrant Rights Real: Nonprofits and the Politics of Integration in San Francisco*. Cornell University Press.
de Graauw, Els, and Shannon Gleeson. 2021. "Labor Unions and Undocumented Immigrants: Local Perspectives on Transversal Solidarity During DACA and DAPA." *Critical Sociology* 47(6): 941–55.
Dey, Eric L. 1996. "Undergraduate Political Attitudes: An Examination of Peer, Faculty, and Social Influences." *Research in Higher Education* 37(5): 535–54.
Dey, Eric L. 1997. "Undergraduate Political Attitudes: Peer Influence in Changing Social Contexts." *Journal of Higher Education* 68(4): 398–413.
Diedenhofen, Birk. 2016. "Cocron: Statistical Comparisons of Two or More Alpha Coefficients." https://CRAN.R-project.org/package=cocron.
Digest of Education Statistics. 2023. "Percentage of Recent High School Completers Enrolled in College, by Race/Ethnicity: 1960 through 2022." National Center for Education Statistics. https://nces.ed.gov/programs/digest/d23/tables/dt23_302.20.asp?current=yes.
Dinas, Elias. 2014. "Why Does the Apple Fall Far from the Tree? How Early Political Socialization Prompts Parent-Child Dissimilarity." *British Journal of Political Science* 44(4): 827–52.

Dinesen, Peter Thisted, and Rasmus Fonnesbæk Andersen. 2022. "The (Re)Socialization of Participatory Political Culture: Immigrants' Political Participation between Their Contemporary Country and Their Ancestral Country." *Political Geography* 98: 1–11. https://doi.org/10.1016/j.polgeo.2022.102650

Downs, Anthony. 1957. *An Economic Theory of Democracy*. Harper.

Dutwin, David, Mollyann Brodie, Melissa Herrmann, and Rebecca Levin. 2005. "Latinos and Political Party Affiliation." *Hispanic Journal of Behavioral Sciences* 27(2): 135–60.

Eckstein, Susan. 2009. *The Immigrant Divide: How Cuban Americans Changed the U.S. and Their Homeland*. Routledge.

Edsall, Thomas B. 2022. "Will Asian Americans Bolt from the Democratic Party?" *New York Times*. https://www.nytimes.com/2022/03/02/opinion/asian-american-voters-democratic-party.html.

Egan, Patrick J. 2012. "Group Cohesion without Group Mobilization: The Case of Lesbians, Gays and Bisexuals." *British Journal of Political Science* 42(3): 597–616.

Erie, Steven P. 1990. *Rainbow's End: Irish-Americans and the Dilemmas of Urban Machine Politics, 1840–1985*. University of California Press.

Facts on U.S. Immigrants. 2018. Pew Research Center. https://www.pewhispanic.org/2018/09/14/facts-on-u-s-immigrants/.

Fernandez, Kenneth E., and Matthew C. Dempsey. 2017. "The Local Political Context of Latino Partisanship." *Journal of Race, Ethnicity, and Politics* 2(2): 201–32.

Fischer, Mary J. 2008. "Does Campus Diversity Promote Friendship Diversity? A Look at Interracial Friendships in College." *Social Science Quarterly* 89(3): 631–55.

Fischer, Mary J. 2011. "Interracial Contact and Changes in the Racial Attitudes of White College Students." *Social Psychology of Education* 14(4): 547–74.

Fong, Dominique. 2021a. "How to Talk to Your Parents About Politics: Part 1." *The Massachusetts Review*. https://massreview.org/node/9886.

Fong, Dominique. 2021b. "How to Talk to Your Parents About Politics: Part 2." *The Massachusetts Review*. https://www.massreview.org/node/9888.

Fong, Eric, and Elic Chan. 2010. "The Effect of Economic Standing, Individual Preferences, and Co-Ethnic Resources on Immigrant Residential Clustering." *International Migration Review* 44(1): 111–41.

Fraga, Bernard L., Paru Shah, and Eric Gonzalez Juenke. 2020. "Did Women and Candidates of Color Lead or Ride the Democratic Wave in 2018?" *PS: Political Science & Politics* 53(3): 435–39.

Fraga, Bernard L., Yamil R. Velez, and Emily A. West. 2025. "Reversion to the Mean, or Their Version of the Dream? Latino Voting in an Age of Populism." *American Political Science Review* 119(1): 517–25.

Frasure, Lorrie, Janelle Wong, Edward Vargas, and Matt Bareto. 2016. "Collaborative Multi-Racial Post-Election Survey (CMPS), United States, 2016: Version 2." Inter-university Consortium for Political and Social Research [distributor]. 2022-05-03. https://doi.org/10.3886/ICPSR38040.V2.

Frendreis, John P., James L. Gibson, and Laura L. Vertz. 1990. "The Electoral Relevance of Local Party Organizations." *American Political Science Review* 84(1): 225–35.

Frost, Jim. 2019. "Using Confidence Intervals to Compare Means." Statistics By Jim. https://statisticsbyjim.com/hypothesis-testing/confidence-intervals-compare-means/.

Frymer, Paul. 2010. *Uneasy Alliances: Race and Party Competition in America*. Revised edition. Princeton University Press.

Frymer, Paul, and Jacob M. Grumbach. 2021. "Labor Unions and White Racial Politics." *American Journal of Political Science* 65(1): 225–40.

Frymer, Paul, and John David Skrentny. 1998. "Coalition-Building and the Politics of Electoral Capture During the Nixon Administration: African Americans, Labor, Latinos." *Studies in American Political Development* 12(1): 131–61.

Galvin, Daniel J. 2009. *Presidential Party Building: Dwight D. Eisenhower to George W. Bush.* Princeton University Press.

Galvin, Daniel J. 2016. "Obama Built a Policy Legacy. But He Didn't Do Enough to Build the Democratic Party." *Washington Post.* https://www.washingtonpost.com/news/monkey-cage/wp/2016/11/16/obama-built-a-policy-legacy-but-didnt-do-enough-to-build-the-democratic-party/.

Gebeloff, Robert, Denise Lu, and Miriam Jordan. 2021. "Inside the Diverse and Growing Asian Population in the U.S." *New York Times.* https://www.nytimes.com/interactive/2021/08/21/us/asians-census-us.html.

Gelman, Andrew. 2009. *Red State, Blue State, Rich State, Poor State: Why Americans Vote the Way They Do.* Expanded edition. Princeton University Press.

Gelman, Andrew. 2012. "Why Aren't Asians Republicans? For One Thing, More than Half of Them Live in California, New York, New Jersey, and Hawaii." *Statistical Modeling, Causal Inference, and Social Science.* https://statmodeling.stat.columbia.edu/2012/11/27/why-arent-asians-republicans-for-one-thing-more-than-half-of-them-live-in-california-new-york-new-jersey-and-hawaii/.

Gershon, Sarah Allen, and Adrian D. Pantoja. 2014. "Pessimists, Optimists, and Skeptics: The Consequences of Transnational Ties for Latino Immigrant Naturalization." *Social Science Quarterly* 95(2): 328–42.

Giles, Michael W., and Marilyn K. Dantico. 1982. "Political Participation and Neighborhood Social Context Revisited." *American Journal of Political Science* 26(1): 144–50.

Gimpel, James G., and Iris S. Hui. 2015. "Seeking Politically Compatible Neighbors? The Role of Neighborhood Partisan Composition in Residential Sorting." *Political Geography* 48: 130–42.

Goldenstein, Taylor. 2022. "First-Ever Muslims Elected to Texas House Reflect on Their Wins: 'A Very Proud Moment.'" *Houston Chronicle.* https://www.houstonchronicle.com/politics/texas/article/First-ever-Muslims-elected-to-Texas-House-reflect-17603981.php.

Goldstein, Harvey, and Michael J. R. Healy. 1995. "The Graphical Presentation of a Collection of Means." *Journal of the Royal Statistical Society. Series A (Statistics in Society)* 158(1): 175–77.

Graber, Doris A. 2001. *Processing Politics: Learning from Television in the Internet Age.* University of Chicago Press.

Graber, Doris. 2004. "Mediated Politics and Citizenship in the Twenty-First Century." *Annual Review of Psychology* 55: 545–71.

Green, Donald P., Bradley Palmquist, and Eric Schickler. 2004. *Partisan Hearts and Minds: Political Parties and the Social Identities of Voters.* Yale University Press.

Greene, Steven. 2004. "Social Identity Theory and Party Identification." *Social Science Quarterly* 85(1): 136–53.

Greenstein, Fred I. 1965. *Children and Politics.* Yale University Press.

Grieco, Elizabeth M. 2001. *Census 2000 Brief: The Native Hawaiian and Other Pacific Islander Population: 2000.* US Census Bureau. https://www.census.gov/library/publications/2001/dec/c2kbr01-14.html.

Grieco, Elizabeth M. 2014. "The 'Second Great Wave' of Immigration: Growth of the Foreign-Born Population Since 1970." US Census Bureau. https://www.census.gov/newsroom/blogs/random-samplings/2014/02/the-second-great-wave-of-immigration-growth-of-the-foreign-born-population-since-1970.html.

Grossmann, Matt, and David A. Hopkins. 2024. *Polarized by Degrees: How the Diploma Divide and the Culture War Transformed American Politics.* Cambridge University Press.

Guarnizo, Luis Eduardo, Alejandro Portes, and William Haller. 2003. "Assimilation and Transnationalism: Determinants of Transnational Political Action among Contemporary Migrants." *American Journal of Sociology* 108(6): 1211–48.

Gurin, Patricia, Eric Dey, Sylvia Hurtado, and Gerald Gurin. 2009. "Diversity and Higher Education: Theory and Impact on Educational Outcomes." *Harvard Educational Review* 72(3): 330–67.

Hajnal, Zoltan L., and Taeku Lee. 2011. *Why Americans Don't Join the Party: Race, Immigration, and the Failure (of Political Parties) to Engage the Electorate*. Princeton University Press.

Hall, Lisa Kahaleole. 2015. "Which of These Things Is Not Like the Other: Hawaiians and Other Pacific Islanders Are Not Asian Americans, and All Pacific Islanders Are Not Hawaiian." *American Quarterly* 67(3): 727–47.

Hamlin, Rebecca. 2008. "Labor Unions at Work: Immigrants and Non-Citizen Members." In *Civic Hopes and Political Realities: Immigrants, Community Organizations, and Political Engagement*, ed. S. Karthick Ramakrishnan and Irene Bloemraad. Russell Sage Foundation, 300–22.

Han, Sungil, Jordan R. Riddell, and Alex R. Piquero. 2022. "Anti-Asian American Hate Crimes Spike During the Early Stages of the COVID-19 Pandemic." *Journal of Interpersonal Violence* 38(3–4): 3513–33.

Hardy-Fanta, Carol, Pei-te Lien, Dianne Pinderhughes, and Christine Marie Sierra. 2016. *Contested Transformation*. Cambridge University Press.

Hassell, Hans J.G., and Neil Visalvanich. 2019. "The Party's Primary Preferences: Race, Gender, and Party Support of Congressional Primary Candidates." *American Journal of Political Science* 63(4): 905–19.

Heath, Anthony F., Stephen D. Fisher, Gemma Rosenblatt, David Sanders, and Maria Sobolewska. 2013. *The Political Integration of Ethnic Minorities in Britain*. Oxford University Press.

Hess, Robert D., and JV Torney. 1967. *The Development of Political Attitudes in Children*. Aldine Publishing Company.

Hillygus, D.S. 2005. "The Missing Link: Exploring the Relationship between Higher Education and Political Behavior." *Political Behavior* 27(1): 25–47.

Hitti, Aline, Laura Elenbaas, Jee Young Noh, Michael T. Rizzo, Shelby Cooley, and Melanie Killen. 2020. "Expectations for Cross-Ethnic Inclusion by Asian American Children and Adolescents." *Group Processes & Intergroup Relations* 23(5): 664–83.

Hobbs, William R. 2019. "Major Life Events and the Age-Partisan Stability Association." *Political Behavior* 41(3): 791–814.

Holbein, John B., and D. Sunshine Hillygus. 2020. *Making Young Voters: Converting Civic Attitudes into Civic Action*. Cambridge University Press.

Hopkins, Daniel J. 2018. *The Increasingly United States: How and Why American Political Behavior Nationalized*. University of Chicago Press.

Hopkins, Daniel J., Cheryl R. Kaiser, Efrén O. Pérez, Sara Hagá, Corin Ramos, and Michael Zárate. 2020. "Does Perceiving Discrimination Influence Partisanship among U.S. Immigrant Minorities? Evidence from Five Experiments." *Journal of Experimental Political Science* 7(2): 112–36.

Hopkins, Daniel J., Cheryl R. Kaiser, and Efrén O. Pérez. 2023. "The Surprising Stability of Asian Americans' and Latinos' Partisan Identities in the Early Trump Era." *Journal of Politics* 85(4): 1321–35.

"How Groups Voted." 2025. Roper Center for Public Opinion Research. https://ropercenter.cornell.edu/how_groups_voted.

Huang, Eric, and Shuran Lee. 2020. "How 12 Asian Americans Are Voting in 1 Swing State." *The Atlantic*. https://www.theatlantic.com/politics/archive/2020/11/asian-american-swing-state-vote/616874/.

Huckfeldt, R. Robert. 1979. "Political Participation and the Neighborhood Social Context." *American Journal of Political Science* 23(3): 579–92.

Huckfeldt, Robert, and John Sprague. 1987. "Networks in Context: The Social Flow of Political Information." *American Political Science Review* 81(4): 1197–216.

Huckfeldt, R. Robert, and John Sprague. 1995. *Citizens, Politics and Social Communication: Information and Influence in an Election Campaign.* Cambridge University Press.

Hyman, Herbert H. 1959. *Political Socialization: A Study in the Posychology of Political Behavior.* Free Press.

"Ideological Gap Widens Between More, Less Educated Adults." 2016. Pew Research Center. https://www.pewresearch.org/politics/2016/04/26/a-wider-ideological-gap-between-more-and-less-educated-adults/.

Irizarry, Giovanni Castro. 2024. "The Influence of Country of Origin in the Process of Party Identification Acquisition." *Journal of Race, Ethnicity, and Politics* 9(1): 80–99.

Iyengar, Shanto, and Donald R. Kinder. [1987] 2010. *News That Matters: Television and American Opinion.* University of Chicago Press.

Iyengar, Shanto, Tobias Konitzer, and Kent Tedin. 2018. "The Home as a Political Fortress: Family Agreement in an Era of Polarization." *Journal of Politics* 80(4): 1326–38.

Jackson, John S., and Robert A. Hitlin. 1981. "The Nationalization of the Democratic Party." *Western Political Quarterly* 34(2): 270–86.

Jarvie, Jenny, and Jennifer Haberkorn. 2020. "Georgia Senate Races May Hinge on a Small but Growing Asian American Voter Population." *Los Angeles Times.* https://www.latimes.com/politics/story/2020-12-10/georgia-senate-runoffs-asian-american-vote.

Jaschik, Scott. 2017. "The Numbers and the Arguments on Asian Admissions." *Inside Higher Ed.* https://www.insidehighered.com/admissions/article/2017/08/07/look-data-and-arguments-about-asian-americans-and-admissions-elite.

Jefferson, Hakeem. 2024. "The Curious Case of Black 'Conservatives': Assessing the Validity of the Liberal-Conservative Scale among Black Americans." *Public Opinion Quarterly* 88(3):909-32.

Jennings, M. Kent, and Richard G. Niemi. 1968. "The Transmission of Political Values from Parent to Child." *American Political Science Review* 62(1): 169–84.

Jennings, M. Kent, and Richard G. Niemi. 1974. *The Political Character of Adolescence: The Influence of Families and Schools.* Princeton University Press.

Jennings, M. Kent, and Richard G. Niemi. 1981. *Generations and Politics: A Panel Study of Young Adults and Their Parents.* Princeton University Press.

Jennings, M. Kent, Laura Stoker, and Jake Bowers. 2009. "Politics across Generations: Family Transmission Reexamined." *Journal of Politics* 71(3): 782–99.

Jo, Moon H., and Michael Roskin. 1990. "Participation Among Asian and Jewish Americans." *International Social Science Review* 65(4): 154–65.

Johnson, Susan M., and Xia Li Lollar. 2010. "Diversity Policy in Higher Education: The Impact of College Students' Exposure to Diversity on Cultural Awareness and Political Participation." *Journal of Education Policy* 17(3): 305–20.

Jones-Correa, Michael. 1998. *Between Two Nations: The Political Predicament of Latinos in New York City.* Cornell University Press.

Jones-Correa, Michael. 2016. "Does Prior Socialization Define Patterns of Integration? Mexican Immigrants and Their Political Participation." In *Just Ordinary Citizens?: Towards a Comparative Portrait of the Political Immigrant*, ed Antoine Bilodeau. University of Toronto Press, 83–96.

Jones-Correa, Michael. 2003. "Under Two Flags: Dual Nationality in Latin America and Its Consequences for Naturalization in the United States." In *Rights and Duties of Dual Nationals: Evolution and Prospects*, ed. David A. Martin and Kay Hailbronner. Brill Nijhoff, 303–33.

Junn, Jane. 1999. "Participation in Liberal Democracy: The Political Assimilation of Immigrants and Ethnic Minorities in the United States." *American Behavioral Scientist* 42(9): 1417–38.

Junn, Jane. 2004. "Diversity, Immigration, and the Politics of Civic Education." *PS: Political Science & Politics* 37(2): 253–55.

Junn, Jane, and Natalie Masuoka. 2008. "Asian American Identity: Shared Racial Status and Political Context." *Perspectives on Politics* 6(4): 729–40.

Just, Aida, and Christopher J. Anderson. 2012. "Immigrants, Citizenship and Political Action in Europe." *British Journal of Political Science* 42(3): 481–509.

Juvonen, Jaana, Guadalupe Espinoza, and Casey Knifsend. 2012. "The Role of Peer Relationships in Student Academic and Extracurricular Engagement." In *Handbook of Research on Student Engagement*, ed. Sandra L. Christenson, Amy L. Reschly, and Cathy Wylie. Springer, 387–401.

Kahne, Joseph, David Crow, and Nam-Jin Lee. 2013. "Different Pedagogy, Different Politics: High School Learning Opportunities and Youth Political Engagement." *Political Psychology* 34(3): 419–41.

Kandel, William, and John Cromartie. 2004. *New Patterns of Hispanic Settlement in Rural America*. United States Department of Agriculture. https://www.ers.usda.gov/publications/pub-details?pubid=47091.

Kao, Jason. 2023. "Where New York's Asian Neighborhoods Shifted to the Right." *New York Times*. https://www.nytimes.com/interactive/2023/03/05/nyregion/election-asians-voting-republicans-nyc.html.

Kaulessar, Ricardo. 2023. "Where Does New Jersey Get Its News? Increasingly, It's from Ethnic Media Outlets." North Jersey Media Group. https://www.northjersey.com/story/news/state/2023/06/16/nj-ethnic-community-media-outlets-growth-montclair-state-report/70312900007/.

Kelly, Mary Louise. 2024. "How Young Republicans and Democrats Are Whipping up Votes in Key Districts." NPR. https://www.npr.org/2024/09/30/nx-s1-5123646/donald-trump-kamala-harris-georgia-election-young-voters.

Kelly, Nathan J., and Jana Morgan Kelly. 2005. "Religion and Latino Partisanship in the United States." *Political Research Quarterly* 58(1): 87–95.

Kenny, Caroline, Kyung Lah, and Kim Berryman. 2020. "Democrats See Reaching Asian American Voters as Key Part of Georgia Runoff Strategy." CNN. https://www.cnn.com/2020/12/03/politics/asian-american-voters-georgia-senate-runoff/index.html.

Khalid, Asma. 2019. "Democrats Used to Talk About 'Criminal Immigrants,' So What Changed The Party?" NPR. https://www.npr.org/2019/02/19/694804917/democrats-used-to-talk-about-criminal-immigrants-so-what-changed-the-party.

Kiang, Peter Nien-Chu. 2001. "Asian Pacific American Youth: Pathways for Political Participation." In *Asian Americans and Politics: Perspectives, Experiences, and Prospects*, ed. Gordon H. Chang. Stanford University Press, 230–57.

Kistner, Michael, and Tanika Raychaudhuri. 2025. "Immigration and Political Incorporation: Asian American Representation in State Legislatures." *State Politics & Policy Quarterly* 25(2): 212-236.

Kim, Claire Jean. 1999. "The Racial Triangulation of Asian Americans." *Politics & Society* 27(1): 105–38.

Kim, Claire Jean. 2023. *Asian Americans in an Anti-Black World*. Cambridge University Press.

Kim, Thomas P. 2007. *The Racial Logic of Politics: Asian Americans and Party Competition*. Temple University Press.

Kinder Institute for Urban Research. 2021. "Kinder Houston Area Survey: Political Affiliations." https://docs.google.com/spreadsheets/d/19vGWWx32vx5QzvP8GKLHsmDsE1TJbeI1GJVmYVfTppk/pubhtml?widget=true&headers=false.

Koch, Jeffrey W. 2017. "Partisanship and Non-Partisanship Among American Indians." *American Politics Research* 45(4): 673–91.

Komisarchik, Mayya, Maya Sen, and Yamil R. Velez. 2022. "The Political Consequences of Ethnically Targeted Incarceration: Evidence from Japanese American Internment during World War II." *Journal of Politics* 84(3): 1497–514. doi:10.1086/717262.

Kremer, Michael, and Dan Levy. 2008. "Peer Effects and Alcohol Use among College Students." *Journal of Economic Perspectives* 22(3): 189–206. doi:10.1257/jep.22.3.189.

Kuo, Alexander, Neil Malhotra, and Cecilia Hyunjung Mo. 2017. "Social Exclusion and Political Identity: The Case of Asian American Partisanship." *Journal of Politics* 79(1): 17–32.

Lah, Kyung, and Jason Kravarik. 2023. "Shift in San Francisco Politics Serves as Warning from Asian American Voters to Democrats in 2024." CNN. https://www.cnn.com/2023/03/22/politics/asian-voters-democrats-warning/index.html.

Lai, James S. 2011. *Asian American Political Action: Suburban Transformations*. Lynne Rienner Publishers.

Lai, James S. 2022a. *Asian American Connective Action in the Age of Social Media: Civic Engagement, Contested Issues, and Emerging Identities*. Temple University Press.

Lai, Stephanie. 2022b. "In Orange County, a House Race Is Testing What Asian Americans Want." *New York Times*. https://www.nytimes.com/2022/09/08/us/elections/orange-county-asian-american-voters.html.

Lai, James S., Wendy K. Tam Cho, Thomas P. Kim, and Okiyoshi Takeda. 2001. "Asian Pacific-American Campaigns, Elections, and Elected Officials." *PS: Political Science and Politics* 34(3): 611–17.

Langton, Kenneth P., and M. Kent Jennings. 1968. "Political Socialization and the High School Civics Curriculum in the United States." *American Political Science Review* 62(3): 852–67.

"Language Access." 2023. Asian Americans Advancing Justice. https://www.advancingjustice-aajc.org/language-access.

Le, Loan Kieu, and Phi Hong Su. 2017. "Party Identification and the Immigrant Cohort Hypothesis: The Case of Vietnamese Americans." *Politics, Groups, and Identities* 6(4): 743–63.

Le Espiritu, Yen. 1992. *Asian American Panethnicity: Bridging Institutions and Identities*. Temple University Press.

Lee, Taeku. 2002. *Mobilizing Public Opinion: Black Insurgency and Racial Attitudes in the Civil Rights Era*. University of Chicago Press.

Leighley, Jan E. 1990. "Social Interaction and Contextual Influences On Political Participation." *American Politics Quarterly* 18(4): 459–75.

Leip, David. 2024. "Dave Leip's Atlas of U.S. Presidential Elections." http://uselectionatlas.org.

Leonhardt, David. 2023. "Asian Americans, Shifting Right." *New York Times*. https://www.nytimes.com/2023/03/06/briefing/asian-americans-conservative-republican.html.

Leung, Vivien. 2022. "Asian American Candidate Preferences: Evidence from California." *Political Behavior* 44(4): 1759–88.

Leung, Vivien, Sara Sadhwani, Tanika Raychaudhuri, Maneesh Arora, Chinbo Chong, and Nathan Chan. 2020. "Omnibus Asian American Survey." https://sites.google.com/view/vivienleung/data.

Li, Wei. 1998. "Anatomy of a New Ethnic Settlement: The Chinese Ethnoburb in Los Angeles." *Urban Studies* 35(3): 479–501.

Li, Wei. 2009. *Ethnoburb: The New Ethnic Community in Urban America*. University of Hawaii Press.

Li, Wei, Emily Skop, and Wan Yu. 2016. "Enclaves, Ethnoburbs, and New Patterns of Settlement among Asian Immigrants." In *Contemporary Asian America (Third Edition): A Multidisciplinary Reader*, ed. Min Zhou and Anthony Christian Ocampo. NYU Press, 193–216.

Lichtenstein, Andrew. 2022. "Asian Americans Favored Democratic Candidates in Midterms, Exit Polls Say." *NBC News*. https://www.nbcnews.com/news/asian-america/asian-americans-favored-democratic-candidates-midterms-exit-polls-say-rcna56659.

Lichter, Daniel T., and Kenneth M. Johnson. 2021. "A Demographic Lifeline to Rural America: Latino Population Growth in New Destinations, 1990–2019." In *Investing in Rural Prosperity*, ed. Andrew Dumont and Daniel Paul Davis. Federal Reserve Bank of St. Louis, 67–80. https://www.stlouisfed.org/-/media/project/frbstl/stlouisfed/files/pdfs/community-development/investing-rural/chapters/chapter04.pdf.

Lien, Pei-te. 1997. *The Political Participation of Asian Americans: Voting Behavior in Southern California*. Routledge

Lien, Pei-te. 2001. *Making Of Asian America: Through Political Participation*. Temple University Press.

Lien, Pei-te. 2004a. "Asian Americans and Voting Participation: Comparing Racial and Ethnic Differences in Recent U.S. Elections." *International Migration Review* 38(2): 493–517.

Lien, Pei-te. 2001. "Pilot National Asian American Political Survey (PNAAPS), 2000–2001: Version 1." 2004-05-05. Inter-university Consortium for Political and Social Research (distributor). https://doi.org/10.3886/ICPSR03832.V1.

Lien, Pei-te. 2008. "Homeland Origins and Political Identities among Chinese in Southern California." *Ethnic and Racial Studies* 31(8): 1381–403.

Lien, Pei-te. 2010. "Pre-Emigration Socialization, Transnational Ties, and Political Participation Across the Pacific: A Comparison Among Immigrants from China, Taiwan, and Hong Kong." *Journal of East Asian Studies* 10(3): 453–82.

Lien, Pei-te, Christian Collet, Janelle Wong, and S. Karthick Ramakrishnan. 2001. "Asian Pacific-American Public Opinion and Political Participation." *PS: Political Science and Politics* 34(3): 625–30.

Lien, Pei-te, M. Margaret Conway, and Janelle Wong. 2004. *The Politics of Asian Americans: Diversity and Community*. Routledge.

Lien, Pei-te, and Nicole Filler. 2022. *Contesting the Last Frontier: Race, Gender, Ethnicity, and Political Representation of Asian Americans*. Oxford University Press.

Lipka, Michael, and Elisa Shearer. 2023. "Audiences Are Declining for Traditional News Media in the U.S.—with Some Exceptions." Pew Research Center. https://www.pewresearch.org/short-reads/2023/11/28/audiences-are-declining-for-traditional-news-media-in-the-us-with-some-exceptions/.

Livingston, Gretchen, and Anna Brown. 2017. "Intermarriage in the U.S. 50 Years After Loving v. Virginia." https://www.pewsocialtrends.org/2017/05/18/intermarriage-in-the-u-s-50-years-after-loving-v-virginia/.

Logan, John R., and Weiwei Zhang. 2013. *Separate But Equal: Asian Nationalities in the U.S.* American Communities Project. https://s4.ad.brown.edu/Projects/Diversity/Data/Report/report06112013.pdf.

Lublin, David, Thomas L. Brunell, Bernard Grofman, and Lisa Handley. 2009. "Has the Voting Rights Act Outlived Its Usefulness? In a Word, 'No.'" *Legislative Studies Quarterly* 34(4): 525–53.

Lublin, David, and Matthew Wright. 2024. "Diversity Matters: The Election of Asian Americans to U.S. State and Federal Legislatures." *American Political Science Review* 118(1): 380–400.

Lung-Amam, Willow. 2017. *Trespassers?: Asian Americans and the Battle for Suburbia*. University of California Press.

Lyons, Jeffrey. 2011. "Where You Live and Who You Know: Political Environments, Social Pressures, and Partisan Stability." *American Politics Research* 39(6): 963–92.

Mahtesian, Charlie, and Madi Alexander. 2023. "'This Is a Really Big Deal': How College Towns Are Decimating the GOP." *Politico*. https://www.politico.com/news/magazine/2023/07/21/gop-college-towns-00106974.

Martinez, Marissa. 2023. "Republicans Are Winning More Latino Votes. But Rising Turnout Still Benefits Dems." *Politico*. https://www.politico.com/news/2023/03/10/republicans-are-winning-more-latino-votes-but-rising-turnout-still-benefits-dems-00086361.

Mason, Melanie. 2024. "This Vietnamese American Candidate Just Blew Up the Democratic Campaign Playbook." *Politico*. https://www.politico.com/news/magazine/2024/12/09/how-derek-tran-flipped-a-gop-district-00192996.

Massey, Douglas S., Camille Z. Charles, Garvey Lundy, and Mary J. Fischer. 2002. *The Source of the River: The Social Origins of Freshmen at America's Selective Colleges and Universities*. Princeton University Press.

Masuoka, Natalie. 2006. "Together They Become One: Examining the Predictors of Panethnic Group Consciousness Among Asian Americans and Latinos∗." *Social Science Quarterly* 87(5): 993–1011.

Masuoka, Natalie, Hahrie Han, Vivien Leung, and Bang Quan Zheng. 2018. "Understanding the Asian American Vote in the 2016 Election." *Journal of Race, Ethnicity, and Politics* 3(01): 189–215.

Masuoka, Natalie, and Jane Junn. 2013. *The Politics of Belonging: Race, Public Opinion, and Immigration*. University of Chicago Press.

Matsaganis, Matthew D., Vikki S. Katz, and Sandra J. Ball-Rokeach. 2011. *Understanding Ethnic Media: Producers, Consumers, and Societies*. SAGE.

McAdam, Doug, and Karina Kloos. 2014. *Deeply Divided: Racial Politics and Social Movements in Postwar America*. Oxford University Press.

McCann, James A., and Katsuo A. Nishikawa Chávez. 2016. "Partisanship by Invitation: Immigrants Respond to Political Campaigns." *Journal of Politics* 78(4): 1196–210.

McClain, Paula D., Jessica D. Johnson Carew, Eugene Walton, and Candis S. Watts. 2009. "Group Membership, Group Identity, and Group Consciousness: Measures of Racial Identity in American Politics?" *Annual Review of Political Science* 12: 471–85.

McDevitt, Michael, and Steven Chaffee. 2002. "From Top-Down to Trickle-Up Influence: Revisiting Assumptions About the Family in Political Socialization." *Political Communication* 19(3): 281–301.

McDonough Annie. 2023. "Democrats Need to Overhaul Their Playbook for Courting Asian American Voters." *City & State New York*. https://www.cityandstateny.com/politics/2023/10/democrats-need-overhaul-their-playbook-courting-asian-american-voters/390931/.

McGraw, Kathleen M., and Milton Lodge. 1996. "Political Information Processing: A Review Essay." *Political Communication* 13(1): 131–38.

Mendelberg, Tali, Katherine McCabe, and Adam Thal. 2017. "College Socialization and the Economic Views of Affluent Americans." *American Journal of Political Science* 61(3): 606–23.

Mendelberg, Tali, Vittorio Mérola, Tanika Raychaudhuri, and Adam Thal. 2021. "When Poor Students Attend Rich Schools: Do Affluent Social Environments Increase or Decrease Participation?" *Perspectives on Politics* 19(3): 807–23.

Merica, Dan. 2018. "Republicans, Democrats See Asian-Americans as Key to Victory in Southern California." *CNNPolitics*. https://www.cnn.com/2018/06/02/politics/california-primary-asian-americans/index.html.

Merriam-Webster. 2023. "Definition of 'Peer.'" https://www.merriam-webster.com/dictionary/peer.

Milkman, Ruth. 2006. *L.A. Story: Immigrant Workers And the Future of the U.S. Labor Movement.* Russell Sage Foundation.
Milkman, Ruth. 2011. "Immigrant Workers, Precarious Work, and the US Labor Movement." *Globalizations* 8(3): 361–72.
Mirilovic, Nikola, and Philip H. Pollock III. 2018. "Latino Democrats, Latino Republicans and Interest in Country of Origin Politics." *Political Science Quarterly* 133(1): 127–49.
Mohsin, Farhan M., Shahmir H. Ali, Stella K. Chong, Roshan S. Parikh, Ralph J. DiClemente, and Lu Hu. 2023. "Social Media Utilization Within Asian American Families and Its Role in Healthy Lifestyle Behavioral Influence: Results From a Nationwide Survey." *Social Media + Society* 9(3): 1–12. https://doi.org/10.1177/20563051231196544.
Mok, Aurelia, Michael W. Morris, Verónica Benet-Martínez, and Zahide Karakitapoğlu-Aygün. 2007. "Embracing American Culture: Structures of Social Identity and Social Networks Among First-Generation Biculturals." *Journal of Cross-Cultural Psychology* 38(5): 629–35.
Mondak, Jeffery J. 1993. "Source Cues and Policy Approval: The Cognitive Dynamics of Public Support for the Reagan Agenda." *American Journal of Political Science* 37(1): 186–212.
Montanaro, Domenico. 2021. "The Growing Power of the AAPI Vote, by the Numbers." NPR. https://www.npr.org/2021/05/22/999345393/the-growing-power-of-the-aapi-vote-by-the-numbers.
Monte, Lindsay M., and Hyon B. Shin. 2022. "20.6 Million People in the U.S. Identify as Asian, Native Hawaiian or Pacific Islander." US Census Bureau. https://www.census.gov/library/stories/2022/05/aanhpi-population-diverse-geographically-dispersed.html.
Morris, Kyle. 2021. "Education Department Expedites Loan Forgiveness for Service Members Following Rare Bipartisan Push." *Fox News.* https://www.foxnews.com/politics/education-department-expedites-loan-forgiveness-for-service-members-following-rare-bipartisan-push.
Mosley, Layna, ed. 2013. *Interview Research in Political Science.* Cornell University Press.
Mummolo, Jonathan, and Clayton Nall. 2016. "Why Partisans Do Not Sort: The Constraints on Political Segregation." *Journal of Politics* 79(1): 45–59.
Museus, Samuel D. 2008. "The Role of Ethnic Student Organizations in Fostering African American and Asian American Students' Cultural Adjustment and Membership at Predominantly White Institutions." *Journal of College Student Development* 49(6): 568–86.
Mutz, Diana C. 2002. "The Consequences of Cross-Cutting Networks for Political Participation." *American Journal of Political Science* 46(4): 838–55.
Mutz, Diana C. 2006. *Hearing the Other Side: Deliberative Versus Participatory Democracy.* Cambridge University Press.
Mutz, Diana C., and Jeffery J. Mondak. 2006. "The Workplace as a Context for Cross-Cutting Political Discourse." *Journal of Politics* 68(1): 140–55.
Nakanishi, Don T. 2001. "Beyond Electoral Politics: Renewing a Search for a Paradigm of Asian Pacific American Politics." In *Asian Americans and Politics: Perspectives, Experiences, Prospects*, ed. Gordon H. Chang. Stanford University Press, 102–29.
Nakanishi, Don T. 2009. "Asian American Politics: An Agenda for Research." *Amerasia Journal* 35(3): 94–124.

Nakanishi, Don T., and James S. Lai. 2003. *Asian American Politics: Law, Participation, and Policy*. Rowman & Littlefield.
NASFAA. 2019. "Former Top ED Official: Republicans Should Support Student Debt Forgiveness." National Association of Student Financial Aid Administrators. https://www.nasfaa.org/news-item/20081/Former_Top_ED_Official_Republicans_Should_Support_Student_Debt_Forgiveness.
National Association of Independent Colleges and Universities. 2021. "National Survey Shows Strong, Bipartisan Support for the Federal Pell Grant Program." https://www.naicu.edu/news-events/news-from-naicu/2021/12/national-survey-shows-strong,-bipartisan-support-for-the-federal-pell-grant-program.
"National Data on Immigrant Students." 2023. Higher Ed Immigration Portal. https://www.higheredimmigrationportal.org/national/national-data/.
Nelsen, Matthew D. 2021a. "Cultivating Youth Engagement: Race & the Behavioral Effects of Critical Pedagogy." *Political Behavior* 43(2): 751–84.
Nelsen, Matthew D. 2021b. "Teaching Citizenship: Race and the Behavioral Effects of American Civic Education." *Journal of Race, Ethnicity, and Politics* 6(1): 157–86.
Neundorf, Anja, Richard G. Niemi, and Kaat Smets. 2016. "The Compensation Effect of Civic Education on Political Engagement: How Civics Classes Make Up for Missing Parental Socialization." *Political Behavior* 38(4): 921–49.
Newcomb, Theodore Mead. 1943. *Personality and Social Change: Attitude Formation in a Student Community*. Dryden Press.
Nguyen, Alex. 2022. "Asian Americans Are One of Texas' Fastest-Growing Demographics. But They Feel Ignored by Politicians." *Texas Tribune*. https://www.texastribune.org/2022/10/14/asian-american-pacific-islander-texas-voters-2022/.
Nguyễn, Sarah, Rachel E. Moran, Trung-Anh Nguyen, and Linh Bui. 2023. "'We Never Really Talked About Politics': Race and Ethnicity as Foundational Forces Structuring Information Disorder Within the Vietnamese Diaspora." *Political Communication* 40(4): 415–39.
Nguyen, Viet Thanh. 2018. "Could Asian-Americans Turn Orange County Blue?" *New York Times*. https://www.nytimes.com/2018/11/05/opinion/asian-americans-orange-county-house-races.html.
Nguyen, Viet Thanh. 2020. "What the Asian-American Coalition Can Teach the Democrats." *New York Times*. https://www.nytimes.com/2020/12/16/opinion/asian-american-democrats.html.
Niemi, Richard G., and Mary A. Hepburn. 1995. "The Rebirth of Political Socialization." *Perspectives on Political Science* 24(1): 7–16.
Niemi, Richard G., and Jane Junn. 2005. *Civic Education: What Makes Students Learn*. Yale University Press.
Niemi, Richard G., R. Danforth Ross, and Joseph Alexander. 1978. "The Similarity of Political Values of Parents and College-Age Youths." *Public Opinion Quarterly* 42(4): 503–20.
Ojeda, Christopher, and Peter K. Hatemi. 2015. "Accounting for the Child in the Transmission of Party Identification." *American Sociological Review* 80(6): 1150–74.
Oliver, J. Eric, and Janelle Wong. 2003. "Intergroup Prejudice in Multiethnic Settings." *American Journal of Political Science* 47(4): 567–82.
Olmos, Antonio, and Priyalatha Govindasamy. 2015. "A Practical Guide for Using Propensity Score Weighting in R." *Practical Assesment, Research & Evaluation* 20(13): 1–8. https://doi.org/10.7275/jjtm-r398.

Ong, Paul M., and David E. Lee. 2001. "Changing of the Guard? The Emerging Immigrant Majority in Asian American Politics." In *Asian Americans and Politics: Perspectives, Experiences, Prospects*, ed. Gordon H. Chang. Stanford University Press, 153–73.

Orfield, Gary, Erica Frankenburg, Jongyeon Ee, and Jennifer B. Ayscue. 2019. *Harming Our Common Future: America's Segregated Schools 65 Years after Brown*. The Civil Rights Project, UCLA. https://www.civilrightsproject.ucla.edu/research/k-12-education/integration-and-diversity/harming-our-common-future-americas-segregated-schools-65-years-after-brown.

Orfield, Gary, and Chungmei Lee. 2006. *Racial Transformation and the Changing Nature of Segregation*. Harvard University. https://escholarship.org/content/qt7519d9sh/qt7519d9sh.pdf.

Pascarella, Ernest T., Christopher T. Pierson, Gregory C. Wolniak, and Patrick T. Terenzini. 2004. "First-Generation College Students: Additional Evidence on College Experiences and Outcomes." *Journal of Higher Education* 75(3): 249–84.

Pascarella, Ernest T., Georgianna L. Martin, Jana M. Hanson, Teniell L. Trolian, Benjamin Gillig, and Charles Blaich. 2014. "Effects of Diversity Experiences on Critical Thinking Skills Over 4 Years of College." *Journal of College Student Development* 55(1): 86–92.

Pascarella, Ernest T., and Patrick Terenzini. 1991. *How College Affects Students: Findings and Insights from Twenty Years of Research*. Jossey-Bass.

Pasek, Josh, Lauren Feldman, Daniel Romer, and Kathleen Hall Jamieson. 2008. "Schools as Incubators of Democratic Participation: Building Long-Term Political Efficacy with Civic Education." *Applied Developmental Science* 12(1): 26–37.

Pérez, Efrén O., and E. Enya Kuo. 2021. *Racial Order, Racialized Responses: Interminority Politics in a Diverse Nation*. Cambridge University Press.

Pettigrew, Thomas F. 1997. "Generalized Intergroup Contact Effects on Prejudice." *Personality and Social Psychology Bulletin* 23(2): 173–85

Pettigrew, Thomas F., and Linda R. Tropp. 2006. "A Meta-Analytic Test of Intergroup Contact Theory." *Journal of Personality and Social Psychology* 90(5): 751–83.

Phan, Ngoc, and John A. Garcia. 2009. "Asian-Pacific-American Partisanship: Dynamics of Partisan and Nonpartisan Identities∗." *Social Science Quarterly* 90(4): 886–910.

Phan, Ngoc T., and Kevin Lujan Lee. 2022. "Toward a Decolonial Quantitative Political Science: Indigenous Self-Identification in the 2019 Native Hawaiian Survey." *Journal of Race, Ethnicity, and Politics* 7(1): 90–118.

Plummer, Deborah L., Rosalie Torres Stone, Lauren Powell, and Jeroan Allison. 2016. "Patterns of Adult Cross-Racial Friendships: A Context for Understanding Contemporary Race Relations." *Cultural Diversity and Ethnic Minority Psychology* 22: 479–94.

Portes, Alejandro, Cristina Escobar, and Renelinda Arana. 2008. "Bridging the Gap: Transnational and Ethnic Organizations in the Political Incorporation of Immigrants in the United States." *Ethnic and Racial Studies* 31(6): 1056–90.

Potochnick, Stephanie, and Mary Stegmaier. 2020. "Latino Political Participation by Citizenship Status and Immigrant Generation." *Social Science Quarterly* 101(2): 527–44.

Prior, Markus. 2007. *Post-Broadcast Democracy: How Media Choice Increases Inequality in Political Involvement and Polarizes Elections*. Cambridge University Press.

Proctor, Andrew. 2022. "Coming out to Vote: The Construction of a Lesbian and Gay Electoral Constituency in the United States." *American Political Science Review* 116(3): 777–90.

"Proprietary Panel." 2025. *Bovitz*. https://www.bovitzinc.com/capabilities/proprietary-panel/.

Qian, Zhenchao, Sampson Lee Blair, and Stacey D. Ruf. 2001. "Asian American Interracial and Interethnic Marriages: Differences by Education and Nativity." *International Migration Review* 35(2): 557–86.

Qin, Amy. 2022. "In Nevada, Both Parties Court a Booming Vote Bloc: Asian Americans." *New York Times*. https://www.nytimes.com/2022/11/04/us/nevada-asian-voters-midterms.html.

"Race/Ethnicity: 1980–2010 City of Houston." 2012. Planning and Development Department. https://www.houstontx.gov/planning/Demographics/docs_pdfs/Cy/coh_race_ethn_1980-2010.pdf.

Ramakrishnan, S. Karthick. 2005. *Democracy in Immigrant America: Changing Demographics and Political Participation*. Stanford University Press.

Ramakrishnan, Karthick. 2016. "How Asian Americans Became Democrats." *The American Prospect*. https://prospect.org/article/how-asian-americans-became-democrats-0.

Ramakrishnan, Karthick. 2017. "The Asian American Vote in 2016: Record Gains, but Also Gaps." *AAPI Data Blog*. https://aapidata.com/blog/voting-gains-gaps/.

Ramakrishnan, Karthick. 2020. "Exercise Caution in Interpreting Asian American Exit Polls." *AAPI Data Blog*. https://aapidata.com/blog/exit-polls-caution/.

Ramakrishnan, Karthick. 2021. "In 2020, AAPIs Saw the Highest Increases in Voter Turnout." *AAPI Data Blog*. https://aapidata.com/blog/2020-record-turnout/.

Ramakrishnan, Karthick, Janelle S. Wong, Taeku Lee, and Jennifer Lee. 2016. *Asian American Voices in the 2016 Election: Report on Registered Voters in the Fall 2016 National Asian American Survey*. http://naasurvey.com/wp-content/uploads/2016/10/NAAS2016-Oct5-report.pdf.

Ramakrishnan, S. Karthick, and Irene Bloemraad, eds. 2008. *Civic Hopes and Political Realities: Immigrants, Community Organizations, and Political Engagement*. Russell Sage Foundation.

Ramakrishnan, S. Karthick, Jane Junn, Taeku Lee, and Janelle Wong. 2008. "National Asian American Survey (NAAS), [United States] 2008." Inter-university Consortium for Political and Social Research [distributor]. 2012-07-19. https://doi.org/10.3886/ICPSR31481.v2.

Ramakrishnan, S. Karthick, Jennifer Lee, Taeku Lee, and Janelle Wong. 2016. "National Asian American Survey (NAAS) Post-Election Survey, [United States] 2016." 2020-01-30. Inter-university Consortium for Political and Social Research [distributor]. https://doi.org/10.3886/ICPSR37380.v1.

Raychaudhuri, Tanika. 2018. "The Social Roots of Asian American Partisan Attitudes." *Politics, Groups, and Identities* 6(3): 389–410.

Raychaudhuri, Tanika. 2020. "Socializing Democrats: Examining Asian American Vote Choice with Evidence from a National Survey." *Electoral Studies* 63: 1–10. https://doi.org/10.1016/j.electstud.2019.102114.

Reflective Democracy Campaign. 2021. *#advance AAPI Power: Asian American Pacific Islander (AAPI) Political Leadership*. Women Donors Network. https://wholeads.us/wp-content/uploads/2021/05/reflectivedemocracy-AdvanceAAPIPower-may2021.pdf.

"Republican Party on Education." 2021. *On the Issues*. https://www.ontheissues.org/celeb/republican_party_education.htm.

"Republican Party Platform of 1988." 2023. The American Presidency Project. https://www.presidency.ucsb.edu/documents/republican-party-platform-1988.

Rice, Tom W., and Jan L. Feldman. 1997. "Civic Culture and Democracy from Europe to America." *Journal of Politics* 59(4): 1143–72.

Rim, Kathy H. 2009. "Latino and Asian American Mobilization in the 2006 Immigration Protests." *Social Science Quarterly* 90(3): 703–21.

Rooney, Kimberly. 2021. "Pittsburgh Asian Organizations Offer Community, Support, and Education for Local AAPI Residents." *Pittsburgh City Paper*. https://www.pghcitypaper.com/news/pittsburgh-asian-organizations-offer-community-support-and-education-for-local-aapi-residents-19445121.

Rosentiel, Tom. 2008. "Young Voters in the 2008 Election." Pew Research Center. https://www.pewresearch.org/2008/11/13/young-voters-in-the-2008-election/.

Ross, Ashley D., and Stella M. Rouse. 2022. "(Young) Generations as Social Identities: The Role of Latino∗Millennial/Generation Z in Shaping Attitudes About Climate Change." *Political Behavior* 44(3): 1105–24.

Rouse, Stella M., Betina Cutaia Wilkinson, and James C. Garand. 2010. "Divided Loyalties? Understanding Variation in Latino Attitudes Toward Immigration." *Social Science Quarterly* 91(3): 856–82.

Roy, Sandip, and Sandy Close. 2007. "Ethnic Media in USA: Giant Hidden in Plain Sight." In *Transnational Lives and the Media: Re-Imagining Diaspora*, ed. Olga G. Bailey, Myria Georgiou, and Ramaswami Harindranath. Palgrave Macmillan, 263–67.

Rubinstein, Dana, and Stefanos Chen. 2024. "New York City Is Still a Democratic Town. But Trump Made Inroads." *New York Times*. https://www.nytimes.com/2024/11/06/nyregion/trump-nyc-voters.html.

Ruiz, Neil G., Luis Noe-Bustamante, and Sono Shah. 2023a. "Appendix: Demographic Profile of Asian American Adults." Pew Research Center. https://www.pewresearch.org/race-and-ethnicity/2023/05/08/asian-american-identity-appendix-demographic-profile-of-asian-american-adults.

Ruiz, Neil G., Luis Noe-Bustamante, and Sono Shah. 2023b. "Diverse Cultures and Shared Experiences Shape Asian American Identities." Pew Research Center. https://www.pewresearch.org/race-ethnicity/2023/05/08/diverse-cultures-and-shared-experiences-shape-asian-american-identities/.

Ryan, Camille, and Kurt Bauman. 2016. *Educational Attainment in the United States: 2015*. US Census Bureau. https://www.census.gov/content/dam/Census/library/publications/2016/demo/p20-578.pdf.

Saavedra Cisneros, Angel. 2017. *Latino Identity and Political Attitudes: Why Are Latinos Not Republican?* Palgrave Macmillan.

Sadhwani, Sara. 2022. "Asian American Mobilization: The Effect of Candidates and Districts on Asian American Voting Behavior." *Political Behavior* 44(1): 105–31.

Saiz, Martin. 1999. *Do Political Parties Matter in U.S. Cities?* Routledge.

Samson, Carl. 2024. "How Trump Won More Asian American Voters in 2024." Yahoo News. https://ca.news.yahoo.com/trump-won-more-asian-american-201944810.html.

Sanchez, Gabriel R., and Natalie Masuoka. 2010. "Brown-Utility Heuristic? The Presence and Contributing Factors of Latino Linked Fate." *Hispanic Journal of Behavioral Sciences* 32(4): 519–31.

Sanchez, Gabriel R., and Edward D. Vargas. 2016. "Taking a Closer Look at Group Identity: The Link between Theory and Measurement of Group Consciousness and Linked Fate." *Political Research Quarterly* 69(1): 160–74.

Santoro, Wayne A., and Gary M. Segura. 2011. "Generational Status and Mexican American Political Participation: The Benefits and Limitations of Assimilation." *Political Research Quarterly* 64(1): 172–84.

Sapiro, Virginia. 2004. "Not Your Parent's Political Socialization: Introduction for a New Generation." *Annual Review of Political Science* 7(1): 1–23.

Schaffner, Brian F., Stephen Ansolabehere, and Sam Luks. 2021. "Cooperative Election Study Common Content, 2020." Harvard Dataverse. https://doi.org/doi:10.7910/DVN/E9N6PH.

Schickler, Eric. 2016. Racial Realignment *Racial Realignment: The Transformation of American Liberalism, 1932–1965*. Princeton University Press.
Sears, David O., and Carolyn L. Funk. 1999. "Evidence of the Long-Term Persistence of Adults' Political Predispositions." *Journal of Politics* 61(1): 1–28.
Second-Generation Americans: A Portrait of the Adult Children of Immigrants. 2013. Pew Research Center. https://www.pewsocialtrends.org/2013/02/07/chapter-5-intergroup-relations/.
Segura, Gary M. 2012. "Latino Public Opinion & Realigning the American Electorate." *Daedalus* 141(4): 98–113.
Seitz-Wald, Alex. 2022. "Democrats Target Asian Americans with New Super PAC." *NBC News*. https://www.nbcnews.com/politics/2022-election/democrats-target-asian-americans-new-super-pac-rcna29875.
"Sep 2024 AAPI Voter Survey." 2024. AAPI Data. https://aapidata.com/surveys/sept-2024-aapi-voter-survey/.
Sesin, Carmen. 2022. "Why Florida Latinos Turned out in Favor of Republicans." *NBC News*. https://www.nbcnews.com/news/latino/florida-latinos-turned-favor-republicans-rcna57167.
Settle, Jaime E. 2018. *Frenemies: How Social Media Polarizes America*. Cambridge University Press.
Shah, Sono, and Karthick Ramakrishnan. 2018. "Where Can AAPI Voters Have Maximum Impact in 2018?" *AAPI Data Blog*. https://aapidata.com/blog/aapi-voters-2018-impact/.
Sidanius, James, Shana Levin, Colette Van Laar, and David O. Sears. 2008. *The Diversity Challenge: Social Identity and Intergroup Relations on the College Campus*. Russell Sage Foundation.
Sinclair, Betsy. 2012. *The Social Citizen: Peer Networks and Political Behavior*. University of Chicago Press.
Sismaet, Kyrie. 2022. "10 Bay Area AAPI Organizations to Support and Show Solidarity With." *San Francisco Magazine*. http://sanfran.com/sf-bay-area-aapi-organizations-to-support.
Smith, Candis Watts, Tehama Lopez Bunyasi, and Jasmine Carrera Smith. 2019. "Linked Fate over Time and across Generations." *Politics, Groups, and Identities* 7(3): 684–94.
Sparacino, Anthony. 2021. "The Democratic and Republican Governors Associations and the Nationalization of American Party Politics, 1961–1968." *Studies in American Political Development* 35(1): 76–103.
Stamm, Stephanie, and Aaron Zitner. 2022. "Where Democrats' Grip on Minority Voters Could Slip in Midterm Elections." *Wall Street Journal*. https://www.wsj.com/articles/where-democrats-grip-on-minority-voters-could-slip-in-midterm-elections-11664500307.
Staton, Jeffrey K., Robert A. Jackson, and Damarys Canache. 2007. "Dual Nationality Among Latinos: What Are the Implications for Political Connectedness?" *Journal of Politics* 69(2): 470–82.
Stevens, Mitchell L., Elizabeth A. Armstrong, and Richard Arum. 2008. "Sieve, Incubator, Temple, Hub: Empirical and Theoretical Advances in the Sociology of Higher Education." *Annual Review of Sociology* 34(1): 127–51.
Stinebrickner, Ralph, and Todd R. Stinebrickner. 2006. "What Can Be Learned About Peer Effects Using College Roommates? Evidence From New Survey Data and Students from Disadvantaged Backgrounds." *Journal of Public Economics* 90(8–9): 1435–54.
Street, Alex, Chris Zepeda-Millán, and Michael Jones-Correa. 2015. "Mass Deportations and the Future of Latino Partisanship." *Social Science Quarterly* 96(2): 540–52.

Sui, Mingxiao, and Newly Paul. 2017. "Transnational Political Engagement: Asian Americans' Participation in US Politics and in the Politics of Their Nation of Origin." *Asian Journal of Comparative Politics* 2(3): 273–92.
Taber, Charles S. 2003. "Information Processing and Public Opinion." In *Oxford Handbook of Political Psychology*, ed. Leonie Huddy, David O Sears, Jack S. Levy. Oxford University Press, 433–76.
Taber, Charles S., and Milton Lodge. 2006. "Motivated Skepticism in the Evaluation of Political Beliefs." *American Journal of Political Science* 50(3): 755–69.
Takaki, Ronald. 1998. *Strangers from a Different Shore: A History of Asian Americans*, Updated and Revised Edition. Little, Brown, and Company.
Tausanovitch, Chris, and Christopher Warshaw. 2014. "Representation in Municipal Government." *American Political Science Review* 108(3): 605–41.
Tedin, Kent L. 1980. "Assessing Peer and Parent Influence on Adolescent Political Attitudes." *American Journal of Political Science* 24(1): 136–54.
Tesler, Michael. 2016. *Post-Racial or Most-Racial?: Race and Politics in the Obama Era*. University of Chicago Press.
The Ethnic Media in America: The Giant Hidden in Plain Sight. 2005. NPR. https://legacy.npr.org/documents/2005/jul/ncmfreport.pdf.
The State of Latino News Media. 2019. The City University of New York: Craig Newmark Graduate School of Journalism. https://thelatinomediareport.journalism.cuny.edu/latino-news-consumers/.
Tichenor, Daniel J. 2002. *Dividing Lines: The Politics of Immigration Control in America*. Princeton University Press.
Tourangeau, Roger, Brad Edwardds, Timothy P. Johnson, Kirk M. Wolter, and Nancy Baates, eds. 2014. *Hard-to-Survey Populations*. Cambridge University Press.
Tran, Alisia G. T. T., and Richard M. Lee. 2011. "Cultural Socialization as a Moderator of Friendships and Social Competence." *Cultural Diversity and Ethnic Minority Psychology* 17(4): 456–61.
Tyler, Matthew, Justin Grimmer, and Shanto Iyengar. 2022. "Partisan Enclaves and Information Bazaars: Mapping Selective Exposure to Online News." *Journal of Politics* 84(2): 1057–73.
Tyler, Matthew, and Shanto Iyengar. 2023. "Learning to Dislike Your Opponents: Political Socialization in the Era of Polarization." *American Political Science Review* 117(1): 347–54.
Ulloa, Jazmine. 2023. "As Haley and Ramaswamy Rise, Some Indian Americans Have Mixed Feelings." *New York Times*. https://www.nytimes.com/2023/09/25/us/politics/haley-ramaswamy-indian-americans.html.
US Census. n.d. "U.S. Census Population Estimates—County Level." Duke University Library. Research Data Repository. https://library.duke.edu/data/sources/popest.
US Census Bureau. 2020a. "Race 1980-2020. Harris County and Fort Bend County, Texas" https://www.socialexplorer.com/data/C2020/metadata?ds=SE&table=T005.
US Census Bureau. 2020b. "Real Median Household Income by Race and Hispanic Origin: 1967 to 2000." https://www.census.gov/content/dam/Census/library/visualizations/2021/demo/p60-273/figure2.pdf.
US Census Bureau. 2021a. "Asian by Specific Origin (Asian with One Asian Category for Selected Groups). Houston-The Woodlands-Sugar Land, TX Metro Area; Texas." https://www.socialexplorer.com/data/ACS2021_5yr/metadata?ds=SE&table=A03002.
US Census Bureau. 2021b. "Asian Alone or in Combination by Selected Groups, American Community Survey 1-Year Estimates," Table B02018. https://data.census.gov/table?q=B02018&y=2021.
US Census Bureau. 2023a. "Decennial Census of Population and Housing." https://www.census.gov/programs-surveys/decennial-census/decade.html.

US Census Bureau. 2023b. "2023 National Population Projections Tables: Main Series." https://www.census.gov/data/tables/2023/demo/popproj/2023-summary-tables.html.
US Census Bureau. 2024a. "American Community Survey 1-Year Data (2005–2023)." https://www.census.gov/data/developers/data-sets/acs-1year.html.
US Census Bureau. 2024b. "American Community Survey 5-Year Data (2009–2023)." https://www.census.gov/data/developers/data-sets/acs-5year.html.
US Department of Education. 2022. "Biden-Harris Administration Continues Fight for Student Debt Relief for Millions of Borrowers, Extends Student Loan Repayment Pause." https://www.ed.gov/news/press-releases/biden-harris-administration-continues-fight-student-debt-relief-millions-borrowers-extends-student-loan-repayment-pause.
Valenzuela, Ali Adam. 2014. "Tending the Flock: Latino Religious Commitments and Political Preferences." *Political Research Quarterly* 67(4): 930–42.
Venkatraman, Sakshi. 2023. "Biden Campaign Releases First TV Ad Speaking to Asian Americans and Pacific Islanders." *NBC News*. https://www.nbcnews.com/news/asian-america/biden-campaign-releases-first-tv-ad-speaking-asian-americans-pacific-i-rcna123922.
Verba, Sidney, Kay Lehman Schlozman, and Henry E. Brady. 1995. *Voice and Equality: Civic Voluntarism in American Politics*. Harvard University Press.
Vespa, Jonathan, Lauren Medina, and David M. Armstrong. 2018. *Demographic Turning Points for the United States: Population Projections for 2020 to 2060*. US Census Bureau. https://www.census.gov/content/dam/Census/library/publications/2020/demo/p25-1144.pdf.
Vestal, Allan James, Andrew Briz, Annette Choi, Beatrice Jin, Andrew McGill, and Lily Mihalik. 2021. "Live Election Results: 2020 Pennsylvania Results." *Politico*. https://www.politico.com/2020-election/results/pennsylvania/.
Võ, Linda Trinh. 2004. *Mobilizing an Asian American Community*. Temple University Press.
Wals, Sergio C. 2011. "Does What Happens in Los Mochis Stay in Los Mochis? Explaining Postmigration Political Behavior." *Political Research Quarterly* 64(3): 600–11.
Wals, Sergio C. 2013. "Made in the USA? Immigrants' Imported Ideology and Political Engagement." *Electoral Studies* 32(4): 756–67.
Wang, Xinyue, Stephanie L. Haft, and Qing Zhou. 2023. "Reasons for Migration, Post-Migration Sociocultural Characteristics, and Parenting Styles of Chinese American Immigrant Families." *Children* 10(4): 612.
Wattenberg, Martin P. 1991. *The Rise of Candidate-Centered Politics: Presidential Elections of the 1980s*. Harvard University Press.
White, Ismail K., and Chryl N. Laird. 2020. *Steadfast Democrats: How Social Forces Shape Black Political Behavior*. Princeton University Press.
White, Stephen, Neil Nevitte, André Blias, Elisabeth Gidengil, and Patrick Fournier. 2008. "The Political Resocialization of Immigrants: Resistance or Lifelong Learning?" *Political Research Quarterly* 61(2): 268–81.
Willeck, Claire, and Tali Mendelberg. 2022. "Education and Political Participation." *Annual Review of Political Science* 25(1): 89–110.
Winter, Ethan. 2020. *Voters Support Accountability for Predatory Colleges and Executives, Support Tackling Student Debt Issues*. Data for Progress. https://www.defendstudents.org/news/body/docket/100-Day-Docket-Policy-Poll-Memo.pdf.
Wong, Carolyn. 2017. *Voting Together: Intergenerational Politics and Civic Engagement among Hmong Americans*. Stanford University Press.

Wong, Janelle S. 2000. "The Effects of Age and Political Exposure on the Development of Party Identification Among Asian American and Latino Immigrants in the United States." *Political Behavior* 22(4): 341–71.
Wong, Janelle S. 2005. "Mobilizing Asian American Voters: A Field Experiment." *The Annals of the American Academy of Political and Social Science* 601: 102–14.
Wong, Janelle S. 2006. *Democracy's Promise: Immigrants and American Civic Institutions*. University of Michigan Press.
Wong, Janelle S. 2015. "The Role of Born-Again Identity on the Political Attitudes of Whites, Blacks, Latinos, and Asian Americans." *Politics and Religion* 8(4): 641–78.
Wong, Janelle S. 2018. *Immigrants, Evangelicals, and Politics in an Era of Demographic Change*. Russell Sage Foundation.
Wong, Janelle S., Pei-te Lien, and M. Margaret Conway. 2005. "Group-Based Resources and Political Participation among Asian Americans." *American Politics Research* 33(4): 545–76.
Wong, Janelle S., and Karthick Ramakrishnan. 2023. "Asian Americans and the Politics of the Twenty-First Century." *Annual Review of Political Science* 26(1): 305–23.
Wong, Janelle S., Karthick Ramakrishnan, Taeku Lee, and Jane Junn. 2011. *Asian American Political Participation: Emerging Constituents and Their Political Identities*. Russell Sage Foundation.
Wong, Janelle, and Ricardo Ramirez. 2006. "Non-Partisan Asian American and Latino Contactability and Voter Mobilization." In *Transforming Politics, Transforming America: The Political and Civic Incorporation of Immigrants in the United States*, ed. Taeku Lee, Karithik Ramakrishnan, and Ricardo Ramírez. University of Virginia Press, 89–105.
Wong, Janelle, and Vivian Tseng. 2008. "Political Socialisation in Immigrant Families: Challenging Top-Down Parental Socialisation Models." *Journal of Ethnic and Migration Studies* 34(1): 151–68.
Yam, Kimmy. 2020. "Asian American 1st-Time Voters Who Helped Flip GOP District Mobilize for Georgia Runoff." *NBC News*. https://www.nbcnews.com/news/asian-america/how-asian-american-1st-time-voters-who-helped-flip-gop-n1251175.
Yam, Kimberly. 2024. "Asian Americans Favored Harris but Shifted Right by 5 Points." *NBC News*. https://www.nbcnews.com/news/asian-america/asian-americans-exit-poll-harris-trump-rcna179005.
Yang, Alan, and Rodolfo O. de la Garza. 2017. "Americanizing Latinos, Latinoizing America: The Political Consequences of Latino Incorporation∗." *Social Science Quarterly* 98(2): 690–727.
Yoo, Jo-Ann, and Sandra Ung. 2022. "Empowering New York City's Asian American Voters." *Gotham Gazette*. https://www.gothamgazette.com/130-opinion/11656-empowering-new-york-city-asian-american-voters.
"Youth Studies Series." 2021. Inter-university Consortium for Political and Social Research [distributor]. https://www.icpsr.umich.edu/web/ICPSR/series/138.
Zarate, Maria Estela, and Rebeca Burciaga. 2010. "Latinos and College Access: Trends and Future Directions." *Journal of College Admission*. 209: 24-9.
Zeleny, Jeff. 2024. "In Razor-Thin Georgia, Harris Campaign Eyeing Asian American Voters." *CNN*. https://www.cnn.com/2024/09/30/politics/asian-american-voters-georgia-harris-trump/index.html.
Zheng, Bang Quan. 2019. "The Patterns of Asian Americans' Partisan Choice: Policy Preferences and Racial Consciousness." *Social Science Quarterly* 100(5): 1593–608.

Zhou, Min, and Yang Sao Xiong. 2005. "The Multifaceted American Experiences of the Children of Asian Immigrants: Lessons for Segmented Assimilation." *Ethnic and Racial Studies* 28(6): 1119–52.

Zingher, Joshua N. 2022. "TRENDS: Diploma Divide: Educational Attainment and the Realignment of the American Electorate." *Political Research Quarterly* 75(2): 263–77.

Zong, Jie. 2022. "A Mosaic, not a Monolith: A Profile of the U.S. Latino Population, 2000–2020." Latino Policy & Politics Institute. https://latino.ucla.edu/research/latino-population-2000-2020/.

Index

For the benefit of digital users, indexed terms that span two pages (e.g., 52–53) may, on occasion, appear on only one of those pages.

Tables, figures, and boxes are indicated by an italic *t*, *f*, or *b*.

abortion, college student views on, 144
Abrajano, Marisa, 102
acculturation, political socialization and, 26
advocacy groups, political socialization and, 98–99
African Americans
   civic education and political engagement among, 131–132
   college peer influence hypothesis and, 134, 135*t*, 136
   college student political attitudes among, 138–142, 139*t*, 141*f*
   cross-racial friendships among, 16, 57–58, 134, 138, 142–146
   Democratic party support among, 9, 10*f*, 12, 27
   linked fate theory and political behavior of, 72
   parental influence on, 134
   partisanship development in, 27
   partisan views in peer networks of, 21, 130
   in political office, 30
   political socialization among, 27
Aleksynska, Mariya, 55
American Community Survey, 41–42
Andersen, Kristi, 35–36
Asian American Political Participation: Emerging Constituents and Their Political Identities (Wong, Ramakrishnan, Lee & Junn), 29–30, 31–32
Asian Americans
   citizenship status of, 7–8, 12
   civic engagement among, 29–33
   college enrollment data on, 128–129, 129*f*, 132–133
   college political ideology impact on, 146–148, 147*f*
   college student political orientation among, 133, 138–142, 139*t*, 141*f*, 180–181
   cross-racial friendships among, 16, 57–58, 133, 138, 142–146
   defined, 1n.1
   Democratic Party support among, 3–5, 31–33, 107–109, 108*f*
   ethnic media consumption among, 56
   ethnic subgroups within, 3–4, 16–18
   foreign-born percentages for, 17, 34–35
   geographic distribution of, 3
   Houston, TX demographics for, 41–46
   income disparity among, 12n.5
   national origin groups within, 16–17
   nonpartisanship among, 12, 28, 74–75
   nonvoters among, 12
   pan-ethnic identification among, 17–18
   partisanship among, 29–33
   peer networks among, 40–46, 130, 151–152, 152*f*, 180
   peer social endorsement treatment effects among, 172
   political influence of, 1–8, 177–178, 184–186
   political learning among, 41–46, 178–181
   population statistics for, 1–3, 2*f*, 18, 41, 186–187
   residential settlement patterns of, 63
   respondent race hypothesis and Republican Party preference among, 172–174, 173*t*
   vote choice by national origin, 9, 11*f*
   voter turnout among, 17, 29–30
   voting trends among, 8–13, 21–22, 187–188
Asian American Voter Survey (AAVS), 9, 31
"Asian Donorgate" scandal, 7
Asians Making America Great Again, 177
The Atlantic magazine, 68–69
authoritarian regimes, political preference of immigrants from, 12, 31, 72

Bangladeshi Americans, vote choice among, 9, 11*f*
Behind the Mule: Race and Class in African-American Politics (Dawson), 27
Between Two Nations: The Political Predicament of Latinos in New York City (Jones-Correa), 53–54
Biden, Joseph, 3–4, 177–178, 187–189
   Asian American support for, 4–5, 9, 32–33, 68
Bovitz survey research firm, 105
Bowers, Jake, 34

Callahan, Rebecca, 131
Cambodian Americans, vote choice among, 9, 11*f*
campus belonging hypothesis, peer group partisan endorsement and, 160, 172–174
candidate-centered campaigns, immigrant mobilization and, 35, 37–38
Carlos, Robert, 51–52, 101
Carlson, Taylor, 102
Carmines, Edward, 6
Chan, Nathan, 32–33
Chang, Michael, 7
Chen, Jay, 5, 187
Chinese Americans
   Democratic support among, 70, 76*f*, 76, 78, 79*f*, 80, 107–109, 108*f*, 115
   family interactions on politics and, 94
   frequency of family and peer political discussion among, 110
   in Houston, TX, 41–42
   lack of parental political socialization among, 47–48
   partisan preference among, 31, 72
   population growth of, 1–3, 2*f*
   residential patterns and population share, 82*f*, 83*f*, 83–84
   second-generation peer networks among, 61
   vote choice among, 9, 11*f*
Chow F-test, 143n.8
Cooperative Institutional Research Program (CIRP), 129–130, 136–137
Citizens, Politics, and Social Communication: Information and Influence in an Electoral Campaign (Huckfeldt & Sprague), 39
citizenship status
   of Asian Americans, 7–8, 42, 46
   legal restrictions on, 36
civic engagement
   Asian American patterns of, 29–30
   national origin and, 53

partisan acquisition and role of, 101, 186
peer groups and youth political engagement and, 131–132
pre-migration socialization and re-socialization and, 54–55
Civil Rights Act of 1964, 6
class dynamics, Latino partisan preference linked to, 28
Clinton, Bill, Asian American support for, 31
Clinton, Hillary, 42
   Asian American support for, 9, 32
co-ethnic voters, minority candidate elections and, 30
Collaborative Multi-Racial Post-Election Survey (CMPS), 9, 20–21, 31–32, 130, 148–152
college peer influence hypothesis
   cross-racial interactions and political views and, 142–146, 144*f*
   summary of, 135*t*, 136
College Pulse research firm, 164
college student peer groups. *See also* peer groups
   campus social networks and, 156–158
   changing political attitudes among, 138–142, 139*t*, 141*f*, 180–181
   college political ideology and, 146–148, 147*f*
   demographic variables in surveys with, 165–166
   discrimination within, 33
   Latino political socialization and, 134, 135*t*, 136, 138, 139*t*, 140, 183
   longitudinal national survey data on, 136–138
   media infographics influence on, 161–163
   non-Asian groups, 20–21, 182
   partisan views among, 19–20n.9, 60–63, 158–160
   party mobilization and, 37
   political endorsements from, 156–158
   political learning on campus and, 127–130, 153–155
   race, political discussion, and sense of belonging and, 172–174
   social effects on students of, 133
   social transmission through, 21, 50, 129–130, 133–136
   summary of hypotheses on, 133–136, 135*t*
Collet, Christian, 29
Communist regimes, political preference of immigrants from, 12, 31, 72
community interaction and organization

immigrant political mobilization and, 35, 37–38, 98–99, 184–185
peer networks and, 50
social transmission and role of, 63–64
conservative ideology, Asian American identification with, 12, 14–15, 14–15n.7
Converse, Philip E., 138–139
Conway, Margaret, 32
Cooperative Election Study (CES) surveys, 14–15n.7, 71
Cooperative Institutional Research Program (CIRP), 129–130, 136–138
Cornwell, Elmer, 35
COVID-19 pandemic
anti-Asian messaging during, 32–33
Asian American discrimination during, 12
Cramer, Katherine, 101–102
cross-racial interactions. *See also* race
partisanship and role of, 16
political views and influence of, 16, 57–58, 134, 138, 142–146, 144f, 154

Dawson, Michael, 27
Democracy's Promise: Immigrants and American Civic Institutions (Wong), 22, 36, 186
Democratic Party
African American support for, 9, 10f, 12, 27, 134
Asian American support for, 4–5, 6–13, 33, 76f, 76–80, 158, 175, 177–179, 185–189
college student support for, 37, 62–63
decline in recruitment by, 98–99
discrimination linked to support for, 12, 16, 32–33
failure of state and local level mobilization by, 36–37
higher education linked to support for, 62–63, 140–141
Houston-area Asian American identification with, 42–43
immigrant political mobilization by, 35–36
Latino support for, 28
local partisan context and support for, 76–80, 80f
minority group support for, 6
peer partisan influence hypothesis and preference for, 103, 113–114, 113t, 114t
peer social endorsement treatment effects on ratings of, 169–172, 170f, 171f, 175
policy proposals linked to, 159t, 161–162, 167
positive peer messages from, 157–158

racial group influence hypothesis and support for, 122–123, 123f
social transmission as predictor of support for, 63–64, 184
vote share by race for, 9, 10f
demographic variables
in college student surveys, 165–166
Houston-based Asian Americans, 41–46
Dempsey, Matthew C., 183
Dey, Eric, 132
discrimination experience
partisan preference and, 12, 16, 32–33, 71–72, 99
summary of, 73t
Downsian theory, policy preference and partisanship in, 65

educational settings. *See also* higher education
Asian American educational achievement and, 62
Asian American partisanship and, 32, 132–133
ideological gap and, 62–63
partisan acquisition and role of, 101
partisan statements on higher education and, 161–162
peer network diversity in, 60–63
transitional and second-generation Asian American political views in, 60–63, 97
youth political engagement and peer groups in, 131–132
electoral politics
Asian American influence in, 1–8, 177–178, 187–188
Asian American vote choice in, 8–13
immigration law and policy and, 6–7
Erie, Steven, 35–36
ethnic media, immigrant political learning and, 56
ethno-racial minorities
civic education impact on, 131
minority voter support for candidates from, 30
partisanship development among, 27–28
political mobilization of, 35–39
Europe, immigrant political socialization in, 54–55
European immigrants, pre-migration socialization and re-socialization among, 54–55
Evangelical Christianity
Asian American identification with, 12

Evangelical Christianity (*Continued*)
  Asian American partisan preference and, 71–72
exit polling, Asian American vote choice and limits of, 9

familial influence. *See also* parental influence
  frequency of political discussions and, 102, 107, 109–113, 110*f*, 111*f*, 173–174
  lack of political socialization linked to, 46–49, 182
  limits of influence on partisan choice in, 118–119, 119*t*, 123
  OAAS study of partisan acquisition and, 105–107
  partisan acquisition and, 34–35, 98–104, 124
  on partisan choice, 13–14, 113–119, 115*t*, 117*f*
  peer networks *vs.*, 20, 104*t*, 105–107
  polarization and role of, 182–183
  political learning and, 34–35
  second-generation Asian American political views and, 98–104
  social networks and, 58–60
family political discussion hypothesis, peer group partisan endorsement and, 159*t*, 160, 173–174
Feldman, Jan, 54
Fernandez, Kenneth E., 183
Filipino Americans
  Democratic partisanship among, 107–109, 108*f*, 115
  in Houston, TX, 41–42
  local partisan context impact on, 86
  population growth of, 1–3, 2*f*
  Republican Party affiliation among, 109
  residential patterns and population share, 82*f*, 83*f*, 83–84
  subgroup variation hypothesis and, 80
  Trump support among, 68
  vote choice among, 9, 11*f*, 76*f*, 76, 78, 79*f*, 86
first-generation Asian Americans
  defined, 17–18
  Democratic support among, 107–109, 108*f*
  peer influence among, 58–60, 103, 106, 180
  peer network racial homogeneity among, 15–16, 57–58
  population data on, 15
Fong, Dominique, 94, 97, 112
Fort Bend County, Texas, Asian American political affiliation in, 41–46

Forthright panel, 105
frequency of political discussion measures
  Democratic Party ratings and, 113*t*, 114–115, 115*t*, 115*f*
  family influence and, 102, 107, 109–113, 110*f*, 111*f*
  limits of influence on partisan choice and, 118–119, 119*t*
  partisan choice and, 113–119
  peer influence and, 102, 107, 109–113, 110*f*, 111*f*, 117–118, 118*f*
full model of vote choice, 86–88, 87*f*
Fung, Margaret, 4–5, 177

Galvin, David, 37
García Bedolla, Lisa, 102
generational status
  Asian American partisanship and, 32, 98–104
  defined, 17–18
  Democratic support among Asian Americans and, 107–109, 108*f*
  Latino partisan preference linked to, 28
  OAAS sample variation by, 106
  NAAS sample variation by, 74
  peer group racial composition and, 57–58, 98, 103, 104*t*, 120–123, 121*f*
  social transmission and, 26, 57–58
geographic Asian American population centers, 14, 81*f*, 81, 82*f*
Georgia
  Asian American community in, 3–4
  Asian American political influence in, 1–8, 177

Hajnal, Zoltan, 6, 12, 27–28, 31–32, 34–36, 101
Hamlin, Rebecca, 37
Harris, Kamala, 9, 42, 177–178, 188–189
Harris County, Texas, Asian American political affiliation in, 41–46
Hess, Robert, 101
higher education. *See also* college peer influence hypothesis; college student peer groups; educational settings
  Asian American college enrollment, 128–129, 129*f*
  Asian American partisanship and, 32, 132–133
  Asian American political learning in, 132–133
  partisan policies on, 159*t*, 161–162
  summary of hypotheses on, 133–136, 135*t*

Higher Education Research Institute
    (HERI), 129–130
Hmong Americans, voter turnout and civic
    engagement among, 30
Hochul, Kathy, 188
Hopkins, Dan, 33
Houston, Texas
    Asian American partisan composition
        in, 19–20n.10, 26–27, 41–46
    population data on Asian Americans in, 43,
        43n.9, 44*f*, 45*f*
"How to Talk to Your Parents about Politics"
    (Fong), 94
Huckfeldt, Robert, 39–40

ideological change hypothesis
    changes in college student political attitudes
        and, 140–142, 141*f*
    college student political views and, 134,
        135*t*, 140–142
ideological context hypothesis, 135*t*, 136,
    146–148, 147*f*, 153
immediate discussion networks, vote choice
    and, 40
immigrants and immigration. *See also*
    generational status
    Asian American experience with, 12, 17, 33
    college students from immigrant
        families, 132–133, 140
    decline in party focus on, 36–37
    electoral politics and role of, 22
    familial influence on political views
        and, 98–104
    labor union political mobilization and, 37
    law and policy on, electoral politics and, 6–7
    local partisan context and vote choice
        among, 90–92, 91*f*
    Muslim immigrants to Europe, 55
    parties' engagement and recruitment
        and, 58–60, 98
    partisan acquisition and, 25, 98–104
    partisanship acquisition and, 14, 27–28, 39
    peer influence among, 58–60, 140
    political socialization and, 181–184
    pre-migration socialization and
        re-socialization and, 54–55
    reverse intergenerational political
        socialization among, 34
    rural settlement by, 184
    social transmission and, 49–58, 140
Immigration and Nationality Act of 1965, 6
Indian American Impact, 4–5
Indian Americans
    Democratic partisanship among, 53, 70,
        76*f*, 76, 78, 79*f*, 80, 107–109, 108*f*, 115
    familial influence on political learning
        among, 49, 59, 96
    frequency of family and peer political
        discussion in, 110
    in Houston, TX, 41–42
    population growth of, 1–3, 2*f*
    residential patterns and population
        share, 82*f*, 83*f*, 83–84
    vote choice among, 9, 11*f*
infographics
    college student endorsements and, 161–163,
        166, 175
    peer social endorsement treatment effects
        and, 168–171, 169*f*, 170*f*, 171*f*
    respondents' understanding of, 167
information processing theory, policy
    preferences and, 65–66n.11
intergenerational transmission
    Asian American political mobilization
        and, 185
    partisan acquisition and role of, 34–35,
        98–104
*Issue Evolution: Race and the Transformation of
    American Politics* (Carmines &
    Stimson), 6

Japanese Americans
    acculturation of, 26
    Democratic partisanship among, 53, 76*f*,
        76, 78, 79*f*, 80, 107–109, 108*f*, 115
    frequency of family and peer political
        discussion in, 110–111
    population decline of, 1–3, 2*f*
    residential patterns and population
        share, 82*f*, 83*f*, 83–84
    vote choice among, 9, 11*f*
Jennings, Kent, 34, 131–132
Johnson, Lyndon, 6
Jones-Correa, Michael, 53–54
Junn, Jane, 29–30
Justice Unites Us (political action
    committee), 5

Kao, Jason, 188
Kim, Jae Yeon, 32–33
Kim, Thomas, 7
Kinder Houston Area Survey (2020), 42–43
Korean Americans
    college peer interactions among, 127
    Democratic party support among, 53, 70,
        72, 107–109, 108*f*, 115

Korean Americans (*Continued*)
  frequency of family and peer political discussion in, 110
  in Houston, TX, 41–42
  parental lack of political socialization in families of, 47
  population growth of, 1–3, 2*f*
  residential patterns and population share, 82*f*, 83*f*, 83–84
  transitional generation peer networks, 61
  vote choice among, 9, 11*f*, 76*f*, 76, 78, 79*f*
Kuh, George, 156
Kuo, Alexander, 25, 32–33

labor unions, political mobilization among, 37
Laird, Cheryl, 27
Langton, Kenneth, 131–132
Latinos
  civic education and political engagement among youth in, 131–132
  college student peer influence and, 134, 135*t*, 136, 138, 139*t*, 140
  college student political orientation among, 134, 138–142, 139*t*, 141*f*, 183
  cross-racial friendships among, 57–58, 142–146
  naturalization delay among, 53–54
  nonpartisanship among, 28
  partisan preferences among, 28
  peer networks among, 20–21
  political socialization of, 183
Le, Anne, 1
Lee, David, 29, 33
Lee, Taeku, 6, 12, 27–28, 29–30, 31–32, 34–36, 101
Leung, Vivien, 32–33, 105
Levin, Shana, 133
LGBT community, social transmission and, 21, 66, 184
Lien, Pie-te, 29, 32
linked fate hypothesis
  Asian American partisan preference and, 72
  summary of, 73*t*
local Asian American context
  Asian American population size and, 75, 81*f*, 82*f*
  vote choice and, 81–84, 83*f*
local partisan context hypothesis
  accounting for alternative explanations for vote choice, 86–88
  Asian American vote choice and, 71, 76–80, 84–86
  immigrant residential selection and vote choice and, 90–92, 91*f*
  NAAS evidence for, 72–75
  national origin vote choice and, 76–80, 79*f*, 80*f*
  peer partisan influence hypothesis and, 103
  political motivation for residential selection, 88–92, 89*t*
  summary of, 73*t*
  vote choice prediction and, 75, 84–86, 85*f*
local partisan norms
  Asian American vote choice and, 20, 39–40, 68–72, 76–80
  political socialization within, 39–40
  residential and environmental factors in, 64
  social transmission and, 25–26, 70–72
  subgroup variation hypothesis, 71

machine politics, immigrant mobilization through, 35–39
main model of vote choice, 86–88, 87*f*
mainstream media, immigrant political learning and, 55–56
majority-party districts, Asian American vote choice and, 86–88, 87*f*
Makhija, Neil, 4–5
Malhotra, Neil, 25, 32–33
Masuoka, Natalie, 32, 75
McCain, John, Asian American support for, 76
McCann, James, 38
mediated political communication, immigrant political learning and, 55–57
Mexican immigrants
  candidate-centered campaign focus on, 38
  pre-migration socialization and re-socialization and, 54
Milkman, Ruth, 37
Mo, Cecilia, 25, 32–33
Muller, Chandra, 131
Mummolo, Jonathan, 64

naive model of vote choice, 86–88, 87*f*
Nall, Clayton, 64
National Asian American Post-Election Survey, peer network diversity in, 57
National Asian American Survey (NAAS)
  Asian American partisanship data, 19n.8
  civic engagement and partisanship data from, 29–30
  geographical indicators in, 74
  local partisan dynamics and Asian American vote choice, 69–70, 72–75
  partisan preference data, 31–32

on transnational political activity, 54
vote share data in, 9
national origin
  Asian American population percentages and, 81–83, 82f
  Asian American subgroups, 16–17
  civic engagement and, 53
  Democratic support and, 76f, 76, 108f, 109
  frequency of peer and family political discussion and, 109–113, 110f
  of Houston, TX Asian Americans, 46
  local partisan dynamics and, 73–74, 76–80, 79f, 80f
  partisan preference and, 31, 53, 71–72, 99
  social transmission and role of, 26
  summary of, 73t
  vote choice and, 9, 11f, 88
National Populations Project, 186–187
Native Americans, partisanship patterns among, 28
naturalization status for immigrants
  of Houston, Texas Asian Americans, 46
  party machine facilitation of, 35–36
neighborhood characteristics, partisan socialization and, 39–40
Nelsen, Matthew, 131
Neundorf, Anja, 131
news coverage, immigrant political learning and, 55–56
Niemi, Richard, 34, 131
Nishikawa Chávez, Katsuo, 38
non-Asian peer networks
  college peer groups, 20–21, 175–176
  political influence on Asian Americans of, 64–65, 122–123, 123f
nonimmigrant groups, political socialization in, 181–183
nonpartisanship
  among Asian Americans, 12, 28–30
  among ethno-racial minorities, 27–28
  among immigrants, 34–35
  among Latinos, 28
  intended vote choice and, 74–75

Obama, Barack
  Asian American support for, 9, 20, 31, 76f, 76
  immigrant-focused campaigning by, 38
  state and local politics impact of election of, 36–37
Omnibus Asian American Survey (OAAS) (2020), 19n.8, 97, 105–107
Ong, Paul, 29, 33

Open Science Framework (OSF), 163
Ossoff, Jon, Asian American support for, 1, 4–5

Pakistani Americans
  in Houston, TX, 41–42
  peer networks among, 60–62
  vote choice among, 9, 11f
pan-ethnic Asian American coalition, 17–18
parental influence. *See also* familial influence
  political discussion hypothesis and, 102
  political socialization and, 99–100
  youth political engagement and peer groups and, 131–133
Park, Sam, 4–5
partisan acquisition
  college student mobilization and, 37, 127
  familial influence on, 34–35, 98–104
  peer group influence on, 98–104, 104t, 113–119
  pre-migration socialization and re-socialization and, 54–55
  social transmission through peer networks and, 40–46
partisan preference (partisan choice)
  affective influences on, 158
  age and length of residence linked to, 51–52
  college peer influence on, 19n.9, 21, 156–158, 166, 168–172
  Democratic trend among Asian Americans, 31–33
  discrimination impact on, 12, 16
  ethno-racial minorities and immigrants and development of, 27–28
  familial influence on, 13–14, 106–107, 113–119
  frequency of political discussion linked to, 113–119
  of Houston area Asian Americans, 41–46
  immigrant experience and, 14
  limits of family influence on, 118–119, 119t
  local norms and, 14–15, 20
  national origin and, 53
  neighborhood demographics and, 39–40
  peer group influence on, 13–16, 98–104, 104t, 106–107, 117–118, 118f
  peer social endorsement treatment effects on, 169f, 169–172, 170f, 171f
  policy preference and, 65
  political socialization and, 13–16
party system, immigrant mobilization through, 35–39
peer endorsement hypothesis, 159t, 160

peer endorsement hypothesis (*Continued*)
    policy support and partisan preferences
        and, 169*f*, 170*f*, 171*f*
peer groups. *See also* college student peer
        groups; political socialization
    Asian American political learning
        and, 180–181, 185
    candidate mobilization of, 22
    civic education and youth political
        engagement and, 131–132
    Democratic Party ratings across discussions
        with, 113–114, 113*t*, 114*t*, 117*f*
    diversity in, 57–58, 60–63, 130, 133–136
    familial influence *vs.*, 20, 104*t*, 105–107
    frequency of political discussion in, 102,
        107, 109–113, 110*f*, 111*f*, 117–118
    generational status and composition
        of, 57–58, 98, 103, 120–123, 121*f*
    immigrant networks, 58–60
    influence on partisan choice in, 118–119,
        119*t*
    media consumption and, 56–57
    national origin and, 53
    non-Asian peers, political influence
        of, 64–65, 122–123
    nonimmigrant political socialization
        and, 182
    OAAS study of partisan influence
        of, 105–107
    partisan acquisition and, 19–20, 101–102,
        104*t*, 123–124
    partisan endorsements by, 158–160, 159*t*
    policy views, influence on, 65–66
    political discussion hypothesis
        and, 102–104, 104*t*, 109–113
    racial homogeneity in Asian American
        networks, 15–16
    social transmission through, 13–16, 25–26,
        40–46, 49–58
    transitional and second-generation Asian
        Americans and, 57–58, 60–63, 97
peer partisan influence hypothesis, 102–103,
        104*t*, 113–119, 117*f*
peer political discussion hypothesis, 159*t*, 160
Phan, Nicole, 1
Pilot National Asian American Political Survey
        (PNAAPS), 31–32
polarization
    familial influence and, 182–183
    political socialization and, 182
policy endorsements, 156–158, 161–162, 166,
        168–172
political crystallization hypothesis

changes in college student political
        orientation, 138–140, 139*t*
    college student political views and, 134, 135*t*
political discussion hypothesis, families and
    peer groups and, 102, 104*t*, 109–113
political learning
    among Asian Americans, 41–46, 178–181
    college peers and, 127–130
    familial influence on, 34–35, 58–60,
        109–113
political mobilization
    of Asian Americans, 184–186
    civic education and, 131
    co-ethnic candidates and, 30
    decline in, 36–37
    of immigrants, 35–39
    of labor unions, 37
    social transmission theory and, 21
political socialization
    acculturation and, 26
    Asian American college students
        and, 156–158
    Asian American partisanship and, 13–16
    Black voters and, 27
    college peer groups and, 133–136, 135*t*
    familial influence on, 34, 97, 102–104,
        109–113, 110*f*
    of immigrants, 183–184
    immigrants and process of, 140, 181–183
    institutions' role in, 98
    local partisan composition and, 39–40, 104
    mediated political communication
        and, 55–57
    in nonimmigrant groups, 181–183
    origins of, 13–14
    parental influence on, 97, 99–100
    research on, 19–20, 25
Progressive Era, party politics in, 36
protest activities, Asian American participation
        in, 29–30
Providence, Rhode Island, ethnic political
        mobilization in, 35

race. *See also* cross-racial interactions
    college peer groups and, 134, 138, 182
    college peer influence hypothesis and, 135*t*,
        136
    college political ideology and student
        political views and, 146–148, 147*f*
    neighborhood demographics, 39–40
    partisanship development role of, 27
    peer group diversity and, 26, 57–58, 130,
        133–134

political views and cross-racial interactions, 142–146, 144f
social transmission and role of, 15, 103
racial composition hypothesis, 103, 104t
racial group influence hypothesis, 104t
  Asian American partisan acquisition and, 103–104, 124
  political discussion and partisan choice and, 64–65, 122–123, 123f, 124
racial moderator hypothesis, 135t, 136
  cross-racial interactions and, 145
Ramakrishnan, Karthick, 17, 29–30
Reagan, Ronald, 6–7, 37–38
registered voters, Asian Americans as, 30
religion hypothesis, partisan preference and, 71–72, 88
Republican Party
  anti-Asian messages from, 32–33
  Asian American support for, 5–13, 14–15, 21–22, 31, 88, 158, 177–179, 185–189
  Black voters and, 27
  college student mobilization by, 37
  decline in recruitment by, 98–99
  Filipino American support for, 68
  focus on state and local level mobilization by, 36–37
  Houston-area Asian American identification with, 42–43
  Latino support for, 28
  majority-Republican local politics and Asian American support for, 70
  peer social endorsement treatment effects on ratings of, 169–172, 170f, 171f
  policy proposals linked to, 159t, 161–162
  positive peer messages from, 157–158
  respondent race hypothesis and support for, 172–174, 173t
residential selection
  Asian American preferences in, 18, 63–64, 88–92
  immigrant preferences and vote choice and, 90–92, 91f
  local partisan norms and Asian American vote choice linked to, 88–89
  political motivation for, 88–92
  social transmission and, 184
respondent race hypothesis
  partisan preference and, 172–174, 173t
  peer endorsements and, 160
reverse intergenerational political socialization
  familial influence on political views and, 96
  in immigrant families, 34, 49

Rice, Tom, 54
Rim, Kathy, 29

Sears, David, 133
second-generation Asian Americans
  ages of, 128
  college peer interactions among, 127–128
  defined, 17–18
  Democratic support among, 107–109, 108f
  family interactions on politics and, 98–104
  in Houston, Texas, 46
  parental lack of political socialization in, 46–49
  peer and family influence in partisan acquisition and, 60–63, 106, 180
  peer network diversity among, 16, 57–58, 60–63
  population data on, 15
Sidanius, James, 133–134, 138–139
Sinclair, Betsy, 102
Singaporean Americans, familial influence on political learning among, 59–60
Smets, Kaat, 131
social endorsement treatment effects, 169f, 169–172, 170f, 171f
"Social Exclusion and Political Identity" (Kuo, Malhotra & Mo), 25
social media
  college student endorsements and, 161–163
  immigrant political learning and, 56
social transmission theory
  Asian American partisan dynamics and, 43–46, 64–65, 66, 179–180
  college peer interactions and, 129–130, 133–136
  community interaction and, 63–64
  Democratic party preference and, 63–64
  experimental testing of, 21, 158–160, 159t
  generational status and, 57–58
  geographic specificity in, 70–71
  local partisan socialization and, 39–40, 69–72
  mediated political communication, 55–57
  national origin and, 53
  overview of, 25–26
  parental influence on lack of partisanship and, 46–49
  partisan acquisition and, 13–16, 66–67
  peer influence on partisanship and, 13–16, 26, 40–46, 49–60, 116
  policy endorsements and, 65–66, 157–158
  political influence of Asian Americans and, 64–65

social transmission theory (*Continued*)
  political mobilization and, 21
  pre-migration socialization and re-socialization and, 54–55
  race and, 15, 103
  scope conditions of, 183–184
  subgroups of Asian Americans and, 16–18, 71
  transnational political and social ties, 53–54
  vote choice and political interest predictors and, 88–92, 89t, 90t
socioeconomic status hypothesis
  Asian American partisanship and, 12, 39–40
  partisan preference and, 71–72
  summary of, 73t
Sprague, John, 39–40
state partisan politics
  comparisons of Republican and Democratic mobilization in, 36–37
  peer group influence on partisan acquisition and, 103
Steadfast Democrats: How Social Forces Shape Black Political Behavior (White & Laird), 27
Steel, Michelle, 5, 187–188
Stimson, James, 6
Stoker, Laura, 34
subgroup variation hypothesis, 71
  Asian American Democratic vote choice and, 78–80, 79f, 80f
  summary of, 73t
  vote choice and local partisan context and, 84–86, 85f

Talking about Politics: Informal Groups and Social Identity in American Life (Cramer), 101–102
Talking Politics: Political Discussion Networks and the New American Electorate (Carlson, Abrajano & García Bedolla), 102
Tammany Hall political machine, 35–36
The Social Citizen: Peer Networks and Political Behavior (Sinclair), 102
third-generation Asian Americans
  defined, 17–18
  peer and family influence in partisan acquisition and, 60–63, 180
  peer network diversity among, 16
  population data on, 15
third parties
  Black voters and, 27
  ethno-minority lack of support for, 28

Torney, JV, 101
Tran, Derek, 187–188
transitional generation Asian Americans
  college peer interactions of, 127
  defined, 17–18
  familial influence on political views for, 96
  parental lack of political socialization in, 46–49
  peer influence among, 60–63, 180
transnational politics
  Asian American social ties and, 53–54
  immigrant focus on, 48
Trump, Donald, 177, 189
  Filipino American support for, 68
tuition debt forgiveness policy
  college student endorsements of, 161–162
  diverse student peer group endorsement of, 163
tuition grant policy
  college student endorsements of, 161–162
  national student sample, endorsement by, 164–165

Van Laar, Colette, 133
Vietnamese Americans
  college peer interactions among, 127–128
  Democratic support among, 107–109, 108f, 115
  in Houston, TX, 41–42
  parental lack of political socialization among, 47–48
  partisan preference among, 31, 72, 187–188
  population growth of, 1–3, 2f
  Republican partisanship among, 53, 109
  residential patterns and population share, 82f, 83f, 83–84
  subgroup variation hypothesis and vote choice of, 80
  transitional generation peer networks, 60–61
  vote choice among, 9, 11f, 76f, 76, 78, 79f
vote choice
  Asian American nonpartisanship and, 74–75
  Democratic trend in, 31–33
  familial influence on, 34
  immediate discussion networks and, 40
  individual-level mechanisms in, 20
  local Asian American population context and, 81–84
  local partisan context and, 71, 76–80, 83f, 84–88, 85f
  local partisan norms and, 20, 39–40, 68–72

voter registration drives, on college campuses, 37
voter turnout
  Asian American levels of, 29–30
  of Asian Americans, 1, 17
  neighborhood demographics and, 39–40

Wals, Sergio, 54
Warnock, Raphael, 1
  Asian American support for, 4–5
Wattenburg, Martin, 37–38
weighted models, 89–90, 115–116n.10
White, Ismail, 27
white Americans
  changing political attitudes among college students, 138–142, 139t, 141f
  civic education and political engagement among, 131–132
  college enrollment data on, 62–63, 128, 129f
  college peer influence and, 20–21, 134
  college political ideology and student political views among, 146–148, 147f
  cross-racial friendships among, 16, 57–58, 134, 138, 142–146

  Democratic party support among, 9, 10f, 12
  family influence on partisan choice among, 64–65
  local partisan context hypothesis and, 71
  parental influence on political views of, 134
Why Americans Don't Join the Party: Race, Immigration, and the Failure (of Political Parties) to Engage the Electorate (Hajnal & Lee), 6–7, 27–28
Why We Vote: How Schools and Communities Shape Our Civic Life (Campbell), 131–132
Wong, Janelle, 22, 29–30, 32, 36, 53, 186
workplace, peer networks in, 62

Youth Parent Political Socialization Study, 100
Youth Parent Socialization Panel Study, 131
youth political engagement
  civic education and peer groups and, 131–132
  partisan preference and, 88
  party mobilization of, 37

www.ingramcontent.com/pod-product-compliance
Ingram Content Group UK Ltd.
Pitfield, Milton Keynes, MK11 3LW, UK
UKHW020729111125
464865UK00039B/355